# Lecture Notes in Bioinformatics 5167

Subseries of Lecture Notes in Computer Science

T0213110

Ana L.C. Bazzan   Mark Craven
Natália F. Martins (Eds.)

# Advances in
# Bioinformatics and
# Computational Biology

Third Brazilian Symposium on Bioinformatics, BSB 2008
Santo André, Brazil, August 28-30, 2008
Proceedings

Springer

Series Editors

Sorin Istrail, Brown University, Providence, RI, USA
Pavel Pevzner, University of California, San Diego, CA, USA
Michael Waterman, University of Southern California, Los Angeles, CA, USA

Volume Editors

Ana L.C. Bazzan
Instituto de Informática, UFRGS
Porto Alegre, RS, Brazil
E-mail: bazzan@ufrgs.br

Mark Craven
University of Wisconsin
Madison, Wisconsin, USA
E-mail: craven@biostat.wisc.edu

Natália F. Martins
EMBRAPA, Recursos Genéticos e Biotecnologia
Brasília, DF, Brazil
E-mail: natalia@cenargen.embrapa.br

Library of Congress Control Number: 2008932956

CR Subject Classification (1998): H.2.8, F.2.1, I.2, G.2.2, J.2, J.3, E.1

LNCS Sublibrary: SL 8 – Bioinformatics

ISSN        0302-9743

ISBN        978-3-540-85556-9 Springer Berlin Heidelberg New York

Springer is a part of Springer Science+Business Media

springer.com

© Springer-Verlag Berlin Heidelberg 2008

Typesetting: Camera-ready by author, data conversion by Scientific Publishing Services, Chennai, India
Printed on acid-free paper     SPIN: 12453382      06/3180      5 4 3 2 1 0

# Preface

The Brazilian Symposium on Bioinformatics (BSB) 2008 was held at Santo André (São Paulo), Brazil, August 28–30, 2008. BSB 2008 was the third symposium in the BSB series, although BSB was preceded by the Brazilian Workshop on Bioinformatics (WOB). This previous event had three consecutive editions in 2002 (Gramado, Rio Grande do Sul), 2003 (Macaé, Rio de Janeiro), and 2004 (Brasília, Distrito Federal). The change from workshop to symposium reflects the increasing quality and interest behind this meeting.

For BSB 2008, we had 41 submissions: 32 full papers and 9 extended abstracts, submitted to two tracks: the main track on Computational Biology and Bioinformatics, and the track Applications of Agent Technologies and Multiagent Systems to Computational Biology. The current proceedings contain 14 full papers and 5 extended abstracts that were accepted. These papers and abstracts were carefully refereed and selected by an international Program Committee of 35 members, with the help of 13 additional reviewers. We believe that this volume represents a fine contribution to current research in computational biology and bioinformatics, as well as in molecular biology.

The editors would like to thank: the authors for submitting their work to this symposium; the Program Committee members as well as additional reviewers for their support in the review process; the symposium sponsors (see list in this volume); and Springer for agreeing to print this volume. We thank especially the General and Local Chairs André C.P.L.F. de Carvalho (USP/São Carlos), Ana Carolina Lorena and Luis Paulo Barbour Scott (UFABC), and Katti Faceli (UFSCar/Sorocaba), as well as Maria Emilia M.T. Walter (UnB) who has given us valuable hints out of her experience with last year's proceedings, and the other members of the local organization, all from UFABC (André Fonseca, Claudia Barros Monteiro-Vitorello, Cláudio Nogueira de Meneses, Hana Masuda, Jiri Borecky, Leonardo Maia, Maria das Graças Marietto, Mauricio Coutinho, and Paula Homem de Melo). Without their support and hard work this symposium would not have been held.

Ana L. C. Bazzan
Mark Craven
Natália Martins

# Organization

BSB 2008 was organized by the CMCC of UFABC (Universidade Federal do ABC) in Santo André, Brazil.

## Executive Committee

Conference Chair        André C.P.L.F. de Carvalho
USP/São Carlos
Brazil

Local Chairs        Ana Carolina Lorena (UFABC)
Luis Paulo Barbour Scott (UFABC)
Katti Faceli (UFSCar/Sorocaba)
Brazil

## Scientific Program Committee

Program Chairs        Ana L. C. Bazzan
Instituto de Informática, UFRGS
Brazil

Mark Craven
University of Wisconsin
USA

Natalia F. Martins
Embrapa Genetic Resources and Biotechnology
Brazil

## Program Committee

| | |
|---|---|
| Aaron Cohen | Oregon Health and Science University |
| Adelinde Uhrmacher | University of Rostock |
| Adelmo Cechin | UNISINOS |
| Alba Melo | UnB |
| Alberto Apostolico | Georgia Tech |
| Alexandre Caetano | Embrapa |
| Ana Freitas | Technical University of Lisbon |
| Antonio Miranda | Fiocruz |
| Bernard Maigret edam | UHP-NANCY |
| Carlos Eduardo Ferreira | USP |
| Carlos H. Inacio Ramos | UNICAMP |
| Celia Ralha | UnB |

| | |
|---|---|
| Colin Dewey | University of Wisconsin |
| David Sankoff | University of Ottawa |
| Daniel Huson | Tuebingen University |
| Dominique Cellier | Université de Rouen |
| Edson Cáceres | UFMS |
| Emanuela Merelli | Università di Camerino |
| Fernando Von Zuben | UNICAMP |
| Frank DiMaio | University of Washington |
| Gad Landau | University of Haifa |
| Gunnar Klau | Freie Universität Berlin |
| Irene Ong | University of Wisconsin Madison |
| João Setubal | Virginia Tech |
| José Carlos Mombach | UFRGS |
| Karl Tuyls | University of Maastricht |
| Gunnar Klau | Freie Universität Berlin |
| Marcilio de Souto | UFRGN |
| Marie-Dominique Devignes | LORIA |
| Marta Mattoso | COPPE/UFRJ |
| Melissa Lemos | PUC/Rio |
| Nadia Pisanti | University of Pisa |
| Nalvo Almeida | UFMS |
| Ney Lemke | UNESP |
| Osmar Norberto de Souza | PUCRS |
| Paulo Moscato | University of Newcastle |
| Ryan Lilien | University of Toronto |
| Satoru Miyano | University of Tokyo |
| Siang Song | USP |
| Stacia Wyman | Fred Hutchinson Cancer Research Center |
| Wellington Martins | UCG |

## Sponsors

Brazilian Computer Society (SBC)
Fundação de Apoio à Pesquisa do Estado de São Paulo (FAPESP)
Conselho Nacional de Desenvolvimento Científico e Tecnológico (CNPq)
Coordenação de Aperfeiçoamento de Pessoal de Nível Superior (CAPES)
Universidade Federal do ABC
CLC bio
SGI

# Table of Contents

## Selected Articles

## Extended Abstracts

# Multi-label Hierarchical Classification of Protein Functions with Artificial Immune Systems

Roberto T. Alves[1], Myriam R. Delgado[1], and Alex A. Freitas[2]

[1] Programa de Pós-Graduação em Engenharia Elétrica e Informática Industrial, UFTPR
Av. Sete de Setembro, 3165, CEP: 80230-901, Curitiba – PR – Brazil
roberto.t.alves@gmail.com, myriamdelg@utfpr.edu.br
[2] Computing Laboratory and Centre for BioMedical Informatics, University of Kent,
CT2 7NF, Canterbury, U.K.
A.A.Freitas@kent.ac.uk

**Abstract.** This work proposes two versions of an Artificial Immune System (AIS) - a relatively recent computational intelligence paradigm – for predicting protein functions described in the Gene Ontology (GO). The GO has functional classes (GO terms) specified in the form of a directed acyclic graph, which leads to a very challenging multi-label hierarchical classification problem where a protein can be assigned multiple classes (functions, GO terms) across several levels of the GO's term hierarchy. Hence, the proposed approach, called MHC-AIS (Multi-label Hierarchical Classification with an Artificial Immune System), is a sophisticated classification algorithm tailored to both multi-label and hierarchical classification. The first version of the MHC-AIS builds a global classifier to predict all classes in the application domain, whilst the second version builds a local classifier to predict each class. In both versions of the MHC-AIS the classifier is expressed as a set of IF-THEN classification rules, which have the advantage of representing comprehensible knowledge to biologist users. The two MHC-AIS versions are evaluated on a dataset of DNA-binding and ATPase proteins.

**Keywords:** Artificial Immune System, Hierarchical and Multi-label Classification, Prediction of Protein Function.

## 1 Introduction

Artificial Immune Systems (AIS) are one of the most recent natural computing approaches to emerge from computer science. The immune system is a distributed system, capable of constructing and maintaining a dynamical and structural identity, learning to identify previously unseen invaders and remembering what it has learnt. These computational techniques have many potential applications, such as in distributed and adaptive control, machine learning, pattern recognition, fault and anomaly detection, computer security, optimization, and distributed system design [1].

In data mining, ideally the discovered knowledge should be not only accurate, but also comprehensible to the user [2]. This work addresses the multi-label hierarchical classification task of data mining, where the goal is to discover a classification model

A.L.C. Bazzan, M. Craven, and N.F. Martins (Eds.): BSB 2008, LNBI 5167, pp. 1–12, 2008.
© Springer-Verlag Berlin Heidelberg 2008

that predicts more than one class for an example (data instance) across several levels of a class hierarchy, based on the values of the predictor attributes for that example.

Bioinformatics is an inter-disciplinary field, involving the areas of computer science, mathematics, biology, etc. [3]. Among many bioinformatics problems, this paper focuses on the prediction of protein functions from information associated with the protein's primary sequence. As proteins often have multiple functions which are described hierarchically, the use of multi-label hierarchical techniques for the induction of classification models in Bioinformatics is a promising research area. At present, the biological functions that can be performed by proteins are defined in a structured, standardized dictionary of terms called the Gene Ontology (GO) [4].

The AIS algorithms proposed in this paper combine the adaptive global search of the AIS paradigm with advanced concepts and methods of data mining (hierarchical and multi-label classification), in order to solve a challenging bioinformatics problem (protein function prediction – assigns GO terms (classes) to proteins). The AIS presented in this paper discovers knowledge interpretable by the user, in the form of IF-THEN classification rules, unlike other methods proposed in the literature, whose classification model is typically a "black box" which normally does not provide any insight to the user about interesting hidden relationships in the data [5].

## 2  Multi-label Hierarchical Classification

The classification task of data mining [2] consists of building, in a training phase, a classification model that maps each example $t_i$ to a class $c \in C$ of the target application domain, with $i = 1, 2, ..., n$, where $n$ represents the number of examples in the training set.

The majority of classification algorithms cope with problems where each example $t_i$ is associated with a single class $c \in C$. These algorithms are called single label. However, some classification problems are considerably more complex because each example $t_i$ is associated with a subset of classes $C$ is contained in $C$ of the application domain. Protein function prediction is a typical case of this type of problem, since a protein can perform several biological functions. Algorithms for coping with this kind of problem are called multi-label [6].

There has been a very large amount of research on conventional "flat" (non-hierarchical) classification problems, where the classes to be predicted are not hierarchically organized. However, in some problems the classes are hierarchically organized, which makes the classification problem much more challenging. Problems of this type are known as hierarchical classification problems [7].

In hierarchical classification problems, typically the classes are hierarchically organized in one of the following two forms: as a tree (where each class has at most one parent class) or as a direct acyclic graph (DAG), where each class can have more than one parent. In bioinformatics, two of the most well-known hierarchical structures for classifying protein functions are the enzyme commission hierarchy [8] – organized in the form of a tree and GO [4] – organized in the form of a DAG. The GO consists of a dictionary that defines gene products independent from species. GO actually consists of 3 separate "domains" (very different types of GO terms): molecular function, biological process and cellular component. The GO is structurally organized in the form of a direct acyclic graph (DAG), where each GO term represents a node of the hierarchical structure.

In hierarchical classification, there are basically two types of classifiers that can be built to cope with the full set of classes to be predicted: local or global classifiers. In local classifiers, for each class $c \in C$ a (local) classifier is built to predict whether or not each class $c$ is associated with an example $t_i$. After all classifiers are built, an example $t_i$ is submitted to all those classifiers (one for each class) in order to determine which classes are predicted for that example. In global classifiers, a single (global) classifier is built to discriminate among all classes of the application domain and so $t_i$ is submitted to a single (potentially very complex) classifier [7].

# 3   Multi-label Hierarchical Classification with an Artificial Immune System

The immune system as a biological complex adaptive system has provided inspiration for a range of innovative problem solving techniques, including classification tasks [9]. In this paper, the construction of a immune-based learning algorithm is explored whose recognition, distributed, and adaptive nature offer many potential advantages over more traditional models. The AIS algorithm used in this paper is called MHC-AIS (Multi-label Hierarchical Classification with an Artificial Immune System). MHC-AIS is based on the following natural immunology principles: clonal selection, immune network and somatic hypermutation [10,11]. In AIS, antibodies (*ab*) represent candidate solutions to the target problem, whilst antigens (*ag*) represent specific instances of the problem. In the context of this work, *ab*´s represent IF-THEN classification rules and *ag*´s represent proteins in the training set whose classes have to be predicted by the AIS.

In essence, in the clonal selection theory antibodies are cloned in proportion to their degree of matching ("affinity") to antigens, so that the antibodies which are better in recognizing antigens produce more clones of themselves. The just-generated clones are then subject to a process of somatic hypermutation, where the rate of mutation applied to a clone is inversely proportional to its affinity with the antigens. In computer science terms, the best antibodies are cloned more often and undergo a smaller rate of mutation (have fewer parts of their candidate solution modified) than the worst antibodies. With time this process of clonal selection and hypersomatic mutation leads to better and better candidate solutions to the target problem.

In essence, the theoretical immunology principle of immune networks states that antibodies can recognize not only antigens but also other antibodies. The first kind of recognition stimulates antibody production, but the latter suppresses antibodies, which in computer science terms means a candidate solution tends to suppress other similar candidate solutions, which has the effect of improving the diversity of the search for a (near-)optimal candidate solution.

The training phase of MHC-AIS is performed by two major procedures, called Sequential Covering (SC) and Rule Evolution (RE) procedures. The SC procedure iteratively calls the RE procedure until (almost) all "antigens" (proteins, examples) are covered by the discovered rules. The RE procedure essentially evolves artificial "antibodies" (IF-THEN classification rules) that are used to classify antigens. Then, the best evolved antibody is added to discovered rule set. Each antibody (candidate classification rule) consists of two parts: the rule antecedent (IF part), represented by a vector of conditions (attribute-value pairs), and the rule consequent (THEN part) that represents the classes predicted by the rule. In this work the classes correspond to GO terms denoting protein functions. This work proposes two versions of the MHC-AIS, viz.: local and global versions (more details in the following subsections).

## 3.1 Global Version

In biological databases a protein is annotated only with its most specific GO term. Given the semantics of the GO's functional hierarchy, this implicitly means the protein also contains all the functional classes of its ancestral GO terms in the GO's DAG. Hence, in a data preprocessing step, MHC-AIS explicitly assigns to each antigen (protein) both its most specific class(es) (GO term(s)) and all its ancestral classes. MHC-AIS also considers the semantics of the GO's functional hierarchy when creating classification rules – i.e., it guarantees that, if a rule predicts a given GO term, all its ancestral GO terms are also predicted by the rule.

Fig. 1 shows the high-level pseudocode of the SC procedure.

```
Input: full protein training set;
Output: set of discovered rules;
DiscoveredRuleSet = ∅ ;
TrainSet = {set of all protein training examples};
Re-label TrainSet regarding GO's functional class hierarchy;
WHILE |TrainSet| > MaxUncovExamp
        BestRule = RULE-EVOLUTION(TrainSet); //based on AIS
        DiscoveredRuleSet = DiscoveredRuleSet U BestRule;
        updateCoveredClasses(TrainSet, BestRule)
        removeExamplesWithAllClassesCovered(TrainSet);
END WHLE
```

**Fig. 1.** Sequential Covering (SC) procedure

First, it initializes the set of discovered rules with the empty set and initializes the training set with the set of all original training examples. Next, each example in the training set is extended to contain both the original class and all its ancestral classes in the GO hierarchy. Thereafter, the algorithm starts a WHILE loop which, at each iteration, calls the RE procedure. The latter receives, as parameters, the current training set and use AIS algorithm to discover classification rules. The RE procedure returns the best classification rule discovered by the AIS for the current training set. Then the SC procedure adds that rule to the discovered rule set and removes the training examples covered by that rule, as follows. In conventional rule induction algorithms for single-label classification, examples correctly covered by the just discovered rule are removed from the training set. However, in multi-label classification this process is more complex, since different rules and different training examples have different numbers of classes. In the global version of the AIS, the process of example removal works as follows. First, the training examples covered by the just-discovered rule (i.e. examples satisfying the rule's antecedent) are identified.

For each of those examples, its annotated (true) classes which are predicted by the just-discovered rules are marked as covered. As more and more rules are discovered, more and more of the annotated classes of each example will be covered. Only when all the classes of an example are covered that example is removed from the training set. The process of rule discovery terminates when the number of examples in the current training set becomes smaller than a user-defined parameter called *MaxUncovExamp*. Such procedure avoids the discovery of rules covering too few examples, unlikely to generalize well to the test set [12].

Fig. 2 shows the high-level code of the RE procedure, where rules are obtained by the proposed MHC-AIS. First, the initial population of antibodies $AB_{t=0}$ is created, where the consequent of each rule contains (initially) all GO classes in the data being mined. At the end of the evolutionary process, the AIS updates the consequent of the discovered rule (to be returned by the RE procedure) to contain only a subset of classes, representing the classes predicted by that rule, as will be explained later.

```
Input: current TrainSet;   Output: the best evolved rule;
AB_{t=0} = Create initial population of antibodies at random;
Computefitness(AB_{t=0},TrainSet);
FOR t = 1 to Number of Generations
        CL = ProduceClones(AB_{t-1});
        CL* = MutateClones(CL);
        AB_t = AB_{t-1} U CL*;
        Computefitness(AB_t,TrainSet);
        Suppresion(AB_t);
        Elitism(AB_{t+1});
END FOR t;
Determine the final subset of classes of the best antibody found so far;
return(best antibody);
```

**Fig. 2.** Rule Evolution (RE) procedure

After its creation, the fitness (quality measure) of each antibody $ab_i^{t=0}$ of the initial population is calculated on the training set, where each example represents an antigen $ag_j$. The fitness of each $ab_i$ is computed in two stages. First, a fitness value is associated with each $k$th-class $c_k^i$ contained in the consequent of rule (antibody) $ab_i$. The value of this fitness is computed according to the following equation:

$$fit\left(c_k^i\right) = \frac{TP_{c_k^i}}{TP_{c_k^i} + FN_{c_k^i}} \times \frac{TN_{c_k^i}}{TN_{c_k^i} + FP_{c_k^i}} \tag{1}$$

where:

- TP (true positives) = number of training examples satisfying affinity$(ab_i,ag_j) \geq \delta_{AF}$ and having the annotated class $c_k^i$.
- TN (true negatives) = number of training examples satisfying affinity$(ab_i,ag_j) < \delta_{AF}$ and not having the annotated class $c_k^i$.
- FP (false positives) = number of training examples satisfying affinity $(ab_i,ag_j) \geq \delta_{AF}$ and not having the annotated class $c_k^i$.
- FN (false negatives) = number of training examples satisfying affinity $(ab_i,ag_j) < \delta_{AF}$ and having the annotated class $c_k^i$.

The function *affinity* $(ab_i, ag_j)$ returns the degree of matching between the rule $ab_i$ and the training example $ag_j$. The value of the parameter $\delta_{AF}$ represents the minimum degree of matching required for the antigen $ag_j$ to be deemed as classified by the rule $ab_i$. It is important to note that $\delta_{AF}$ is a user-specified parameter, which gives more flexibility to the use of the algorithm, allowing the use of a partial or total degree of matching ($\delta_{AF} = 1.0$) in the classification process. MHC-AIS is a hierarchical classification algorithm, and so it must consider the hierarchical structure of classes in the classification process, to reduce classification errors. A common hierarchical classification error occurs when a classifier correctly predicts a given class $c$ for an example but does not predict an ancestral class of $c$. Recall that all the ancestral classes of a given predicted class must also be predicted by the trained classifier, due to the semantics of the class hierarchy in the GO. Some hierarchical classification algorithms try to correct hierarchical classification errors after the classifier has been built, in a post-processing phase. By contrast, MHC-AIS maintains a set of consistent hierarchical classifications during the construction of the global classifier. This kind of consistency is given by equation (2):

$$fit\left(c_{k*}^i\right) = \max\left[\, fit\left(c_{k*}^i\right), fit\left(c_k^i\right)\right], \quad c_{k*}^i \in Ancestors(c_k^i) \tag{2}$$

Hence, if the fitness of some ancestral class $c_{k*}^i$ is smaller than the fitness of its descendant class $c_k^i$, then the fitness of $c_k^i$ is assigned to its ancestral class, therefore maintaining the consistency of hierarchical classifications during training.

The fitness of an entire rule (computed as an aggregated value of the fitness of all the classes predicted by the rule) is calculated by equation (3):

$$fitness(ab_i) = \frac{1}{n}\sum fit\left(c_k^i\right), \quad fit\left(c_k^i\right) > \delta_{FT} \tag{3}$$

where $n$ indicates the number of classes $c_i^k$ with fitness greater than the value of the parameter $\delta_{FT}$.

Next, the AIS starts to evolve the population of antibodies. Once the global fitness of the entire rule has been calculated for each $ab_i$, the algorithm executes the clonal expansion process, typical in AIS [1]. Each $ab_i$ produces *NumCl* clones of itself, where *NumCl* is proportional to the fitness of $ab_i$. The number of clones to be produced for each $ab_i$ is determined by equation (4):

$$NumCl_i = \text{int}\left( fitness\left(ab_i\right) \times NumMaxCl \times ClRate\right) \tag{4}$$

where the value of *NumCl* $\in$ [1,*NumMaxCl*]. The parameter *NumMaxCl* represents the maximum number of clones that can be generated for a given *ab*. The function *int* truncates the fractional part of its parameter. The *ClRate* is calculated in every iteration with the goal of controlling the size of the antibody population, stimulating or inhibiting the production of clones. The value of *ClRate* is given by equation (5):

$$ClRate = \begin{cases} HyperClRate & \text{if } |AB| < nIP \\ 0 & \text{if } |AB| > nMaxP \\ 1 - \left( \dfrac{|AB| - nIP}{nMaxP - nIP} \right) & otherwise \end{cases} \qquad (5)$$

where *HyperClRate*, *nIP* and *nMaxP* are specified in the beginning of the execution of the algorithm and indicate, respectively, clonal hyper-expansion rate, initial antibody population size and maximum antibody population size. It is important to emphasize that the parameter *nMaxP* does not represent the maximum size that the antibody population *AB* can take during the evolution. Rather, it indicates that, if the size of *AB* is greater than the value of that parameter, the generation of clones proportional to antibody fitness is turned off. Next, the population *CL* of clones undergoes a process of somatic hypermutation just on the IF part of the rule. A mutation rate applied to each clone *cl* is inversely proportional to the fitness of the antibody *ab* from which the clone was produced. The mutation rate is determined by equation (6):

$$MutRate_{cl} = mutMin + (mutMax - mutMin) \times (1 - fitness(cl)) \qquad (6)$$

where *MutMin* and *MutMax* indicate, respectively, the minimum and maximum mutation rates to be applied to a clone *cl*; and the function fitness(*cl*) is presented in equation (3). The *MutRate* represents the probability that each gene (rule condition – IF antecedent) will undergo mutation. The population $CL^*$, which is formed only by clones that underwent some mutation, is then inserted in *AB*. Other procedures are also applied to *AB* during the rule evolution procedure: suppression of antibodies and elitism. The suppression procedure, characteristic of AIs based on the immune network theory, removes from $AB_t$ similar antibodies. More precisely, if two antibodies $ab_i$ and $ab_i^*$ have a similarity degree greater than or equal to the value of $\delta_{SIM}$, then, out of those two antibodies, the one with the smallest fitness is removed. The degree of similarity between two antibodies is computed as the number of conditions (attribute-value pairs) in the rule antecedents of both antibodies divided by the number of conditions in the rule antecedent of the antibody with the greatest number of conditions – which produces a measure of antibody similarity normalized in the range from 0 (no rule conditions in common) to 1 (identical rule antecedents). Elitism, a mechanism quite common in evolutionary algorithms [13], selects the antibody with the best fitness to be included in the next-iteration population $AB_{t+1}$.

During the rule evolution procedure all the classes occurring in the data being mined are represented in the consequent. The choice of the final subset of classes to be assigned to the consequent of the best discovered rule is given by equation (7):

$$PC = \bigcup c_k \in C \, | \, fit(c_k) > \delta_{FT} \qquad (7)$$

where PC represents the set of classes predicted by the best discovered rule whose fitness value is greater than $\delta_{FT}$.

## 3.2 Local Version

Like the global MHC-AIS, the local MHC-AIS consists of the SC (Fig. 3) and RE procedures, but with some differences. In the local version, the SC procedure labels the training examples as positive or negative. Positive examples represent examples associated with the class of the current node of the GO's DAG (a classifier is trained for each node of the GO's DAG), denoted class Y, whilst examples that do not have the class Y are labeled as negative examples. MHC-AIS is an algorithm for constructing hierarchical classifiers, and therefore the hierarchical structure has to be coped with like in the global version. Hence, all training examples labeled with any descendant class or ancestor class of the current class Y are labeled as positive class. Concerning the latter type of positive examples, it is often the case that, when a hierarchical classifier is being built, examples annotated with an ancestor class of the current class Y are removed, since they are considered as ambiguous – they do not have an annotation suggesting that they have class Y, but maybe they actually have class Y, which was not annotated yet simply due to the lack of evidence for its presence (note that "absence of evidence is different from evidence of absence"). However, in this work we use examples with an annotated class that is an ancestral of the current class Y in order to increase the number of positive examples and so hopefully increase the predictive accuracy of the algorithm.

```
Input: full training set; Output: set of discovered rules;
DiscoveredRuleSet = ∅ ;
FOR EACH class c
       TrainSet = {set of all training examples};
       WHILE |TrainSet| > MaxUncovExamp
          BestRule = RULE-EVOLUTION(TrainSet, class c);//based on AIS
          DiscoveredRuleSet=DiscoveredRuleSet ∪ BestRule;
          TrainSet = TrainSet - {examp. correctly covered by BestRule};
       END WHILE;
END FOR EACH class;
```

**Fig. 3.** Sequential Covering (SC) procedure for Local Version

In this local version, MHC-AIS first discovers as many classification rules as necessary in order to cover the positive examples. Next, the algorithm discovers as many rules as necessary to cover the negative examples. Every time that a given rule is discovered, all the examples correctly covered by that rule (i.e. examples satisfying the conditions in the rule antecedent and having the class predicted by the rule consequent) are removed from the current training set, as usual in rule induction algorithms. This iterative process of rule discovery and removal of training examples is repeated until the number of examples in the current training set becomes smaller than a user-defined threshold *MaxUncovExamp*.

The other procedures of the local MHC-AIS are the same as in the global version of the algorithm, described in the previous subsection.

# 4 Computational Results

The two versions of the MHC-AIS were evaluated on a dataset of proteins created from information extracted from the well-known UNIPROT database [14]. This dataset contains two protein families: DNA-binding and ATPase [15]. These two protein families were chosen for our experiments because there are many proteins that belong to both families, increasing the difficult of the problem of building a multi-label classifier. The dataset used in the experiments contains 7877 proteins, where each protein (example) is described by 40 predictor attributes, 38 of which are PROSITE[1] patterns and 2 of which are continuous attributes (molecular weight and the number of amino acids in the primary sequence). In total, the dataset contains 214 classes (GO terms) to be predicted.

As previously discussed, in data mining the discovered knowledge should be not only accurate, but also comprehensible to the user [2,5]. In this spirit, the results can be evaluated according to two criteria, viz. the predictive accuracy and simplicity of the discovered rule set. In this paper, the predictive accuracy is evaluated by the F-measure (adapted to the scenario of multi-label hierarchical classification), which involves computing the precision and recall of the discovered rule set on the test set (unseen during training). Interpretability will be measured in terms of the size of the discovered rule set, an approach which is not ideal but is still used in the literature.

In the global version, the set of GO terms predicted for a test example $t$, denoted *PredGO(t)*, consists of the union of all GO terms in the consequent of all rules covering $t$ – i.e. all rules whose conditions are satisfied by $t$'s attribute values.

In the local version of MHC-AIS, each test example $t$ is submitted to the $n$ trained classifiers. Each classifier consists of a set of discovered rules. The class predicted by each classifier is the class represented in the consequent of the rule with the greatest fitness value (computed during training) out of all rules discovered by that classifier that cover the example $t$. If no discovered rule covers the example $t$, the latter is classified by the default rule, which predicts the majority class in the training set. Hence, *PredGO(t)* consists of all GO terms whose trained classifiers predicted their corresponding positive class for the example $t$.

MHC-AIS computes the Precision and Recall for a test example $t$ – denoted $P(t)$ and $R(t)$, respectively – as per equations (8) and (9), where *TrueGO(t)* is the set of true GO terms for test example $t$.

$$P(t) = |PredGO(t) \cap TrueGO(t)| / PredGO(t) \qquad (8)$$

$$R(t) = |PredGO(t) \cap TrueGO(t)| / TrueGO(t) \qquad (9)$$

Thus, precision is the proportion of true classes among all predicted classes, whilst recall is the proportion of predicted classes among all true classes. The F-measure for a test example $t$ is given by equation (10), the harmonic mean of $P$ and $R$.

$$F(t) = (2 \times P(t) \times R(t)) / (1 + P(t) + R(t)) \qquad (10)$$

---

[1] PROSITE patterns are motifs well-known in bioinformatics [16] and they are represented as binary attributes – i.e., each attribute indicates whether or not the corresponding PROSITE pattern occurs in the sequence of amino acids of a protein.

Finally, once $P(t)$ and $R(t)$ have been computed for each test example $t$, the system computes the overall F-measure over the entire test set $\mathbf{T}$ by equation (11), where $|\mathbf{T}|$ denotes the cardinality of the test set $\mathbf{T}$.

$$\text{Predictive Accuracy} = F(\mathbf{T}) = (\Sigma_{t \in \mathbf{T}} F(t)) / |\mathbf{T}| \qquad (11)$$

Table 1 shows the predictive accuracy for precision, recall and F-measure for global and local version. The numbers after the "±" symbol represent the standard deviations associated with a well-known 10-fold cross-validation procedure [2]. In the columns F-measure, the best result (out of both version of MHC-AIS) is shown in bold. The results presented in Table 1 consider different affinity (matching) thresholds  for both versions of MHC-AIS, to evaluate the predictive performance of the algorithms using partial matching ($\delta_{AF} < 1.0$)  or total matching ($\delta_{AF} = 1.0$).

**Table 1.** Predictive accuracy (%) of MHC-AIS versions on the used protein data set

| Affinity Threshold | Global Version | | | Local Version | | |
|---|---|---|---|---|---|---|
| | Precision | Recall | F-Measure | Precision | Recall | F-Measure |
| 0.8 | 45.93±2.71 | 98.23±0.61 | **58.35±2.23** | 80.58±1.01 | 44.65±1.59 | 55.65±1.45 |
| 0.9 | 50.79±3.18 | 92.86±3.76 | 58.34±2.86 | 75.61±1.12 | 52.57±2.35 | **59.75±1.77** |
| 1.0 | 28.91±1.31 | 99.50±0.12 | 42.84±1.37 | 58.56±1.01 | 69.91±1.13 | **61.37±0.82** |

Table 1 shows that the global MHC-AIS performed worst (according to the F-measure) when using total matching. Note that the global MHC-AIS obtained the worst results for the precision measure with all affinity threshold values. By contrast, the global MHC-AIS obtained very good recall values with all affinity thresholds. This performance behavior of global MHC-AIS indicates that the trained global classifier has a bias favoring the prediction of a large number of classes, mainly because the set of classes predicted for a test example consists of the union of all classes in the consequents of all rules covering that example - regardless of the fitness of the individual rules in question and the fact that the predictions of some of those rules might be inconsistent with each other. This tends to predict more classes than the actual number of true classes for a given test example, which tends to increase recall but reduce precision (given the definition of these terms).

In both cases of MHC-AIS, as the value of the affinity threshold $\delta_{AF}$ increases the value of precision is reduced, showing a disadvantage in the use of total matching. As expected, due to the trade-off between precision and recall, the local version of the algorithm had the opposite performance behavior in the case of recall, where the largest value was obtained with total matching.

**Table 2.** Simplicity of the discovered rule set of MHC-AIS versions

| Threshold Affinity | Global Version | | Local Version | |
|---|---|---|---|---|
| | #rules | #Conditions | #rules | #Conditions |
| 0.8 | **63.90±1,59** | **1164,30±28.20** | 788.00±3.68 | 2901.30±42.83 |
| 0.9 | **58.09±3.08** | **1066.60±53.39** | 1016.80 ±8.09 | 4829.80±67.44 |
| 1.0 | **79.90±1.83** | **1361.00±41.16** | 1232.90±16.07 | 7069.53±18298 |

Table 2 shows the results of both local and global versions of MHC-AIS with respect to the simplicity (interpretability) of the discovered rule set. This simplicity was measured by the number of discovered rules and total number of rule conditions (in all rules). The averages were computed over 10-fold cross-validation.

Note that, as shown in Table 2, the global MHC-AIS obtained much better results concerning rule set simplicity than the local MHC-AIS, in all experiments. This advantage of the global MHC-AIS is probably due to the fact that, by building a single set of rules predicting all classes in a single run of the algorithm, the algorithm can avoid the need for discovering redundant rules covering the same set of true classes for some examples. In particular, when the local version discovers rules predicting the "negative" class at each node of the GO's DAG, it should be noted that those rules predicting the negative class tend to be redundant with respect to rules predicting positive classes in other nodes of the GO's DAG, since some of the negative class examples for a given GO node will inevitably be positive class examples in another GO node. An example of a rule discovered rule by global MHC-AIS in the used data set is presented below:

IF (PS00676 == 1) and (PS00390 == 1) and (MOLECULAR_WEIGHT < 29353)
then (5488, 5515, 51087)

The biological interpretation of this rule is: if a protein presents "Sigma-54 interaction domain signatures and profile" and "Sodium and potassium ATPases beta subunits signatures" signatures and "molecular weight is less than 29353" then the predicted classes (biological functions) are: "binding" (5488) and "protein binding" (5515) and "chaperone binding" (51087). Note that the GO hierarchy was considered, i.e. the true hierarchical path is 5488 → 5515 → 51087 (from shallower to deeper nodes).

## 5  Conclusion and Future Work

This work described an artificial immune system (AIS)-based rule induction algorithm to the prediction of protein function. The paper proposed two versions of the AIS algorithm, a global version, where a single global classifier is built predicting all classes of the application domain; and a local version, where a local classifier is built for each node of the GO class hierarchy. Both versions have the advantage of discovering IF-THEN classification rules, constituting a type of knowledge representation that can, in principle, be easily interpretable by biologist users. The global and local versions of the AIS have different (roughly dual) advantages and disadvantages with respect to predictive accuracy, but the global version at least has the advantage of discovering much simpler (smaller) rule sets.

Future work involves: (a) comparing the predictive performance of both versions of the AIS with other classification algorithms designed for hierarchical classification (e.g. [17]); (b) investigating new criteria for selecting, out of all classes in the consequent of the rules covering a test example in the global approach, which classes should be actually predicted for the test example; (c) incorporating an explicit mechanism during the training phase to improve the rules' interpretability (d) analyzing the biological relevance of the discovered rules; and (e) evaluating the proposed AIS in datasets of other protein families and other types of predictor attributes.

# References

1. De Castro, L.N., Timmis, J.: Artificial Immune Systems: A New Computational Intelligence Approach. Springer, Berlin (2002)
2. Witten, I.H., Frank, E.: Data Mining: Practical Machine Learning Tools and Techniques, 2nd edn. Morgan Kaufmann, San Mateo (2005)
3. Fogel, G.B., Corne, D.W.: Evolutionary Computation in Bioinformatics. Morgan Kaufmann Publishers, San Franciso (2003)
4. The Gene Ontology Consortium. The Gene Ontology (GO) Database and Informatics Resource. Nucleic Acids Research 32(1), 258–261 (2004)
5. Freitas, A.A.: Data Mining and Knowledge Discovery with Evolutionary Algorithms. Springer, Berlin (2002)
6. Tsoumakas, G., Katakis, I.: Multi-Label Classification: An Overview. International Journal of Data Warehousing and Mining 3(3), 1–13 (2007)
7. Sun, A., Lim, E.-P., Ng, W.-K.: Performance Measurement Framework for Hierarchical Text Classification. Journal of the American Society for Information Science and Technology 54(11), 1014–1028 (2003)
8. E. Nomenclature, of the IUPAC-IUB. American Elsevier Pub. Co., New York, NY 104 (1972)
9. Freitas, A.A., Timmis, T.: Revisiting the foundations of artificial immune systems for data mining. IEEE Trans. on Evolutionary Computation 11(4), 521–540 (2007)
10. Ada, G.L., Nossal, G.V.: The Clonal Selection Theory. Scientific American 257, 50–57 (1987)
11. Jerne, N.K.: Towards a Network Theory of Immune System. Ann. Immunol (Inst. Pasteur) 125C, 373–389 (1974)
12. Alves, R.T., Delgado, M.R., Lopes, H.S., Freitas, A.A.: An artificial immune system for fuzzy-rule induction in data mining. In: Yao, X., Burke, E.K., Lozano, J.A., Smith, J., Merelo-Guervós, J.J., Bullinaria, J.A., Rowe, J.E., Tiño, P., Kabán, A., Schwefel, H.-P. (eds.) PPSN 2004. LNCS, vol. 3242, pp. 1011–1020. Springer, Heidelberg (2004)
13. Goldberg, D.E.: Genetic Algorithms in Search Optimization and Machine Learning. Addison-Wesley, Reading (1989)
14. The UniProt Consortium. The Universal Protein Resource (UniProt). Nucleic Acids Res. 35, D193–D197 (2007)
15. Alberts, B., Johnson, A., Lewis, J., Raff, M., Roberts, K., Water, P.: Molecular Biology of the Cell, 4th edn. Garland Science, New York (2002)
16. Hulo, N., Bairoch, A., Bulliard, V., Cerutti, L., De Castro, E., Langendijk-Genevaux, P.S., Pagni, M., Sigrist, C.J.A.: The PROSITE Database. Nucleic Acids Res. 34, D227–D230 (2006)
17. Wolstencroft, K., Lord, P.W., Tabernero, P., Brass, P., Stevens, R.: Protein classification using ontology classification. Bioinformatics 22, 530–538 (2006)

# Operon Prediction in Bacterial Genomes*

Matheus B.S. Barros, Simone de L. Martins, and Alexandre Plastino

Departamento de Ciência da Computação – Universidade Federal Fluminense (UFF)
24210-240 – Niterói – RJ – Brasil
matheusbersotsb@gmail.com, {simone,plastino}@dcc.ic.uff.br

**Abstract.** Operons are sets of adjacent genes that encode proteins with related metabolic functions. Operon prediction may be useful for understanding the systems of regulation and for genome annotation. In this work, we present an extension of the PROCSIMO tool to allow the operon prediction in bacterial genomes based on the similarity evaluation between pairs of genes. Computational experiments were made to validate this new functionality. With the use of this tool, we expect to enlarge the number of known operons in bacterial organisms.

## 1   Introduction

The genes of bacterial genomes are organized in operons which are sets of genes transcribed into a single mRNA sequence. Operons form the fundamental transcriptional units within a bacterial genome, so defining these structures may help in examining transcriptional regulation. In addition, operons often contain genes that are functionally related and required by the cell for a certain process or pathway and, thus, they are highly predictive of biological networks. For these reasons, identifying the genes that are grouped together into operons may enhance our knowledge of gene regulation and function, and such information is an important addition to genome annotation [1,2,3].

The PROCSIMO tool [4] was developed to identify similarity between operons. The main contribution of this work is to add a new functionality to this tool, which enables the operon prediction in new sequenced genomes.

A variety of prediction algorithms has been developed in recent years. Craven et al. [5] present an approach which uses machine learning methods to induce predictive models from a variety of data types including sequence data, gene expression data, and functional annotations associated with genes. The learned models are used to individually predict promoters, terminators and operons themselves and a dynamic programming method uses these predictions to map every known and putative gene in a given genome into its most probable operon. This method is more suitable to highly characterized genomes, such as the E. coli K-12 genome, because it needs lots of input data.

Another method, proposed in [2], is based on finding gene clusters in which gene order and orientation are conserved in two or more genomes. This approach

---

* Work sponsored by CNPq.

A.L.C. Bazzan, M. Craven, and N.F. Martins (Eds.): BSB 2008, LNBI 5167, pp. 13–22, 2008.

does not rely on experimental data, but instead uses the genome sequence and gene locations. They developed a computational and statistical method which finds such conserved gene clusters and assigns to each one its probability of being an operon. They consider that genes, which may belong to an operon, should not be separated by more than 200 base pairs and should be on the same strand.

The method presented in [6] uses log-likelihoods derived from the distribution of intergenic distances to predict operons. They obtained an accuracy of 82% for E. coli and B. subtilis genomes.

Okuda et al. [7] developed a tool[1] which uses four types of associations between genes to determine an operon: intergenic distances, functional links in biological pathways, gene co-expression obtained from microarray data and the conservation of gene order across multiple genomes. Given a specific species, predicted operons that may exist within that species are returned. There are two options that are available: simple and advanced prediction mode. For simple mode, users can obtain prediction results based on default parameter values that have been validated by known operons. In advanced prediction mode, users can freely change these parameter values, which are based on the four types of information described above.

Bergman et al. [1] constructed a Bayesian hidden Markov model which incorporates comparative genomic data into traditional predictors, such as intergenic distances. They applied the algorithm to the Bacillus anthracis genome and found that it successfully predicted all previously verified B. anthracis operons.

In this study, we propose to predict new operons in complete sequenced genomes using the similarity among genes from these genomes and genes from known operons. Therefore, we need a representative database of known operons to obtain accurate results. We used data stored in the Operon DataBase [7] which provides a data retrieval system of known operons documented in literature and also putative operons which are conserved in terms of known operons.

In Section 2, we present the criteria used to define the similarity between operons. The PROCSIMO tool is described in Section 3 and, in Section 4, we describe some experiments performed to show the accuracy of the operon prediction method. In the last section, we discuss the obtained results and show directions to improve the method.

## 2   Similarity Criteria

Azevedo [4] proposed a method to evaluate the similarity between two operons. First, each pair of genes from two operons, $O_1$ and $O_2$, are compared using the sequence comparison tool BLAST [8]. The gene pairs that present an acceptable similarity, according to BLAST, are used to evaluate the similarity between operons $O_1$ and $O_2$. The parameters adopted to define the similarity level are E-value, which is reported by BLAST, and Coverage, which is derived from the parameter Identities also reported by BLAST.

---

[1] Available in http://odb.kuicr.kyoto-u.ac.jp/

The E-value reported by BLAST, between two genes, $G_1$ and $G_2$, is a parameter that describes the number of hits one can expect to see by chance when searching genes of a particular size [9]. BLAST($G_1$,$G_2$) represents this value and lower values indicates that the number of hits is more significant.

The Coverage, represented by Cover($G_1$,$G_2$) indicates the pairwise alignment percentage, and has values in the interval $[0$ , $\frac{Identities}{number\_bases(G_2)} \times 100$ $]$, where $number\_bases(G_1) \leq number\_bases(G_2)$ and $Identities$ is a value reported by BLAST, which represents the extent to which two sequences are invariant.

For evaluating the similarity between operons $O_1$ and $O_2$, based on all pairs of genes that were considered similar according to limit values for E-value ($emax$) and Coverage ($cmin$), Azevedo [4] proposed the following similarity criteria:

– Number of Similar Genes (NSG). Two operons $O_1$ and $O_2$ present similarity level k, according to criterion NSG, if there are k similar gene pairs ($G_1$,$G_2$), where $G_1$ is a gene from $O_1$ and $G_2$ is a gene from $O_2$ or its inversion. The same gene or its inversion must not appear in more than one of these k gene pairs.
– Average E-value (AEV). The similarity level r among two operons $O_1$ and $O_2$, according to criterion AEV, is defined as the average of the E-values of the k similar gene pairs.
– Inversions Number (IN). Consider that the k similar gene pairs ($G_{11}$,$G_{21}$), ($G_{12}$,$G_{22}$), ..., ($G_{1k}$,$G_{2k}$) are organized in such a way that ($G_{1i}$,$G_{2i}$) precedes ($G_{1j}$,$G_{2j}$) if and only if $G_{1i}$ appears before $G_{1j}$ in $O_1$. In this way, the genes from $O_2$ which belong to the k pairs do not have to be in the same order and direction as they are in operon $O_2$. $O_1$ and $O_2$ present similarity level s, according to criteria IN, if s inversion operations should be made in chain $G_{21} G_{22} \ldots G_{2k}$ to obtain the same order and direction in which they are in $O_2$.
– Size Difference (SD). The similarity level d between operons $O_1$ and $O_2$, according to criteria SD, is defined as the modulus of the difference between the size of operons $O_1$ and $O_2$, where the size of an operon is considered as the number of its bases.
– Difference of Intergenic Regions (DIR). The similarity level u between operons $O_1$ and $O_2$, according to criteria DIR, is defined as the difference modulus between the average intergenic regions of operons $O_1$ and $O_2$, where an intergenic region of an operon is considered as the number of its bases located between a pair of operon genes.

# 3   The PROCSIMO Tool

In this Section, we present the functionality of the PROCSIMO tool [4] and describe how the operon prediction function was added to this tool.

## 3.1   The Tool Functionality

The PROCSIMO tool, as defined in [4], was developed to identify operons, stored in a database, which are similar to an input operon. We added a new functionality to this tool, which predict operons in complete genomes, using the same similarity criteria described in the previous section.

The tool has two modules: the Search Module and the Consult Module. The first one implements the basic tool functions: the similarity search among operons stored in a database and an input operon, and the operon prediction in complete genomes. The second one allows the user to access information about the operons stored in the database, and the genes which compose these operons.

The present tool database stores operons extracted from the Operon Database [7], and the base sequences of the operon genes were obtained from GenBank [10]. The tool administrator may include, exclude or update any database component (organism, operon or gene).

The tool was projected to enable its access via Internet using a navigator, such as Mozilla Firefox. We use the following free software tools: PERL 5.0 [11], the database server MySQL 5.0 Server [12] and the webserver Apache 2.0 [13].

## 3.2  Operon Prediction

The main contribution of this work is to add the operon prediction functionality to the PROCSIMO tool. This new functionality aims to predict operons in an input complete genome by comparing the similarity among genes from the complete genome to genes from the operon database.

The pseudo-code in Figure 1 illustrates the main steps of the developed procedure to implement this new functionality.

This procedure uses as input data: $CompleteGenome[]$, which contains the $n$ gene sequences of the complete genome; $OperonDatabase[]$, which contains the gene sequence $S[]$, the number of genes in $S[]$ ($size$), and an identifier ($IdOp$) for each of the $k$ operons; values $emax$ and $cmin$, defined by the user and used to filter the genes from the complete genome that may be in an operon.

From line 4 to line 17, all genes from $CompleteGenome[]$ are pairwise compared to all genes from $OperonDatabase[]$ using BLAST. The pairs which present $E\_value > emax$ and $Cover < cmin$ are discarded. The other pairs are inserted in $SimilarGenePairs$. From line 18 to line 22, the pairs from $SimilarGenePairs$ are grouped in subsets according to the operon identifier. Then, from line 23 to 25, for each subset, all genes from the complete genome are combined in order to find possible operons.

To exemplify this procedure execution, consider an operon $O_D$ from the database composed of genes $S_1 S_2 S_3 S_4$ and an input complete genome $CG_I$ composed of genes $G_A G_B G_C G_D G_E G_F$. After making a BLAST pairwise comparison of $(G_A, S_1), \ldots, (G_A, S_4), \ldots, (G_F, S_4)$, the gene pairs $(G_A, S_1)$, $(G_D, S_1)$, $(G_B, S_2)$, $(G_C, S_3)$, $(G_F, S_3)$, $(G_E, S_4)$ are considered similar according to values $emax$ and $cmin$. As all genes $S_i$ belong to operon $O_D$, these pairs are grouped in one subset as illustrated in Figure 2. Genes $G_A$ and $G_D$ are similar to gene $S_1$, which is located at the first position of database operon $O_D$. Gene $G_B$ is similar to gene $S_2$ located at the second position of operon $O_D$. Genes $G_C$ and $G_F$ are similar to gene $S_3$, which is located at the third position of database

```
procedure OperonPrediction(CompleteGenome[], OperonDatabase[], emax, cmin)
1.    idpairs ← 0;
2.    InvertedGenes ← Invert(CompleteGenome);
3.    CompleteGenome ← CompleteGenome ∪ InvertedGenes;
4.    for i = 1, . . . , 2n do
5.        Seq_1 ← CompleteGenome[i];
6.        for j = 1, . . . , k do
7.            for g = 1, . . . , OperonDatabase[j].size do
8.                Seq_2 ← OperonDatabase[j].S[g];
9.                Id_op ← OperonDatabase[j].IdOp;
10.               Call_BLAST(Seq_1, Seq_2, E_value, Cover);
11.               if E_value ≤ emax and Cover ≥ cmin then
12.                   Insert(SimilarGenePairs[idpairs], Seq_1, Seq_2, Id_op);
13.                   idpairs ← idpairs + 1;
14.               endif;
15.           end_for;
16.       end_for;
17.   end_for;
18.   num_subsets ← 0;
19.   for each different IdOp in SimilarGenePairs[] do
20.       SubSet[num_subset] ← GroupPairs(SimilarGenePairs[], IdOp);
21.       num_subsets ← num_subsets + 1;
22.   end_for;
23.   for i = 1, . . . , num_subsets do
24.       Operons ← Operons ∪ FindOperons(SubSet[i]);
25.   end_for;
26.   return Operons;
end.
```

**Fig. 1.** Operon prediction procedure

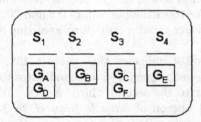

**Fig. 2.** Gene pairs arrangement in a subset

operon $O_D$, and gene $G_E$ is similar to gene $S_4$ located at the fourth position of operon $O_D$.

After identifying this subset, all genes $G_x$ are combined to build possible operons. These combinations should follow the order that these genes appear in the subset. For each possible operon position, the genes $G_x$, similar to gene $S_y$ in this position, are permuted.

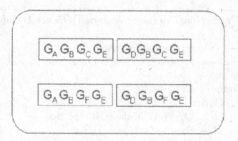

**Fig. 3.** Predicted operons

| Operon | Organism | AEV | IN | SD | DIR | Gene1 | Gene2 | Gene3 | Gene4 | Gene5 | Gene6 | Gene7 |
|--------|----------|-----|-----|-----|-----|-------|-------|-------|-------|-------|-------|-------|
| putative_11 | Shigella flexneri 2a 2457T | 0 | 0 | 13759 (putative_11>) | 2693 | X | t2139 | t2140 | t2141 | t2142 | t2143 | t2144 |
| ulaABCDEF | Escherichia coli K12 | 0 | 0 | 32 (ulaABCDEF <) | 46 | t4434 | t4435 | t4436 | t4437 | t4438 | t4439 | |
| spoT | Escherichia coli K12 | 0 | 5 | 63 (spoT <) | 1 | t3778 | t3777 | t3776 | t3775 | t3774 | | |

**Fig. 4.** Operon prediction for organism *Salmonella typhy* Ty2

Figure 3 shows all possible combinations for the subset presented in Figure 2. For this example, we have four predicted operons.

After that, for each predicted operon and its similar database operon, the tool evaluates the values associated to each similarity criterion, and the results are shown according to a precedence order defined by the user.

Figure 4 illustrates the results obtained for predicting operons of organism *Salmonella typhy* Ty2. In practice, many operons were found, so we show only three of these operons. For this example, values 0.5 and 70% were used for *emax* and *cmin* and the precedence criteria order for visualizing results is: NSG, AEV, IN, SD and DIR.

The first line of Figure 4 indicates that genes t2139, t2140, t2141, t2142, t2143 and t2144 of *Salmonella typhy* Ty2 are candidates to compose an operon. These genes were similar to the second, third, fourth, fifth, sixth and seventh genes of the putative_11 operon of *Shigella flexneri* 2a 2457T. The first gene of the putative_11 operon was not similar to any gene from the input complete genome and this is represented by 'X'. The columns AEV and IN present the value 0, which indicates a great similarity between this predicted operon and the putative_11 operon according to these criteria. Value 0 in column IN also indicates that there are no changes in order or direction among the genes of these two operons. The value 13759(*putative_11* >) in column SD indicates that the operon *putative_11* has 13759 more bases than the predicted operon. The value 2693 in column DIR indicates the average intergenic regions difference between the two operons.

The second line indicates that genes t4434, t4435, t4436, t4437, t4438 and t4439 compose a predicted operon and are similar to all genes of the operon *ulaABCDEF*. The value 0 in columns AEV and IN indicates a maximum similarity degree for these two criteria. The value $32(ulaABCDEF <)$ in column SD indicates that operon *ulaABCDEF* has 32 less bases than the predicted operon. Value 46 in column DIR indicates the average intergenic region difference between the two operons.

The third line indicates that genes t3774, t3775, t3776, t3777 and t3778 of *Salmonella typhy* Ty2 compose another predicted operon. The genes of this operon are all similar to genes of operon *spoT* from *Escherichia coli* k12. The value 0 in column AEV indicates maximum level of similarity according to this criterion. The value 5 in column IN indicates that five inversion operations should be made in the chain of the predicted operon, so that its genes present the same order and direction of genes from operon *spoT*. The value $63(spoT <)$ indicates that operon *spoT* has 63 less bases than the predicted operon and the value 1 indicates a significant level of similarity, according to DIR criterion.

# 4    Experimental Results

In this section, we present results obtained from experiments executed to validate the new functionality of PROCSIMO tool developed to predict operons in complete sequenced genomes. All base gene sequences and operons stored in the tool database were obtained from GenBank [10] and Operon DataBase [7].

For all experiments, the tool database stores genes and operons from the following 16 organisms: *Escherichia coli* K12, *Escherichia coli* O157:H7 Sakai, *Acinetobacter sp.* ADP1, *Haemophilus influenzae* KW20 Rd, *Legionella pneumophila* Paris, *Pseudomonas putida* KT2440, *Shewanella oneidensis* MR-1, *Shigella flexneri* 2a 2457T, *Vibrio parahaemolyticus* RIMD 2210633, *Xylella fastidiosa* 9a5c, *Methylococcus capsulatus* Bath, *Photorhabdus luminescens* TTO1, *Yersinia pestis* KIM, *Erwinia carotovora*, *Legionella pneumophila* Philadelphia 1 and *Vibrio vulnificus* CMCP6.

The criteria similarity order used to present the results is: (1) Number of Similar Genes (NSG) , (2) Average E-value (AEV), (3) Inversions Number (IN), (4) Size Difference (SD) and (5) Difference of Intergenic Regions (DIR).

In Sections 4.1, 4.2 and 4.3, we present obtained results of operon prediction for organisms *Salmonella typhy* Ty2, *Legionella pneumophila* Lens e *Escherichia coli* O157:H7 Sakai.

## 4.1    *Salmonella Typhy* Ty2

In this experiment, the complete genome from *Salmonella typhi* Ty2 is the input data to PROCSIMO tool. The aim is to verify the number of operons that PROCSIMO can correctly identify.

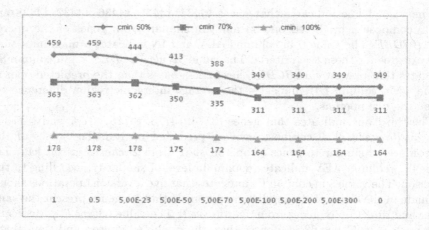

**Fig. 5.** Number of predicted operons for *Salmonella typhy* Ty2

This experiment was done using several values for *emax*: 1, 0.5, 5e-023, 5e-050, 5e-070, 5e-100, 5e-200, 5e-300 and 0, and three different values for *cmin*: 50%, 70% and 100%. Thus, combining these values, 27 queries were submitted to PROCSIMO. According to Operon Database [7], Salmonella typhi Ty2 has 191 operons.

Figure 5 shows the obtained results. Each curve represents the queries executed for the same *cmin* value and different *emax* values. Each point indicates the number of predicted operons. For example, for query using *emax* equal to 1 and *cmin* equal to 50%, the tool identified 459 operons for the organism *Salmonella typhy* Ty2.

To verify the tool accuracy, we evaluated the number of the predicted operons which are indeed real operons from *Salmonella typhy* Ty2. Figure 6 illustrates the obtained results. Using *emax* = 1 and *cmin* = 50%, 459 operons were predicted by the tool, among which 98 are real operons of *Salmonella typhy* Ty2.

We observe in Figures 5 and 6 that, as we decrease *emax* and increase *cmin*, the number of predicted operons and the number of real operons returned by the tool decrease, because these parameter values make queries more restrictive.

To verify the efficiency of this tool compared to another operon prediction tool, we used the tool proposed in [7], which is available via Internet, for the same input organism *Salmonella typhy* Ty2. This tool predicted 857 operons, in simple mode execution, among which only 71 were real operons.

Thus, we can conclude that, for this experiment, PROCSIMO tool returns less false positives and more real operons than the tool presented in [7].

### 4.2  *Legionella Pneumophila* Lens

In this experiment, the complete genome from *Legionella pneumophila* Lens is the input data to PROCSIMO tool. The values 0 and 100% were used for

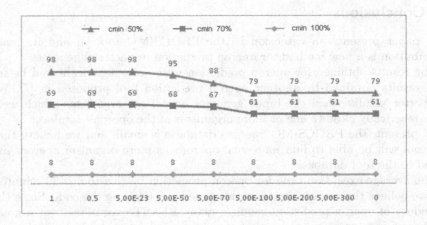

**Fig. 6.** Number of real operons obtained by the tool for *Salmonella typhy* Ty2

*emax* and *cmin*, because they make the query more restrictive and the obtained predicted operons present more similarity to operons database.

According to Operon Database [7], the organism *Legionella pneumophila* Lens has 51 operons. The tool predicted 80 operons, among which 44 are real operons. The tool defined in [7], in simple mode execution, predicted 620 operons, among which 25 are real operons.

The reason for obtaining this significant result by PROCSIMO is that all genes from *Legionella pneumophila* Lens are similar to genes of *Legionella pneumophila* Paris or *Legionella pneumophila* Philadelphia 1. These organisms are phylogenetically close and have the same genus in a taxonomic rank [14].

### 4.3   *Escherichia Coli* O157:H7 Sakai

In this experiment, the complete genome from *Escherichia coli* O157:H7 Sakai is the input data to PROCSIMO tool. For this experiment, the database stores operons of 15 organisms, because the operons from the organism *Escherichia coli* O157:H7 Sakai were excluded from the database. The values 0 and 100% were used for *emax* and *cmin*.

The organism *Escherichia coli* O157:H7 Sakai has 249 operons, according to Operon Database [7]. PROCSIMO obtained 429 predicted operons, among which 186 are real operons.

The tool in [7], in simple execution mode, returned 981 operons, among which 94 are real operons.

We can explain this significant result obtained by PROCSIMO by observing that genes from *Escherichia coli* O157:H7 Sakai are similar to genes from operons of organisms *Escherichia coli* K12 and *Shigella flexneri* 2a 2457T. The organisms *Escherichia coli* K12 and *Escherichia coli* O157:H7 Sakai are from the same species in a taxonomic rank, and the organisms *Escherichia coli* O157:H7 Sakai and *Shigella flexneri* 2a 2457T are from the same family in a taxonomic rank [14].

# 5    Conclusions

This paper presents an extension to the PROCSIMO tool [4] and its main contribution is a new method for operon prediction in bacterial genomes.

The results obtained for operon prediction were quite significant and better than results obtained by another operon prediction tool proposed in [7]. We got better results when the input genomes were from organisms which were phylogenetically close to one or more organisms of the operons database.

At present, the PROCSIMO operons database is small, and we believe that this tool will be able to find more real operons as more organism operons are stored in the tool database.

The average execution time for operon prediction by this tool is 30 minutes, and we believe that we can decrease this time by optimizing the code. Since the procedure of operon prediction requires many BLAST executions over a great number of gene pairs, we think that a code parallelization could be performed in order to decrease the processing time.

# References

1. Bergman, N.H., Passalacqua, K.D., Hanna, P., Qin, Z.S.: Operon prediction for sequenced bacterial genomes without experimental information. Applied and Environmental Microbiology 73, 846–854 (2007)
2. Ermolaeva, M.D., White, O., Salzberg, S.L.: Prediction of operons in microbial genomes. Nucleic Acids Research 29, 1216–1221 (2001)
3. Hodgman, T.C.: A historical perspective on gene/protein functional assignment. Bioinformatics 16, 10–15 (2000)
4. Azevedo, C.V.: Procura de similaridade entre operons. Master's thesis, Departamento de Ciência da Computação, Universidade Federal Fluminense, Niterói (2003)
5. Craven, M., Page, D., Shavlik, J., Bockhorst, J., Glasner, J.: A probabilistic learning approach to whole-genome operon prediction. In: Proceedings of the 8th International Conference on Intelligent Systems for Molecular Biology, pp. 116–127 (2000)
6. Moreno-Hagelsieb, G., Collado-Vides, J.: A powerful non-homology method for the prediction of operons in prokaryotes. Bioinformatics 18, S329–S336 (2002)
7. Okuda, S., Katayama, T., Kawashima, S., Goto, S., Kanehisa, M.: Odb: a database of operons accumulating known operons across multiple genomes. Nucleic Acids Research 34, D358–D362 (2005)
8. Altschul, S.F., Gish, W., Miller, W., Myers, E.W., Lipman, D.J.: Basic local alignment search tool. Journal of Molecular Biology 215, 403–410 (1990)
9. Korf, I., Yandell, M., Bedell, J.: BLAST: An Essential Guide to the Basic Local Alignment Search Tool, 1st edn. O'Reilly & Associates, Sebastopol (2003)
10. Benson, D.A., Karsch-Mizrachi, I., Lipman, D.J., Ostell, J., Wheeler, D.L.: Genbank. Nucleic Acids Research 35, D21–D25 (2007)
11. Perl: The Perl Directory - perl. org. (2005), www.perl.org
12. MySQL: Database server (2005), www.mysql.com
13. Apache: Apache: Servidor WEB (2005), http://httpd.apache.org/
14. NCBI: National Center for Biotechnology Information (2007), http://www.ncbi.nlm.nih.gov/sites/entrez?db=taxonomy

# An Evaluation of the Impact of Side Chain Positioning on the Accuracy of Discrete Models of Protein Structures*

Miguel M.F. Bugalho and Arlindo L. Oliveira

INESC-ID/IST, R. Alves Redol 9, 1000 LISBOA, Portugal
mmfb@kdbio.inesc-id.pt, aml@inesc-id.pt

**Abstract.** Discrete models are important to reduce the complexity of the protein folding problem. However, a compromise must be made between the model complexity and the accuracy of the model.

Previous work by Park and Levitt has shown that the protein backbone can be modeled with good accuracy by four state discrete models. Nonetheless, for ab-initio protein folding, the side chains are important to determine if the structure is physically possible and well packed.

We extend the work of Park and Levitt by taking into account the positioning of the side chain in the evaluation of the accuracy. We show that the problem becomes much harder and more dependent on the type of protein being modeled. In fact, the structure fitting method used in their work is no longer adequate to this extended version of the problem. We propose a new method to test the model accuracy.

The presented results show that, for some proteins, the discrete models with side chains cannot achieve the accuracy of the backbone only discrete models. Nevertheless, for the majority of the proteins an RMSD of four angstrom or less is obtained, and, for many of those, we reach an accuracy near the two angstrom limit. These results prove that discrete models can be used in protein folding to obtain low resolution models. Since the side chains are already present in the models, the refinement of these solutions is simpler and more effective.

**Keywords:** Protein models, discrete state models, side chain positioning, protein folding.

## 1 Introduction

The ab-initio protein folding problem consists in determining the structure of a protein using only the information of its amino acid sequence. Even extremely simplified versions of this problem have been proved to be NP-Hard [1,2,3,4].

In a protein structure there are several structural constrains. For the atomic angles and bond lengths the variation is small and, thus, the majority of the folding algorithms focus on the dihedral angles. In addition to the structural

* Partially supported by project Biogrid POSI/SRI/47778/2002 and by the Portuguese Science and Technology Foundation by grant SFRH/BD/13215/2003.

A.L.C. Bazzan, M. Craven, and N.F. Martins (Eds.): BSB 2008, LNBI 5167, pp. 23–34, 2008.

constrains, the protein structures are defined by the atomic interactions. Although the dihedral angles have optimal values they usually assume different values to allow for interactions between atoms.

In the context of this work, a discrete state model is an all heavy atoms protein model that uses a discrete set for the possible values of the dihedral angles. The atomic bond lengths and angles are considered fixed at the optimal values. Previous work [5] has shown that discrete state models with a limited number of states (four) can describe proteins with relatively good accuracy. In that work the authors have also shown that, for the same degree of complexity, off lattice discrete state models are more accurate than lattice models.

In the work of Park and Levitt only the main chain is used and no consideration is made for clashes between atoms. In this work we will analyze the accuracy of discrete state models using an all heavy atoms representation and disallowing atomic clashes. Using all heavy atoms representations requires positioning of the side chains. A simple positioning method based in rotamer libraries is proposed.

## 1.1  Motivation

Although important studies on the accuracy and application of discrete models were published more then 10 years ago [5,6], discrete models are still being studied and applied to problems in recently published works. Discrete models are used in studies for ab-initio protein folding [7,8]. Recent works also use discrete models for generating ensembles of structures [9,10]. The study of discrete protein models is, therefore, highly relevant. Although the models presented by Park and Levitt are used in protein folding problems, the models were only shown to be accurate for modeling the backbone. Using only backbone models can produce physically impossible models. Moreover, depending on the scoring function, these models may have a high score and may be chosen as the best model. Therefore, to avoid physically impossible models, we have extended this work by considering side chain position and atomic clashes.

Discrete models are particulary fit to perform high level structure search, since the search space is greatly reduced and very similar structures can be more easily avoided. The applicability of the discrete models relies on the solution of three difficulties, since discrete models:

- Require a scoring function that can ignore the atomic details giving high scores to physically inexact, near native structures.
- Need a search technique that can efficiently search the structure space without enumerating all the structures, since the space size is still exponential on the size of the protein.
- Need to use a set of dihedral angle values that can accurately model the protein. An accurate model must have a low root mean square distance to the native structure but must also have feasible physical properties like: secondary structure, atomic contacts and lack of atomic clashes. This is important since the scoring function must be able to find, in the models, characteristics that are similar to the characteristics of native protein.

The first difficulty can be solved using a statistical scoring function. The second is the final step towards finding a near native structure and a number of techniques have been proposed. However, the search will only work if a good discrete model is available. The third difficulty is, therefore, the focus of this work.

As referred before, the model must be able not only to approximate the atomic positions of the native structure, but also to avoid unfeasible structures, *e.g.* structures with atomic clashes or unrealistic side chain conformations. Therefore, we will analyze the accuracy of known discrete models, while considering clashes and side chain positioning.

## 2    Side Chain Positioning

One of the most used methods for side chain positioning is based on the use of rotamers libraries. In this work we used the Dunbrack Backbone-Dependent Rotamer Library [11,12,13,14] which contains information about each amino acid side chain. For each amino acid, the library has the side chain dihedral angle values indexed by the backbone $\phi/\psi$ pairs in slots of 10 degrees. The library also contains the observed frequency of the side chain dihedral angles in the particular slot. To reduce the number of possible conformations we used the frequency information contained in the library to prune less probable configurations. Unless otherwise stated, a 0.04 (4%) frequency cutoff was used.

The decision to use a rotamer method was made for two reasons:

- The method creates a discretized set of highly probable configurations. This avoids the usage of continuous minimization methods.
- Since the rotamers are indexed by $\phi$ and $\psi$ backbone angles, there is no need to verify clashes between atoms of the same amino acid.

In this paper we present a simple positioning algorithm that tests the possible rotamer conformations until a valid conformation is found. The frequency information is used to establish the testing order. Rotamers that occur more frequently in known proteins will be tested first. Notice that we only want to verify if there is a possible side chain configuration and not to set the best one. The best side chain conformation can be set in the end during refinement using, for example, the SCWRL program [15], which sets the side chain using a graph theory based algorithm and an energy function. Since SCWRL does not change the backbone it is essential that sufficient space is left for the side chains.

After choosing a possible configuration, the algorithm continues to construct the protein model by extending the backbone configuration. However, this particular choice of the side chain configuration can be changed latter. The side chain is modified if, afterwards, that particular side chain configuration prevents other side chains from being positioned. When a clash between side chains is detected (no changes in previous backbone atoms are allowed) the algorithm sets the new side chain in the configuration with less conflicts and tries to reconfigure the old side chain. If a new side chain conflict is found the process is restarted

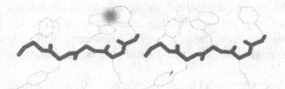

**Fig. 1.** Example of a successful side chain reconfiguration. Both the backbone, stronger lines, and the side chains are represented. The red sphere shows the side chain conflict between the new side chain and a previously set side chain. A new configuration is chosen for the older side chain by rotating it to the opposite side of the new side chain position.

until a predefined threshold for the number of side chain changes is reached. Figure 1 shows a example of successful side chain reconfiguration.

If an unresolvable conflict is found, like a side chain versus backbone conflict, or the backtrack threshold is reached, the algorithm considers that there is not enough space for the side chain and reports a clash. To avoid loops the algorithm does not allow for the same side chain to be changed twice.

## 3  Discrete State Model

Previous work [5] has tested various discrete state models and presented some reasonably accurate sets of states. The test made by Park and Levitt consisted in fitting the discrete models into the backbone of the known structure. The side chains, and possible clashes between atoms, were not considered in the fitting problem. In this section we will analyze some of the models described by Park and Levitt in a test platform that considers side chains and atomic clashes.

Table 1 shows the discrete models previously proposed [5]. We used four of these discrete models: three four states models and one six states model. We have chosen the Rooman et al. six states model since it obtained better results than the one proposed by Park and Levitt. In the four states models, we chose model C because it was the best model, and model A because it obtained the best results for the Alpha and Beta secondary structures. Model G was chosen randomly from the rest.

**Table 1.** Discrete State models used in the work of Park and Levitt [5]. The * signals the models used in this work.

| Name | Set of Pairs of Angles | Name | Set of Pairs of Angles |
|---|---|---|---|
| * A | (-64,-40),(-123,134),(111,-46),(117,105) | B | (-66,-40),(-119,114),(-36,124),(132,-40) |
| * C | (-63,-63),(-132,115),(-42,-41),(-44,127) | D | (-58,-31),(-127,126),(-97,-24),(109,108) |
| E | (-71,-57),(-131,122),(-42,-36),( 107,-25) | F | (-58,-51),(-133,135),(-33,174),(114,-40) |
| * G | (-56,-48),(-129,128),(-108,35),(-31,-109) | H | (-74,-31),(-131,125),(-101,179),(105,-40) |
| 6 states | (-57,-47),(-139,135),(-119,113), | * Rooman | (-65,-42),(-123,139),(-70,138), |
| | (-49,-26),(-106,48),(-101,-127) | et al.[6] | (-87,-47),(77,22),(107,-174) |

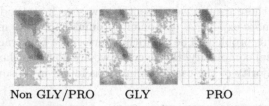

Non GLY/PRO    GLY      PRO

**Fig. 2.** Ramachandran plots for the proline (right), glycine (center) and other types of amino acids (left). Figures taken from the web site of Deniz Yuret (http://www.denizyuret.com/bio/).

If we analyze the angle sets in terms of physical correction, we can notice that only the best model, C, is near the probable zones of the Ramachandran plot [16]. The Ramachandran plots depict the probability distribution for the $\phi$ and $\psi$ angles in known proteins. Although a model might be near the true structure even if the angles in that model fall outside the most probable zone, the torsion angles will probably be very different from the true angles. Figure 2 shows examples of Ramachandran plots. Nevertheless, the torsion angles (or dihedral angles) errors made by the models can be easily corrected in refinement steps. Therefore we will focus on the correction of the overall structure.

## 4 Testing Method

We used an efficient clash detection algorithm [17], and the side chain positioning algorithm presented earlier. To set the side chains we used a maximum number of possible alterations (see section 2) equal to the number of amino acids divided by 10.

We have first tried the algorithm presented by Park and Levitt [5] for testing discrete state models. The algorithm does a simple beam search using the RMSD distance as the scoring function. In a beam search, $n$ states are saved at any given time. Considering that there are $m$ choices in an $m$ state discrete model, the algorithm starts by testing the first $m$ choices. The algorithm then chooses the best $n$ states and tests all the choices for each of those states ($n \times m$ tests). The best $n$ states are chosen and the same steps are iterated until the final configurations are reached.

Although the beam search method obtained good results in the backbone only problem [5], for the problem presented here the results were much worse. In fact, when the protein size was greater than 80 amino acids, a solution with an RMSD near five angstrom was difficult to obtain with this method. The beam search approach is a non exact method. An explanation for this, already presented by Park and Levitt [5] for the backbone fitting problem, is that the neglected search states, although with worse RMSD values at the time they were removed from search, may in reality provide better fits in the long run. With side chains, this problem is greatly aggravated, since many states will prove to be dead ends, because of collisions, or will just be driven away from the best fit because of them. Because of these results we present a new search method that, although computationally more expensive (exponential number of tests instead of $n \times m$ tests), can avoid this problem. The algorithm performs a backtrack search having therefor exponential complexity. However, as we are going to show in the results section, in the majority of the cases a solution is found in reasonable time.

---

**Algorithm 1.** Testing method for the discrete models

---

1: **procedure** FITMODEL(**Pdb,Model**)
2:      **RmsdLimit** = 5
3:      Start with the first amino acid of the sequence
4:      **while** RmsdLimit $> 1$ and there is a possible $(\phi, \psi)$ pair **do**
5:          Choose $argmin_{(\phi, \psi)}$ RMSD ({non tested $(\phi, \psi)$ pairs of **Model**})
6:          **if** RMSD<**RmsdLimit** and no backbone clash with previous atoms **then**
7:              **for all** rotamers indexed by $(\phi, \psi)$ **do**
8:                  **if** the side chain does not clash with any previous atom **then**
9:                      Set the **Next Amino Acid**
10:             **if** no side chain was found **then**
11:                 Choose rotamer with less conflicts and change previous side chains
12:                 **if** no correction is possible **then**
13:                     Execute a **Backtrack**
14:                 **else**
15:                     Set the **Next Amino Acid**
16:         **else**
17:             Execute a **Backtrack**

**procedure** BACKTRACK          ▷ The chosen $(\phi, \psi)$ pair is not a possible configuration
    **if** $\exists$ non tested $(\phi, \psi)$ pairs of **Model then**
        Test the next $(\phi, \psi)$ pair with lowest RMSD (step 5)
    **else**
        Backtrack to previous amino acid,test next lowest RMSD $(\phi, \psi)$ pair (step 4)

**procedure** NEXT AMINO ACID                          ▷ A valid conformation was found
    **if** this is the last amino acid of the sequence **then**
        **RmsdLimit** = **RmsdLimit** - **0.2**
        Re-evaluate this amino acid with the new limit (step 5)
    **else**
        Set the next amino acid (step 4)

---

Each discrete state model is tested by searching in the discrete state search space. Algorithm 1 presents the testing method proposed in this work. The search is performed by fitting the model to the real protein, using a best first approach with backtrack. For each amino acid, if the backbone conformation with lowest RMSD has no conflict with the previously set atoms, and if a non conflicting rotamer configuration is found, the algorithm sets the atoms and tries to set the next amino acid (running the *Next Amino Acid* procedure). During this step, previous side chains may be repositioned to accommodate the new amino acid atoms. If a clash is found that cannot be resolved or if the root mean square distance between the model and the protein exceeds a given threshold, the algorithm backtracks (running the *Backtrack* procedure). While backtracking, one of two actions occurs: if some of the possible configurations for the backbone were not tested the algorithm chooses the next conformation with lowest RMSD; if all configurations were tested the algorithm returns to the previously set amino acid and resumes its main procedure.

The algorithm starts with a minimum RMSD threshold of 5 angstrom and decrements 0.2 angstrom each time a model is found for the previous threshold. The algorithm stops if one of the following conditions is met: a 1 angstrom RMSD threshold limit is reached, no more configurations are possible or a time limit of one hour for each one hundred amino acids is reached. We considered different thresholds for the side chain rotamer library (see section 2). In addition to the 4% default value, we also tried 1%, 0.1% and without any cutoff (complete rotamer library). Since there is a time limit, considering more rotamers or a more complex model may or may not produce better results.

## 5 Results

To test the accuracy of discrete models we compiled a set of protein structures of increasing size. The proteins also differ in terms of secondary structure composition (Alpha Beta, Mainly Alpha and Mainly Beta proteins). Table 2 shows the set of chosen proteins and figure 3 shows the respective structures.

We have chosen different types of proteins and different sizes to study the impact of these features in the precision of the discrete models. We decided to focus our choice in globular proteins which are more packed and therefore more difficult.

Figure 4 shows the results using side chains cutoff of 4% and 1%. Figure 5 shows the results when using 0.1% and the complete rotamer library.

From the results in figure 4 it is possible to verify that, for the majority of the proteins an accurate model can be found. However, for some proteins, it is hard to find a model and, in some cases, no model can be found. For the smaller proteins (less that 100 amino acids), in the cases where an accurate model was found, the

**Table 2.** Protein data set

| Name | Size | Type | Name | Size | Type |
|------|------|------|------|------|------|
| 1r69 | 63 | Mainly Alpha | 1co6 | 107 | Mainly Alpha |
| 1aho | 65 | Alpha Beta | 1a1x | 107 | Manly Beta (beta barrel) |
| 1ctf | 69 | Alpha Beta | 1mai | 120 | Alpha Beta |
| 1hyp | 75 | Manly Alpha | 1vhh | 157 | Alpha Beta |
| 1poh | 85 | Alpha Beta | 1b56 | 134 | Manly Beta (beta barrel) |
| 1opd | 86 | Alpha Beta | 1kao | 167 | Alpha Beta |
| 1o5u | 88 | All Beta (beta helix) | 1pt6 | 192 | Alpha Beta |
| 1tig | 89 | Alpha Beta | 1vec | 206 | Alpha Beta |
| 1bm8 | 100 | Alpha Beta | 1tjy | 316 | Alpha Beta |
| 1e9m | 106 | Alpha Beta | 1pot | 322 | Alpha Beta |

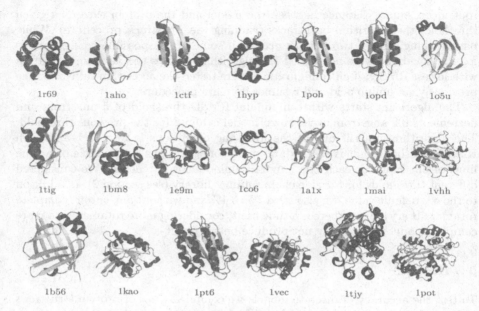

**Fig. 3.** Protein data set

results are consistent with the ones obtained for the backbone fitting problem [5] (2.22 to 2.43 angstrom for the four states models and 1.74 for the six states model). The problem is much easier in this case since the error accumulation in the fitting will be small, and also because many of the side chains can be positioned by choosing a conformation that points to the exterior of the protein.

The side chain will only affect the fit in places where the protein is more compact. In those places, the minor errors in the discrete state models may not provide enough space for the side chains to be positioned. It is possible that a better fit exists even for the larger proteins, however, the fitting problem is NP Hard and the size of the problem does not allow for a complete search. Nevertheless, a less than 5 angstrom fit was found even for the larger proteins.

The cases where the results are worse in the side chain discrete models happen mainly with proteins with a large number of beta structures (1o5u) or that have a dense core (1vhh). In the first case, because the flexibility of the beta structures is harder to model and in the second case, because it is harder to pack the atoms.

We also verify that, for the four states models, the best results are obtained by the A model for the 4% and by the C model for the 1% cutoff. For the results on the 1% cutoff the A model performs better in the proteins with more beta structures. This is expected since the A model dihedral angles represent better the beta structures and the C model the alpha structures. However, the beta structures are flexible and even the A model cannot fully represent them. Therefor the C model will normally perform better then the A model, unless the fitting error in beta structures is too great to be recovered from, or the number of beta structures is high. That is probably the case with the 4% cutoff. In this

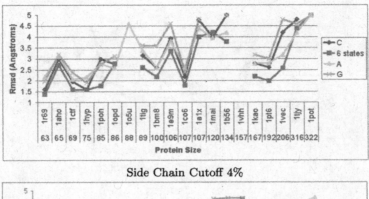

Side Chain Cutoff 4%

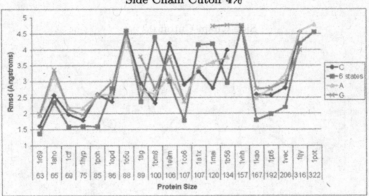

**Fig. 4.** Results of the Discrete State Models Using Side Chain cutoff of 4% and 1%

case, the errors are greater and the search algorithm for the C model cannot a find a reasonable fit for the beta structures (for instance: two strands must be placed further apart because the side chains collide).

The six states model performs better than the four states models. However, the increase in the performance would probably not compensate for the increase in search space in a search procedure. Notice that, in this problem we are using the root mean square distance (RMSD) instead of the scoring functions used in ab-initio folding. The information given by a scoring function is less precise and the space that needs to be searched is much greater, even in a four state model. In a six state model that space will be even greater. We can probably achieve the same result from a four states model after a refinement process and we would benefit greatly from the smaller size of the search space during the search process. From figures 4 and 5 we can see the impact of the size of the rotamer library in the search. The performance of the models usually increases with the size of the rotamer library. However it is possible to verify that, for the bigger or more compact proteins, the performance sometimes decreases. For instance, for the 0.1% cutoff, the C model in 1poh and all models in 1e9m perform worse

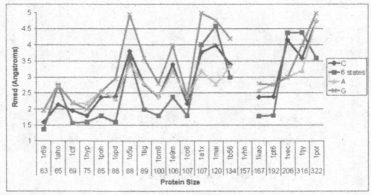

Side Chain Cutoff 0.1%

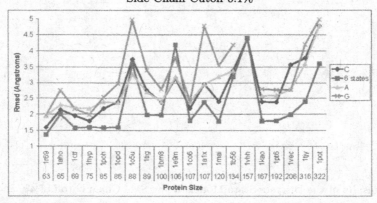

**Fig. 5.** Results of the Discrete State Models Using Side Chain cutoff of 0.1 percent and using all side chains in the rotamer library

than in the 4% cutoff. When we avoid the cutoff we can see this result again (6 state model for the 1e9m protein). This happens because, when we increase the size of the library, a greater number of side chain conformations may be tested. Consequently, although some conflicts may now be avoidable, the cost of the extra tests might not allow for the same number of conformations to be tested. This increase of time for each side chain positioning will have an even greater impact in an ab-initio search algorithm, since no exact measure like the RMSD exists. Without an exact measure, the number of wrong conformations searched will be much greater and the increased computational cost of the enlarged library will further decrease the performance.

The type of model used and the threshold limit will have to be chosen according to the type of proteins (specially their secondary structure and size) and the search algorithm. For a search algorithm, with no specific information, a four states model, specially a generic one like the C model, with a side chain threshold of 1% will probably have best results because of the increase in the size of the searched space. If the protein is small, there are fewer possible conformations, and more detailed models can be found using more rotamers or even using the six states model. For specific cases, where there is some information about the protein, a model that increases the performance can probably be built.

Notice that if we use a threshold limit of, for instance, five angstrom, and we cannot find a model, we cannot be sure that no model can reach a 5 angstrom RMSD. When we stop the model construction, it is above the threshold, but subsequent choices could lower the RMSD. We chose not to pursue an exact solution since we needed to explore an search space that would be exponential to the size of the protein *i.e.* the time needed for the search would be to high even for the smaller proteins.

# 6   Discussion

The results show that, although the discrete models presented previously [5] are well optimized for backbone fitting, when side chains are used and clashes are disallowed the accuracy decreases greatly for some proteins.

For small proteins the problem does not exist, since the side chains may be set to the outside of the structure. However, for larger proteins, especially for proteins with beta sheets, the accuracy is significantly lower than the one obtained for the backbone only tests. However, it is possible to obtain structures with root mean square error close or lower than 4 angstrom, which is still a very good, low detail, representation for the protein and a good starting point for the refinement algorithms. Moreover, for many proteins the results are near the 2 angstrom RMSD value and have, therefore, an accuracy equivalent to the backbone discrete models. The results also show that above a determined protein size the RMSD of the obtained models depends more on the type of the protein than on the size increase *i.e.* even for the bigger proteins good models can be obtained.

Since even low detail structures are very useful to determine protein function, these results show that the presented discrete models may be used in ab-initio protein folding. Furthermore, in the protein folding process, one important aspect is that the scoring function is well adapted to the model that is being used. The model must be able to represent the positive and negative aspects of the structure, in a way that the scoring function can detect. With this work we not only prove that we can obtain a near the native protein structure, but also, by considering side chains and disallowing clashes, we have already obtained physically correct structures. This reduces the noise for the scoring function, since positive aspects of a structure, like the proximity of two amino acids, could be present in a physically impossible structure.

In future work we propose to study efficient algorithms to search near native conformations in the discrete state model space.

# References

1. Fraenkel, A.S.: Complexity of protein folding. Bulletin of Mathematical Biology 55(6), 1199–1210 (1993)
2. Crescenzi, P., Goldman, D., Papadimitriou, C.H., Piccolboni, A., Yannakakis, M.: On the complexity of protein folding. Journal of Computational Biology 5(3), 423–466 (1998)
3. Berger, B., Leighton, T.: Protein folding in the hydrophobic-hydrophilic (HP) is NP-complete. In: Proceedings of the Second Annual International Conference on Computational Molecular Biology, pp. 30–39 (1998)
4. Hart, W.E., Istrail, S.: Robust proofs of NP-hardness for protein folding: general lattices and energy potentials. Journal of Computational Biology 4(1), 1–22 (1997)
5. Park, B.H., Levitt, M.: The complexity and accuracy of discrete state models of protein structure. Journal of Molecular Biology 249, 493–507 (1995)
6. Rooman, M.J., Kocher, J.P., Wodak, S.J.: Prediction of protein backbone conformation based on seven structure assignments. Influence of local interactions. Journal of Molecular Biology 221(3), 961–979 (1991)
7. Gibbs, N., Clarke, A.R., Sessions, R.B.: Ab initio protein structure prediction using physicochemical potentials and a simplified off-lattice model. Proteins Structure Function and Genetics 43(2), 186–202 (2001)
8. Huang, E.S., Koehl, P., Levitt, M., Pappu, R.V., Ponder, J.W.: Accuracy of side-chain prediction upon near-native protein backbones generated by ab initio folding methods. Proteins Structure Function and Genetics 33(2), 204–217 (1998)
9. Ma, B., Nussinov, R.: The Stability of Monomeric Intermediates Controls Amyloid Formation: A $\beta$ 25-35 and its N27Q Mutant. Biophysical Journal 90(10), 3365–3374 (2006)
10. DePristo, M.A., de Bakker, P.I.W., Lovell, S.C., Blundell, T.L.: Ab initio construction of polypeptide fragments: Efficient generation of accurate, representative ensembles. Proteins Structure Function and Genetics 51(1), 41–55 (2003)
11. Dunbrack, R.L., Karplus, M.: Conformational analysis of the backbone-dependent rotamer preferences of protein sidechains. Nature Structural Biology 1(5), 334–340 (1994)
12. Dunbrack Jr., R.L.: Rotamer libraries in the 21st century. Current Opinion in Structural Biology 12(4), 431–440 (2002)
13. Dunbrack Jr., R.L., Cohen, F.E.: Bayesian statistical analysis of protein side-chain rotamer preferences. Protein Science 6(8), 1661–1681 (1997)
14. Dunbrack Jr., R.L., Karplus, M.: Backbone-dependent rotamer library for proteins. Application to side-chain prediction. Journal of Molecular Biology 230(2), 543–574 (1993)
15. Canutescu, A.A., Shelenkov, A.A., Dunbrack, R.L.: A graph-theory algorithm for rapid protein side-chain prediction. Protein Science 12(9), 2001–2014 (2003)
16. Ramakrishnan, C., Ramachandran, G.N.: Stereochemical criteria for polypeptide and protein chain conformations: II. Allowed conformations for a pair of peptide units. Biophysical Journal 5(6), 909 (1965)
17. Bugalho, M., Oliveira, A.L.: An efficient clash detection method for molecular structures. Technical Report 21, INESC-ID (August 2007)

# Top-Down Hierarchical Ensembles of Classifiers for Predicting G-Protein-Coupled-Receptor Functions

Eduardo P. Costa[1], Ana C. Lorena[2], André C.P.L.F. Carvalho[1], and Alex A. Freitas[3]

[1] Depto. Ciências de Computação
ICMC/USP - São Carlos - Caixa Postal 668
13560-970 - São Carlos-SP, Brazil
{ecosta,andre}@icmc.usp.br
[2] Universidade Federal do ABC
09.210-170 - Santo André-SP, Brazil
ana.lorena@ufabc.edu.br
[3] Computing Laboratory and Centre for BioMedical Informatics
University of Kent, Canterbury, CT2 7NF, UK
a.a.freitas@kent.ac.uk

**Abstract.** Despite the recent advances in Molecular Biology, the function of a large amount of proteins is still unknown. An approach that can be used in the prediction of a protein function consists of searching against secondary databases, also known as signature databases. Different strategies can be applied to use protein signatures in the prediction of function of proteins. A sophisticated approach consists of inducing a classification model for this prediction. This paper applies five hierarchical classification methods based on the standard Top-Down approach and one hierarchical classification method based on a new approach named Top-Down Ensembles - based on the hierarchical combination of classifiers - to three different protein functional classification datasets that employ protein signatures. The algorithm based on the Top-Down Ensembles approach presented slightly better results than the other algorithms, indicating that combinations of classifiers can improve the performance of hierarchical classification models.

## 1 Introduction

Proteins are large organic compounds that perform almost all the functions related to cell activity, such as biochemical reactions, cell signaling, structural and mechanical functions. These large molecules consist of long sequences of amino acids, which fold into specific structures so that the protein can function properly.

In functional genomic, an important problem is the prediction of the function of proteins. Due to the recent advances in Molecular Biology methods and the

A.L.C. Bazzan, M. Craven, and N.F. Martins (Eds.): BSB 2008, LNBI 5167, pp. 35–46, 2008.

consequent generation of biological data in large scale, data analysis has become a central issue for the investigation of proteins whose functions are unknown.

An approach that can be used in the prediction of a protein function involves searching against secondary databases, also known as signature databases. These databases contain results of analysis performed in primary databases, which contain linear sequences of amino acids, and can be used to verify the presence of particular patterns in the query proteins. These patterns represent information about conserved motifs in proteins, which are frequently useful to help the prediction of protein functions. Protein signatures can be used to assign a query protein to a specific family of proteins and thus to formulate hypotheses about its function [1]. Examples of signature databases include InterPro [2], Prosite [3], Pfam [4] and Prints [5].

Different strategies can be applied to use protein signatures in the prediction of function of proteins. A sophisticated approach consists of inducing a classification model for this prediction. Accordingly, each protein is represented by an attribute set, describing the presence or absence of patterns in the protein, and a learning algorithm captures the most important relationships between the attributes and the classes involved in the classification problem.

In the context of prediction of protein function, a classification model needs to be induced according to a special kind of classification problem named hierarchical classification, since protein functional data is inherently hierarchical (for example, the Enzyme Commission hierarchy [6]).

In this paper, three protein function datasets are analyzed - each one employing one different kind of protein signature - for a comparative study among six hierarchical classification algorithms. The algorithm based on the Top-Down Ensembles approach - a variation of the Top-Down approach that uses combination of classifiers for the induction of the classification model - presented better results across the three different kinds of protein signatures - Prosite, Pfam and Prints. The main contribution of this paper is to show that combinations of classifiers can improve the performance of hierarchical classification models, a result that was consistent even for different types of protein signatures.

The paper is organized as follows: Section 2 introduces important concepts of hierarchical classification; Section 3 introduces the Top-Down Ensembles approach; Section 4 discusses the materials and methods employed in the experiments performed in this work; Section 5 presents the experimental results; and Section 6 has the main conclusions from this work.

## 2   Hierarchical Classification

Classification is one of the most important problems in Machine Learning (ML) and Data Mining (DM) [7]. Given a dataset composed of $n$ pairs $(\mathbf{x}_i, y_i)$, where each $\mathbf{x}_i$ is a data item (example) and $y_i$ represents its class, a classification algorithm must find a function, through a training or adjustment phase, which maps each data item to its correct class.

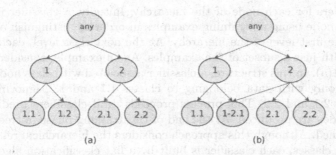

**Fig. 1.** Examples of hierarchies of classes: (a) Tree and (b) DAG

Conventional classification problems involve a finite (and usually small) set of flat classes. Each example is assigned to a class out of this set, in which the classes do not have direct relationships to each other, such as subclass and superclass relationships. For this reason, these classification problems are named flat classification problems. Nevertheless, there are more complex classification problems where the classes to be predicted are hierarchically related [8,9,10]. These problems are known in the ML literature as hierarchical classification problems.

The classes involved in a hierarchical classification problem can be disposed either as a tree or as a Directed Acyclic Graph (DAG). The main difference between these structures is that, in the tree structure (Figure 1.a), each node has just one parent node, while in the DAG structure (Figure 1.b), each node may have more than one parent. The nodes represent the classes involved in the classification problem and the root node corresponds to "any class", denoting a total absence of knowledge about the class of an object.

The deeper the class in the hierarchy, the more specific and useful is its associated knowledge in the classification of a new data item. Hierarchical classification problems often have as objective to assigning a data item into one of the leaf nodes. It may be the case, however, that the classifier does not have the desired reliability to classify a data item into deeper classes. In this case, it would be safer to perform a classification into higher levels of the hierarchy. When all examples must be associated to classes in leaf nodes, the classification problem is named "mandatory leaf node prediction problem". When this obligation does not hold, the classification problem is an "optional leaf node prediction problem".

A simple approach to deal with a hierarchical classification problem consists of reducing it into one or more flat classification problems. This reduction is possible because a flat classification problem may be viewed as a particular case of hierarchical classification, in which there are no subclasses and superclasses. However, the main disadvantage of this approach is to ignore the hierarchical relationships among the classes, which can provide valuable information for the induction of a classification model. Two more sophisticated approaches that consider these relationships are the Top-Down and Big-Bang approaches [8].

The Top-Down approach uses the "divide and conquer" principle to induce the classification model. The main idea of this approach is to produce one or more classifiers for each node of the hierarchy. Initially, a classifier is induced for the root node using all training examples in order to distinguish among the classes at the first level of the hierarchy. At the next class level, each classifier is trained with just a subset of the examples. As an example, consider the class tree of Fig. 1(a). In this structure, a classifier associated with class node 1 would be induced only with data belonging to classes 1.1 and 1.2, ignoring objects from classes 2.1 and 2.2. This process proceeds until classifiers predicting the leaf class nodes are produced. At the end of this training phase, a tree of classifiers is obtained. Although this approach considers the hierarchical relationships between the classes, each classifier is built by a flat classification algorithm. In the test phase, beginning at the root node, an example is classified in a top-down manner, according to the predictions produced by a classifier in each level. An inherent disadvantage of this approach is that errors made in higher levels of the hierarchy are propagated to the most specific levels.

In the Big-Bang approach, a classification model is created in a single run of the algorithm, considering the hierarchy of classes as a whole, presenting then a higher algorithmic complexity. After the classification model induction, the prediction of the class of a new instance is carried out in just one step. For this reason, in contrast to the other approaches, Big-Bang cannot use pure flat classification techniques.

In this paper, only Top-Down algorithms were considered. The aim of the experiments were to compare standard Top-Down algorithms with an algorithm based on a variation of the Top-Down approach, described in the next section.

## 3   The Proposed Top-Down Ensembles Approach

A possible extension of the Top-Down approach consists of using various classifiers in each node of the tree of classifiers, instead of using just one classifier. This can be carried out through the combination of classifiers. This new approach was named Top-Down Ensembles.

Combination methods, also known as ensemble methods, use a set of classifiers to obtain the output (prediction) of the classification model [11]. The main idea behind these methods is to induce various classifiers, also named base classifiers, from the training data. In the test phase, the output for each unseen example is given by the combination of the outputs of the base classifiers.

For the combination of the outputs of the base classifiers, the strategy employed in this paper was to train a meta-classifier to perform this task. Initially, all base classifiers are trained by using training examples. A new training dataset is then produced, in which the input attributes are the outputs of the base classifiers. One alternative to generate this new training data consists of using the original training data as input for the base classifiers and storing the outputs produced by them. These outputs, along with the true class (expected output) for each example, are used to generate the new training dataset. This dataset is then used to induce the meta-classifier, which is in charge of combining the outputs from the base classifiers. In the test phase, the examples are given as inputs for each base classifier and the outputs of these classifiers are given as inputs of the meta-classifier, which performs the final classification.

The main motivation for exploiting Top-Down algorithms based on ensemble methods is the advantage of using the combined power of several techniques instead of choosing just one of them to induce the classifier in each node of the class hierarchy.

## 4   Materials and Methods

This section presents the materials and methods employed in the experiments.

### 4.1   Datasets

Three datasets involving G-Protein-Coupled Receptors (GPCRs) were used in the experiments reported in this paper. In each dataset, the GPCR sequences were described through one kind of protein signature, allowing the comparison of the results of an algorithm across three different protein signatures - Prosite, Pfam and Prints. These datasets were first proposed in [12], but they were modified for the purpose of our experiments, as explained later.

GPCRs are particularly important for medical applications due to the important influence of this type of protein in the chemical reactions within the cell. According to [13], 40% to 50% of current medical drugs interact with GPCRs. The protein functional classes of GPCR are given by unique hierarchical indexes in the GPCRDB [14]. The GPCR classes are arranged in the structure of a tree, with four levels - where the top-level refers to generic classes, which are divided into sub-classes, and so on, up to the fourth level.

In essence, the protein signatures used in the datasets have the following characteristics. Prosite signatures are regular expressions or patterns describing short fragments of protein sequences that can be used to identify protein domains, families and functional sites. Currently, the Prosite database stores patterns and profiles specific for more than a thousand protein families or domains. Each of these signatures comes with documentation providing background information on the structure and function of these proteins [15]. Pfam signatures are based on multiple alignments and Hidden Markov Models (HMMs), which consider probability theory methods, allowing a direct statistical approach to identify and score matches. Prints signatures are based on a pattern recognition approach named "fingerprinting". Such signatures use several motifs to identify an unknown protein rather than just one motif. This renders fingerprinting a powerful diagnostic technique, because there is a higher chance of identifying a distant relative, even though mismatches with some motifs may have occurred.

The three datasets were constructed from data extracted from UniProt [16], a well-known protein database, and GPCRDB [14], a database specialised on GPCR proteins. In each of the three datasets, each protein signature was encoded as a binary attribute, where 1 indicates the presence of a protein signature and 0

**Table 1.** Total number of examples, number of predictor attributes and number of classes per level (number of classes at level 1/2/3/4, respectively) of the three datasets used in the experiments

|         | Examples | Attributes | Classes per level |
|---------|----------|------------|-------------------|
| Prosite | 5728     | 127        | 9/50/79/49        |
| Pfam    | 6524     | 73         | 12/52/79/49       |
| Prints  | 4880     | 281        | 8/46/76/49        |

its absence. Additionally, all datasets contain the attributes "molecular weight" and "sequence length".

Besides the preprocessing steps explained in [12], another preprocessing step was included because a small subset of data belonged only to internal nodes of the hierarchy. As the developed algorithms consider mandatory leaf node prediction, some problems could take place during the evaluation of the classification model. Suppose that an example belonging to an internal node was classified into a class represented by a leaf node. During the evaluation, it would not be possible to answer whether the prediction to the more specific node was successful or not. Therefore, examples belonging to internal nodes were not used in the experiments.

In Table 1, the configuration obtained after preprocessing of the three datasets, regarding the total number of examples, number of predictor attributes and number of classes per level (number of classes at level 1/2/3/4, respectively), are shown. As can be noticed in the table, the fourth level of the class hierarchies contain less classes than the third levels. It occurs because of the presence of several leaf nodes in the third level of these hierarchies. Some leaf-nodes are also present in the first and second levels.

All datasets were divided according to the 5-fold cross-validation methodology. Accordingly, each dataset is divided into five parts of approximately equal size. At each round, one fold is left for test and the remaining folds are used in the classifiers training. This makes a total of five train and test sets. The final accuracy rate of a classification model is given by the mean of the predictive accuracies on the test sets from cross-validation.

## 4.2  Top-Down Hierarchical Classification Techniques

For developing the algorithm based on the hierarchical combination of classifiers, five different ML techniques selected, following distinct learning paradigms: Decision Trees [17], induced with the C4.5 algorithm [18]; Sets of Rules induced by the RIPPER algorithm [19]; Support Vector Machines (SVMs) [20]; K-nearest neighbors (KNN) [21]; and Bayesian Networks (BayesNet) [22]. In order to combine the outputs of the base classifiers, another classifier was used. For each node of the class hierarchies, the technique that induces the meta-classifier is chosen among the ML techniques used to produce the base classifiers - the five ML techniques previously mentioned. The adopted criterion consists of selecting the technique whose classifier presents the highest accuracy for the original training set.

In order to compare the results from the algorithm based on the Top-Down Ensembles approach with the other algorithms, the experiments also included five standard Top-Down hierarchical algorithms: one algorithm for each one of the five ML techniques employed in the hierarchical combination of classifiers.

All the Top-Down algorithms were implemented using packages from the R tool [23]. The following packages were used: e1071 [24] and RWeka [25]. The package e1071 was used to generate classifiers based on SVMs. The package RWeka was used to generate classifiers for the other ML techniques. The default parameters were adopted for all techniques, except for SVM. For this technique, two parameters were modified: the cost was set to 100 and $\gamma$ in the Gaussian Kernel was set to 0.01. These values were adopted because they are often used in previous works involving SVMs, presenting good results. Besides, the continuous attributes were normalized before their use by SVMs. For the other techniques, the normalization was not necessary, either because this procedure does not affect their results or because the technique internally implements this procedure.

### 4.3   Evaluation of the Classification Models

The evaluation of the classification models was carried out level by level in the classification hierarchy. For each hierarchical level, a value resulting from the evaluation of the predictive performance in the level is reported through a measure called depth-dependent accuracy. This measure is based on an approach of attributing misclassification costs proposed in [26].

This approach takes into account that classes closer in the hierarchy tend to be more similar to each other than classes more distant, and that predictions in deeper levels are more difficult. Thus, misclassification costs for classes more distant are higher than misclassification costs for classes closer to each other, and misclassification costs in the shallower levels are higher than in the deeper levels. Accordingly, weights are attributed to the edges of the class tree and the misclassification costs are defined as the shortest weighted path between the true class and the predict class.

In the calculation of the depth-dependent accuracy, the misclassification cost of each prediction is initially estimated through the division of the shortest weighted path between the true class and the predicted class by the value of the farthest weighted path from the node that represents the true class (i.e, the more distant class). After calculating the normalized distance for each misclassification (for each test example), an average of all normalized distances is obtained. This average is the error rate of the classification model. Once the error rate is obtained, the accuracy is defined by the complement of this value. The final accuracy rate of the classification model is then given by the mean of the predictive depth-dependent accuracies on the test sets generated by using 5-fold cross-validation.

The weights used in the edges of the hierarchy for calculating the depth-dependent accuracy were: (0.26,0.13,0.07,0.04), where 0.26 is the weight of an edge between the root node and any of its subclasses (i.e, the classes of the first level), 0.13 is the weight of an edge between a class in the first level and any of its subclasses, and so on. These weights were used originally in [12].

Statistical tests were employed in order to verify statistical significances (at 95% of confidence level) among the results from the several hierarchical classification models induced. The statistical test employed was the corrected t-Student for paired data, which considers the differences of results between pairs of classifiers in the cross-validation test sets [27]. As multiple comparisons are performed, the significance level of the tests was adjusted with the Bonferroni correction strategy [28], so the level of significance was set to 1%.

# 5   Experiments

Experiments were performed in order to evaluate the hierarchical classification methods described in Section 4.2 using the datasets described in Section 4.1.

## 5.1   Results

The results obtained for the investigated algorithms in the GPCR datasets are illustrated in tables 2, 3 and 4. These tables show, for each level of the GPCR hierarchy, the mean depth-dependent accuracy rates of the hierarchical classifiers for the 5-fold cross-validation partitions. The standard deviation rates of the accuracies obtained in the cross-validation data partitions are shown in parentheses. The best results for each dataset and hierarchy level are highlighted in boldface.

**Table 2.** Mean depth-dependent accuracy results in the GPCR dataset that employs Prosite signatures

| TD-KNN | TD-C4.5 | TD-SVM | TD-RIPPER | TD-BayesNet | TD-Ens |
|---|---|---|---|---|---|
| 88.06 (0.51) | 87.92 (0.51) | 84.37 (0.28) | 86.70 (0.69) | 85.00 (0.88) | **88.35 (0.94)** |
| 82.68 (0.65) | 82.36 (0.60) | 77.83 (0.36) | 80.24 (0.78) | 78.37 (0.86) | **82.86 (0.86)** |
| 76.99 (0.52) | 76.68 (0.68) | 70.52 (0.31) | 73.53 (0.87) | 71.88 (0.44) | **76.83 (0.68)** |
| **73.40 (0.41)** | 72.31 (1.26) | 63.77 (0.65) | 70.63 (1.69) | 66.80 (0.83) | 72.73 (0.61) |

**Table 3.** Mean depth-dependent accuracy results in the GPCR dataset that employs Pfam signatures

| TD-KNN | TD-C4.5 | TD-SVM | TD-RIPPER | TD-BayesNet | TD-Ens |
|---|---|---|---|---|---|
| 92.90 (0.50) | 92.66 (0.46) | 92.55 (0.24) | 91.74 (0.30) | 89.88 (0.71) | **93.01 (0.68)** |
| 86.34 (0.44) | 85.99 (0.62) | 82.69 (0.34) | 83.83 (0.51) | 81.16 (0.61) | **86.62 (0.74)** |
| 78.34 (0.56) | 78.03 (0.63) | 75.86 (0.37) | 75.20 (0.60) | 72.77 (0.72) | **78.48 (0.73)** |
| 70.05 (1.25) | 68.51 (1.08) | 57.85 (0.68) | 66.47 (1.00) | 61.25 (1.20) | **70.15 (1.19)** |

**Table 4.** Mean depth-dependent accuracy results in the GPCR dataset that employs Prints signatures

| TD-KNN | TD-C4.5 | TD-SVM | TD-RIPPER | TD-BayesNet | TD-Ens |
|---|---|---|---|---|---|
| 92.52 (0.55) | 91.02 (0.54) | 91.74 (0.75) | 90.43 (0.22) | 86.78 (0.71) | **92.75 (0.57)** |
| 90.72 (0.66) | 88.78 (0.48) | 89.18 (0.84) | 87.38 (0.17) | 83.36 (0.79) | **90.96 (0.69)** |
| **86.25 (0.77)** | 84.11 (0.48) | 84.23 (0.53) | 82.28 (0.13) | 77.24 (1.02) | 86.18 (0.77) |
| 85.25 (1.40) | 81.35 (1.58) | 81.22 (2.26) | 78.10 (1.60) | 72.21 (1.31) | **85.35 (2.40)** |

## 5.2   Discussion

It can be observed from tables 2 to 4 that TD-Ens in general performed better for all levels of the three datasets employed. Only in two cases out of twelve TD-KNN showed a higher accuracy value. These results show that the Top-Down Ensembles approach may be considered promising and that combinations of classifiers can improve the performance of hierarchical classification models. Among the standard Top-Down algorithms, TD-KNN obtained better results than the other algorithms for all datasets.

Comparing statistically the results of the standard top-down hierarchical classifiers to those of TP-Ens, some differences were detected at 95% of confidence. For instance, TD-Ens was better than TD-BayesNet for all levels of all datasets. TD-Ens was better than TD-SVM for all levels of Prosite dataset, for levels two and three from Pfam dataset and for the last level of the Prints dataset. Compared to RIPPER, TD-Ens was better in levels two and three from Prosite dataset, in the third level of Pfam and in all levels of Prints dataset. TD-Ens was also better than TD-C4.5 for levels two and four from Prints dataset. No statistical difference was found between the results of TD-KNN and TD-Ens.

For all algorithms a decrease of performance may also be observed for deeper classes in the hierarchies. This behavior can be attributed to two facts: (1) the propagation of errors from general levels to the specific levels, a characteristics inherent to the Top-Down approach; and (2) the predictions in deeper levels are more difficult.

In an analysis of the predictions of the different classifiers obtained by each classification technique in the test phase, a low diversity of results was observed. In other words, the classifiers commit in general common hits and mistakes, that is, similar predictions. A diversity of predictions is important to improve the predictive performance of an ensemble of classifiers. Although the diversity between the classifiers was not large, it was still useful to improve the predictive performance of TD-Ens compared to the isolate algorithms.

Regarding the results in different datasets, all algorithms showed a similar predictive behavior in terms of accuracy rate. In general, all algorithms performed better for Prints dataset, followed by Pfam and Prosite, in this order. In datasets Pfam and Prints the predictive performances were close in the first layer, but this difference raises for the other levels. The worst results were obtained in Prosite dataset, except from its last level.

## 6   Conclusions

In this paper, we presented a comparative study of six hierarchical classification algorithms for different kinds of protein signatures - Prosite, Pfam and Prints. Five of the algorithms were developed according to the standard Top-Down approach, using the following ML techniques: C4.5, RIPPER, SVMs, KNN and BayesNet. The results from these algorithms were compared with the results of an algorithm based on a variation of the Top-Down approach named Top-Down Ensembles approach, which combines results from classifiers induced by the five ML techniques previously mentioned.

In order to evaluate the performance of these algorithms, experiments were performed using three bioinformatics datasets, which are related with G-Protein-Coupled Receptors (GPCRs). Each dataset was generated based on one of the three protein signatures considered in this work, allowing the comparison of the results of an algorithm across different kinds of protein signatures.

According to the experimental results, TD-Ens outperformed the other algorithms for all datasets, with some exceptions. Therefore, the results of the Top-Down Ensembles approach may be considered promising. This indicates that combinations of classifiers can improve the performance of hierarchical classification models. Among the standard Top-Down algorithms, TD-KNN obtained better results than the other algorithms for all datasets.

As the algorithms investigated in this work were developed to deal with class hierarchies structured as trees, strategies to extend them to the context of hierarchies structured as DAGs should be addressed in future research. Besides, the authors plan to investigate the performance of the hierarchical approaches for optional leaf node predictions, eliminating the restriction that the classifications occur in the leaf nodes only. The authors also plan to investigate the use of diversity measures for the selection of base classifiers in the Top-Down Ensembles approach. Finally, it would be of great interest to investigate the use of different kinds of protein signatures in the same dataset.

**Acknowledgments.** The authors would like to thank the Brazilian research councils FAPESP and CNPq for their financial support and Nicholas Holden for making available the GPCR datasets.

## References

1. E. B. Institute, Protein function (accessed March 07, 2008),
   http://www.ebi.ac.uk/2can/tutorials/function/
2. Apweiler, R., Attwood, T., Bairoch, A., Bateman, A., Birney, E., Biswas, M., Bucher, P., Cerutti, L., Corpet, F., Croning, M., et al.: The InterPro database, an integrated documentation resource for protein families, domains and functional sites. Nucleic Acids Research 29(1), 37–40 (2001)

3. Sigrist, C., Cerutti, L., Hulo, N., Gattiker, A., Falquet, L., Pagni, M., Bairoch, A., Bucher, P.: PROSITE: A documented database using patterns and profiles as motif descriptors. Briefings in Bioinformatics 3(3), 265–274 (2002)
4. Bateman, A., Birney, E., Cerruti, L., Durbin, R., Etwiller, L., Eddy, S., Griffiths-Jones, S., Howe, K., Marshall, M., Sonnhammer, E.: The Pfam Protein Families Database. Nucleic Acids Research 30(1), 276–280 (2002)
5. Attwood, T.: The PRINTS database: A resource for identification of protein families. Briefings in Bioinformatics 3(3), 252–263 (2002)
6. E.Nomenclature, of the IUPAC-IUB, American Elsevier Pub. Co., New York, NY 104 (1972)
7. Mitchell, T.M.: Machine Learning. McGraw-Hill Higher Education, New York (1997)
8. Freitas, A.A., Carvalho, A.C.P.F.: A Tutorial on Hierarchical Classification with Applications in Bioinformatics. In: Taniar, D. (ed.) Research and Trends in Data Mining Technologies and Applications, pp. 175–208. Idea Group (2007)
9. Sun, A., Lim, E.P., Ng, W.K.: Hierarchical text classification methods and their specification. Cooperative Internet Computing 256, 18 p. (2003)
10. Sun, A., Lim, E.P., Ng, W.K.: Performance measurement framework for hierarchical text classification. Journal of the American Society for Information Science and Technology 54(11), 1014–1028 (2003)
11. Kuncheva, L.: Combining Pattern Classifiers: Methods and Algorithms. Wiley-Interscience, Chichester (2004)
12. Holden, N., Freitas, A.A.: Hierarchical Classification of G-Protein-Coupled Receptors with PSO/ACO Algorithm. In: Proceedings of the 2006 IEEE Swarm Intelligence Symposium, pp. 77–84 (2006)
13. Filmore, D.: It's a GPCR world. Modern drug discovery 1(17), 24–28 (2004)
14. GPCRDB, Information system for G protein-coupled receptors (GPCR) (accessed, July 2006), http://www.gpcr.org/7tm/
15. S. I. of Bioinformatics, Prosite - description (accessed March 01, 2008), http://us.expasy.org/prosite/prosite_details.html
16. Apweiler, R., Bairoch, A., Wu, C.H., Barker, W.C., Boeckmann, B., Ferro, S., Gasteiger, E., Huang, H., Lopez, R., Magrane, M., et al.: UniProt: the Universal Protein knowledgebase. Nucleic Acids Research 32, D115–D119 (2004)
17. Quinlan, J.R.: Induction of decision trees. Machine Learning 1(1), 81–106 (1986)
18. Quinlan, J.R.: C4.5: Programs for Machine Learning. Morgan Kaufmann, San Francisco (1993)
19. Cohen, W.: Fast effective rule induction. In: Proceedings of the Twelfth International Conference on Machine Learning, pp. 115–123 (1995)
20. Cristianini, N., Shawe-Taylor, J.: An Introduction to Support Vector Machines and other kernel-based learning methods. Cambridge University Press, Cambridge (2000)
21. Cover, T., Hart, P.: Nearest neighbor pattern classification, Information Theory. IEEE Transactions 13(1), 21–27 (1967)
22. Friedman, N., Geiger, D., Goldszmidt, M.: Bayesian Network Classifiers. Machine Learning 29(2), 131–163 (1997)
23. Venables, W.N., Smith, D.M.: The R Development Core Team, An introduction to R - version 2.4.1 (2006), http://cran.r-project.org/doc/manuals/R-intro.pdf
24. Dimitriadou, E., Hornik, K., Leisch, F., Meyer, D., Weingessel, A.: e1071: Misc Functions of the Department of Statistics (e1071), TU Wien, 1–5 (2006)

25. Hornik, K., Zeileis, A., Hothorn, T., Buchta, C.: RWeka: An R Interface to Weka, R package version 0.2-14, http://CRAN.R-project.org
26. Blockeel, H., Bruynooghe, M., Dzeroski, S., Ramon, J., Struyf, J.: Hierarchical multi-classification. In: Proceedings of the ACM SIGKDD 2002 Workshop on Multi-Relational Data Mining (MRDM 2002), pp. 21–35 (2002)
27. Nadeau, C., Bengio, Y.: Inference for the Generalization Error. Machine Learning 52(3), 239–281 (2003)
28. Salzberg, S.: On Comparing Classifiers: Pitfalls to Avoid and a Recommended Approach. Data Mining and Knowledge Discovery 1(3), 317–328 (1997)

# A Hybrid Method for the Protein Structure Prediction Problem

Márcio Dorn, Ardala Breda, and Osmar Norberto de Souza

Laboratório de Bioinformática, Modelagem e Simulação de Biossistemas – LABIO
Programa de Pós-Graduação em Ciência da Computação - Faculdade de Informática
PUCRS, Av. Ipiranga, 6681- Prédio 32 - Sala 602, CEP 90619-900
Porto Alegre, RS, Brasil
{mdorn,abreda}@inf.pucrs.br, {osmar.norberto}@pucrs.br

**Abstract.** This article provides the initial results of our effort to develop a hybrid prediction method, combining the principles of *de novo* and homology modeling, to help solve the protein three-dimensional (3-D) structure prediction problem. A target protein amino acid sequence is fragmented into many short contiguous fragments. Clustered short templates fragments, obtained from experimental protein structures in the Protein Data Bank (PDB), using the NCBI BLASTp program, were used for building an initial conformation, which was further refined by molecular dynamics simulations. We tested our method with the artificially designed alpha helical hairpin (PDB ID: 1ZDD) starting with its amino acids sequence only. The structure obtained with the proposed method is topologically a helical hairpin, with a Cα RMSD of ~ 5.0 Å with respect to the experimental PDB structure for all 34 amino acids residues, and only ~ 2.0 Å when considering amino acids 1 to 22. We discuss further improvements to the method.

**Keywords:** Protein 3-D structure, *ab initio* prediction, homology modeling, molecular dynamics simulations.

## 1 Introduction

A protein molecule is a covalent chain of amino acids residues that, in physiological condition or native environment, adopt a unique three-dimensional (3-D) structure. This native structure dictates the biochemical function of the protein [1, 2].

Experiments by Anfinsen [3] demonstrated that a protein molecule when denatured, by disrupting conditions in their environment, can be re-folded to their native structure when the physiological condition is restored. Therefore, the amino acid sequence contains all of the information necessary to determine the native structure of the protein. Based on this principle, the native fold of a protein can be predicted computationally using only the physical-chemical information of their amino acids sequence. Protein folding [4] prediction is one of the greatest questions in structural bioinformatics and consists in understanding and predicting how the information coded in the amino acids linear sequence is translated into the 3-D structure of a protein.

A.L.C. Bazzan, M. Craven, and N.F. Martins (Eds.): BSB 2008, LNBI 5167, pp. 47–56, 2008.
© Springer-Verlag Berlin Heidelberg 2008

Many computational methodologies and algorithms have been proposed as a solution to this complex problem [5-8]. Bujnick [5] divide the principal approaches for protein structure prediction in two classes: *de novo* and comparative or homology modeling. *De novo* methods are further divided in two categories: *ab initio* and knowledge-based methods.

*Ab initio* methods are thermodynamics based and rely on the fact that the native structure of a protein corresponds to the global minimum of its Gibbs free energy [6]. This methodology simulates the protein conformational space using an energy function that describes the protein internal energy and its interaction with its surrounding aqueous environment. The objective is to find the global minimum of this free-energy hyper-surface which corresponds to the protein native or functional conformation [7, 9]. Stochastic and deterministic techniques such as Monte Carlo and Molecular Dynamics (MD) Simulations, respectively, are the preferred methodologies employed in *ab initio* prediction [7]. In contrast, knowledge-based methods utilize statistical potentials derived from analysis of folding patterns of known protein 3-D structures in databases [5]. From these statistical features target protein sequences can be predicted when no homologues are available [10]. Fold recognition via threading is the best example of this technique [6, 11].

In comparative modeling, the target sequence is aligned to the sequence of an evolutionarily related template with known 3-D structure in the Protein Data Bank (PDB) [12]. Once homology is detected, usually above the 30% identity threshold, modeling can proceed with copying of coordinates of the template or the average of multiples templates, or using the distance and torsions angles and inter-atomic distances from aligned regions from template as modeling restraints [5, 10]. Comparative modeling is therefore the most accurate prediction [5, 13].

Both methodologies have limitations: comparative modeling can only predict structures that have similar or identical sequences in a database of known structures. With *de novo* (*ab initio* methods) modeling we can obtain novel structures with new folds. However, the complexity and high dimensionality [14] of the search space, even for a small protein molecule, still makes the problem intractable [15], despite the availability of high performance computing.

The aim of this article is to describe a hybrid method we are developing for the protein structure prediction problem. In order to fasten the search for the global minimum of the potential function describing the native, functional structure of a protein we propose a hybrid method that combines the accuracy of homology modeling with a more realistic, force field based, physical-chemical description of a protein, using simulations by the MD method. In our method we split a target amino acid sequence into many short contiguous fragments and for each one of them we obtain templates with known 3-D structures. However, in contrast to most methods developed or under development, we do not use the whole fragment, but only the central amino acid main chain conformation. With these data we build an initial conformation which is then further refined by energy minimization and MD simulations.

In section 2 we detail the proposed method. Sections 3 and 4 provide a case study with results and discussions, and future work, respectively.

## 2 The Proposed Method

In this article we combine principles of *de novo* and comparative modeling to develop a hybrid method that explore the capacity these methods have to predict new (*ab initio* methods) and accurate (homology modeling) structures. Homology modeling is employed such as to reduce the search of the conformational space, but preserve the capacity of predicting novel structures.

A protein structure $X$ can be represented in the form $X = \{x_1, x_2, \ldots, x_n\}$, where $x_i$ is a triplet of torsion angles [$\omega$ (omega), $\phi$ (phi), $\psi$ (psi)] of each amino acid (aa) residue in the protein (Fig. 1). The set of consecutive triplets represent the internal rotations of a protein main chain.

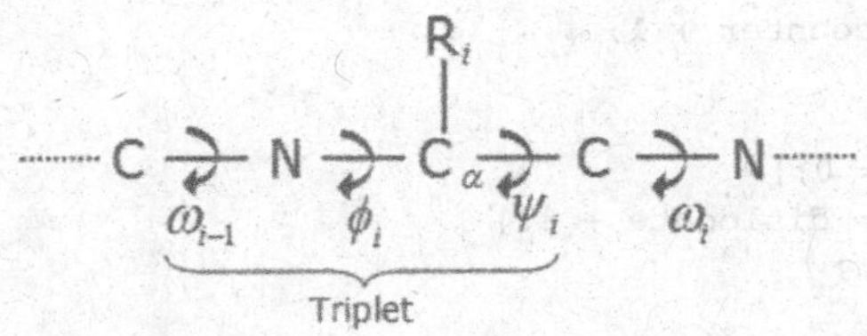

**Fig. 1.** Schematic representation of a model peptide illustrating a triplet of main chain torsion angles. N is nitrogen, C and Cα are carbons and $R_i$ is an arbitrary side-chain. $\omega$ (omega) is the rotation about the peptide bond (C-N) and is fixed to $180^{\circ}$ (trans). $\phi$ (phi) and $\psi$ (psi) are rotations about the N-Cα and Cα-C bonds, respectively.

The method consists of 6 steps: (1) the target sequence is fragmented; (2) template fragments are obtained from a experimental data bank; (3) torsion angles (triplet) from the fragment central amino acid (aa) are calculated; (4) triplets are clusterized; (5) an initial conformation is build, and (6) the initial conformation is refined. These steps are detailed below:

**1. Fragmenting the target sequence:** In this step the target sequence $X$ is fragmented into many short $s_i$ contiguous fragments with $l$ aa each. A set $S$ of contiguous fragments, representing all possible fragments of length $l$, is created and represented as $S = \{s_i, \ldots, s_p\}$, where $s_i$ and $s_p$ are the first and last fragments, respectively. If $n$ is the number of aa in a target sequence $X$ and $l$, the size of each $s_i$ fragment, is an odd value, then the number $p$ of possible fragments obtained within the fragmentation step is given by $p = [n - (l-1)]$. A fragment $s_i$ starts at the $i$th residue and terminates at the $j$th residue, consisting of a set of consecutive triplets of torsion angles $\{ (\omega_{i-1}, \phi_i, \psi_i), \ldots, (\omega_{j-1}, \phi_j, \psi_j) \}$. The triplet of torsion angles is obtained only for the central amino acid of each $s_i$ fragment and an odd value for $l$ guarantees that the central aa in the fragment is flanked by an equal number o amino acid residues. We adopt a default value of $l = 5$ for the fragment lengths in this work. The pseudo code for obtaining all consecutive short $s_i$ fragments from a target sequence $X$ is:

```
Fragmentation (sequence, seqLength, targetSeqLength) {
   fragLength = 5; fragments [((seqLength)-(fragLength-1))];
   end = 1; counter = 0; fragment = "";
   while (end != 0) {
     if ((targetSeqLength-dislocate) >= fragLength) {
       for (i = dislocate; i < fragLength + dislocate; i++) {
             fragment = fragment + sequence[i];}
       fragments[counter] = fragment;
       fragment = "";
       counter = counter + 1;
       end = 1;}
     else {
           end = 0;}
     dislocate = dislocate + 1;}
return fragments;}
```

2. **Searching templates using BLAST:** Each of the $s_i$ fragments of size $l$ obtained in step 1 was used to search the PDB for templates, using the web version of BLASTp for short and near exact matches [16]. Only hits with the same length as the query sequence and with no evolutionary relationship with the target sequence $X$ were retrieved and considered in further analysis. We modified the BioPython library [17] to automate this step. The final result is a list of templates with their PDB accession codes (PDB ID).

3. **Calculating triplets of torsion angles:** For each target fragment $s_i$ a set of template PDB files was obtained. For every central amino acid of all $s_i$ templates triplets of torsion angles were calculated using the program *Torsions* (kindly provided by Dr. Andrew C.R. Martin). Now, each $s_i$ target fragment can be represented as a set of triplet torsion angles $s_i = \{t_1, \ldots, t_n\}$, obtained from all of its $s_i$ templates, where $t_i$ is a triplet of torsion angles of the central aa of the templates. Hence, we may represent the set $S$ of fragments as $S = \{s_i = \{t_i, \ldots, t_n\}, \ldots, s_p = \{t_i, \ldots, t_n\}\}$.

4. **Clustering the triplets:** In this step all $t_i$ elements belonging to one $s_i$ are clustered in order to identify in which region or regions of the Ramachandran plot [18] the triplets are more likely to be. We first generate four clusters because we consider the Ramachandran plot is divided into four major conformational regions. The first region, $-180° < \phi < 0°$, $-100° < \psi < 45°$, is considered to be in a $\alpha$-helix conformation. The second, with $-180° < \phi < -45°$, $45° < \psi < 225°$ is considered to be

in a $\beta$-sheet region. The third, the area between $0°<\phi<180°$, $-90°<\psi<90°$, is called the turn region, and the remaining region, representing 36% of the total area, but containing only 1.9% of the amino acids [19], is the fourth region. We utilize the EM (expectation-maximization) clustering algorithm from WEKA data mining package [20] for processing and finding clusters in all sets of $s_i$ triplet torsion angles. The EM algorithm first calculates the clusters probabilities and, in a second step, it calculates the distribution parameters, maximizing the likelihood of the distributions given a data set [20]. For all clustering tasks a standard seed value of 10 was used. At the end of the clustering step we had, for each $s_i$ set, four clusters, and for each one of them we had an associated mean triplet value and an estimated standard deviation (e.s.d.). In Fig. 2 we illustrate the cluster identification after running the EM algorithm. In this step we have all the information necessary to build an initial conformation for the target sequence $X$. We defined the best cluster of a $s_i$ set as the one with the highest number of $t_i$ elements.

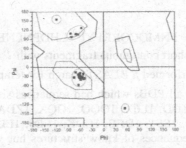

**Fig. 2.** Ramachandran plot of all $t_i$ triplets (phi, psi) of a $s_i$ set. Four clusters (light blue lines) have been identified by WEKA.

**5. Building the initial conformation:** The mean of the triplet torsion angles from the best cluster for each aa is used to build the initial conformation of the target amino acid sequence $X$. We substitute the mean torsion angles of the central triplet of each $s_i$ into the target amino acid sequence $X$. Fragmentation with $l = 5$ results in the loss of the first and last two amino acid residues. The triplet torsion angles for these four residues are obtained from the experimental structure (PDB ID: 1ZDD). The initial conformation was built with the tLeap module of AMBER7 [21]. All $\omega$ torsion angles were set to 180° since the peptide bond is partially rigid and the atoms involved are not free to rotate about it [2].

**6. Refinement with MD simulation:** The initial conformation build for the target sequence $X$ was refined with energy minimization and MD simulation using the SANDER module of the AMBER7 package [21] with the Cornell el al. (22) force field.

# 3  Case Study

To test our method we chose a mini protein composed of 34 amino acids (PDB ID:
1ZDD – Fig. 3A) [23] known to be arranged as two alpha-helices connected by a turn,
a structural motif know as alpha-helical hairpin [24].

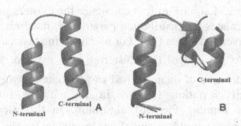

**Fig. 3.** Ribbon representation of the experimental and predicted conformations of 1ZDD. **(A)**
Experimental structure of 1ZDD (PDB ID: 1ZDD). **(B)** Initial (green), minimized (blue) and
MD simulated structure (magenta) of predicted 1ZDD. Amino acids side chains not shown for
clarity.

The target sequence $X$ = FNMQCQRRFYEALHDPNLNEEQRNAKIKSIRDDC
is fragmented into 30 target short contiguous fragments with $l$ = 5 aa (pentapeptides).
For each $s_i$ fragment we performed a BLAST search for template fragments against
the PDB [12]. We removed all PDBs which had sequences similar or were identical
to 1ZDD, namely: 1ZDC, 1ZDD, 1L6X, 1OQO, 1OQX, 1ZDA, 1ZDB, 2SPZ, 1LP1,
1Q2N, 1FC2, 1BDC, 1BDD, 1SS1, 1DEE, 1EDK, 1EDJ, 1EDI, 1EDL. This should
eliminate any bias due to sequences of know structures but very closely related to
1ZDD.

The triplet's torsion angles $t_i$ from the templates for each target $s_i$ are clustered
and its average and estimated standard deviation (e.s.d) are calculated for the $\phi$ and
$\psi$ angles of the best cluster (cluster with most elements). The estimated e.s.d
represents the distance between the maximum and the minimum $\phi$ and $\psi$ angles of
a given cluster. In the next page Table 1 shows the results of this analysis for the best
cluster of each $s_i$ fragment.

The initial structure generated for 1ZDD (Fig. 3B, green) with our method already
had a conformation similar to the expected helical hairpin found in the experimental
structure (Fig. 3A). The C-terminal helix was malformed. This model was submitted
to 500 steps of energy minimization to eliminate structural strains. However, only
very minor changes were observed, with the minimized structure still very similar to
the predicted 1ZDD. A root-mean square deviation (RMSD) of 4.9 Å was measured
between the predicted 1ZDD and the experimental structure, for the main chain atoms
only. When the N-terminal helix only was considered (residues 1 to 22), the RMSD
was 1.9Å.

**Table 1.** The average and e.s.d of $\phi$ and $\psi$ values for each best cluster of a $S_i$ fragment

| $S_i$ fragment | Amino Acid | $\phi_{aver}$ | $\phi_{e.s.d}$ | $\psi_{aver}$ | $\psi_{e.s.d}$ |
|---|---|---|---|---|---|
| FNMQC | M | −64.45 | 3.67 | −39.22 | 8.38 |
| NMQCQ | Q | −64.10 | 7.71 | −42.44 | 8.47 |
| MQCQR | C | −65.71 | 7.59 | −41.19 | 8.67 |
| QCQRR | Q | −61.78 | 2.70 | −42.18 | 2.84 |
| CQRRF | R | −59.89 | 6.78 | −31.96 | 9.48 |
| QRRFY | R | −60.98 | 7.48 | −32.84 | 12.83 |
| RRFYE | F | −59.73 | 1.82 | −38.77 | 4.39 |
| RFYEA | Y | −57.58 | 1.89 | −46.83 | 5.52 |
| FYEAL | E | −66.30 | 2.61 | −42.13 | 3.60 |
| YEALH | A | −66.32 | 4.33 | −36.08 | 4.42 |
| EALHD | L | −65.80 | 4.846 | −38.77 | 10.35 |
| ALHDP | H | −106.20 | 16.57 | 0.60 | 18.15 |
| LHDPN | D | −75.23 | 15.99 | 122.84 | 13.27 |
| HDPNL | P | −58.44 | 3.74 | −35.65 | 22.26 |
| DPNLN | N | −60.47 | 3.29 | −22.71 | 6.46 |
| PNLNE | L | −79.55 | 8.49 | 143.46 | 5.81 |
| NLNEE | N | −88.70 | 25.87 | 142.92 | 29.48 |
| LNEEQ | E | −61.78 | 6.21 | −35.80 | 8.96 |
| NEEQR | E | −61.88 | 2.57 | −48.38 | 5.26 |
| EEQRN | Q | −65.38 | 5.69 | −46.10 | 5.33 |
| EQRNA | R | −65.44 | 5.85 | −40.75 | 5.52 |
| QRNAK | N | −61.40 | 6.02 | −44.98 | 5.37 |
| RNAKI | A | −72.24 | 7.37 | 156.82 | 2.91 |
| NAKIK | K | −70.54 | 2.51 | −32.38 | 6.08 |
| AKIKS | I | −82.52 | 7.93 | 116.37 | 13.62 |
| KIKSI | K | −83.03 | 4.67 | −44.76 | 11.53 |
| IKSIR | S | −68.21 | 15.56 | −38.22 | 20.86 |
| KSIRD | I | −54.73 | 2.73 | −45.87 | 4.21 |
| SIRDD | R | −54.73 | 10.76 | −26.08 | 16.99 |
| IRDDC | D | −66.87 | 10.40 | −32.10 | 11.07 |

The hairpin's second alpha helix, at the predicted 1ZDD C-terminus, is misfolded due to hydrogen bond interactions formed between residues glutamine 22 and arginine 31 (Fig. 3B) that lead to breakage of the typical $i - (i +4)$ hydrogen bonding pattern observed in canonical alpha helices [2].

## The MD Protocol and Structural Analysis

The predicted minimized conformation of 1ZDD was submitted to a further 500 ps MD simulation, at 281.0 K and a 10.0 Å cutoff radius for the evaluation of the long-range van der Waals and electrostatic interactions. The solvent was treated implicitly within the Generalized Born with Surface Area (GBSA) approximation [25]. The SHAKE algorithm [26] was used to restrain all hydrogen-heavy atom bond distances, allowing an integration time-step of 0.002 ps for the equations of motion. The simulation was performed on a PC Pentium 4 (2,4 MHz and 1GB RAM). The atomic positions were saved at every 500 steps (1.0 ps).

The secondary and supersecondary structures, as well as other structural parameters, were monitored based on the RMSD of the predicted 1ZDD MD trajectory with respect to 1ZDD.pdb, the experimental structure [23]. Structure formation was visualized with the Swiss-PdbViewer [27] and PyMol [28] graphics

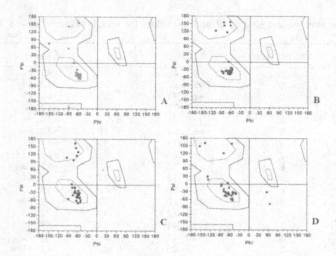

**Fig. 4.** Ramachandran plots for 1ZDD (**A**) experimental, (**B**) predicted by our method, (**C**) predicted minimized and (**D**) MD refined predicted structure. All residues are within allowed regions, being 87%, 100%, 93% and 82% of residues within most favored regions for experimental, initial, minimized and MD refined conformations.

package. $\phi$ and $\psi$ angles distribution as well as other stereochemical analysis and secondary structure calculations were performed with PROCHECK [29] and DSSP [30]. All structure illustrations were prepared with PyMol [28].

The Ramachandran plots [18] show that all residues in the predicted structure (Fig. 4B) are located on allowed regions prior to refinement by energy minimization (Fig. 4c) and MD simulation (Fig. 4D). This illustrates the reliability of the method on limiting spatial search for each of the 1ZDD amino acids.

The secondary structure conformation adopted by the predicted 1ZDD amino acids are in agreement with the experimental structure (1ZDD.pdb) according to the Dictionary of Protein Secondary Structure [18]. The only exception are the residues located at the C-terminus of predicted 1ZDD, from position 25 to 28, that alternatively adopt a bent conformation, as a result of the H-bond pattern that lead to the C-terminal helix misfolding. The final six residues are helically arranged as a $\pi$ or $3_{10}$ helix types.

Alpha helices are known to fold in vitro in the millisecond timescale [31]. For this work we could only simulate 500 ps. It is clear that a correct folded alpha helical hairpin has not been attained at the end of the available MD simulation timescale. Helix number two still presents a kink on the amino acids residues 25 to 28. The RMSD values are ~5.0 Å for all amino acids of the predicted 1ZDD structure, and ~2.0 Å when considering amino acids 1 to 22. The MD simulation refinement did not improve the structure obtained with our proposed structure prediction method (Fig. 3B). This is certainly in part due to the short time course of the simulation. We believe that longer MD simulations with more appropriate protocols will improve these results. In CASP6 the most successful *de novo* prediction method presented RMSD values for proteins of less than 100 residues ranging from 4.0 to 6.0 Å [8], a value comparable to the results presented here, considering the full sequence, but much higher than the one we obtain when the misfolded C-terminal residues are not included in the RMSD calculation.

## 4 Final Considerations and Future Work

The simple protein structure prediction method we are developing was able to generate a predicted structure topologically very close to the desired one and with a processing time of only 3 minutes, after clustering of templates obtained from the PDB. This shows the method's potential for reducing the high dimensionality of the conformational search space for a given protein sequence. At this stage, our MD simulation refinement protocol did not work. As future work to improve our method we will investigate the application of enhanced clustering techniques to the torsion angles triplets, test the effect of different clusters on the initial predicted structure, and develop better MD simulations protocols, including simulations in longer time scales and possibly using explicit salvation.

## Acknowledgements

We thank the reviewers for their useful comments and suggestions to improve the original manuscript. This project was supported by grants from CAPES, FAPERGS, and CNPq to ONS. ONS is a CNPq Research Fellow. MD was supported by a CNPq M.Sc. scholarship. AB was supported by a CAPES scholarship.

## References

1. Baxevanis, A.D., Ouellette, B.F.F.: Bioinformatics: A Practical Guide to the Analysis of Genes and Proteins, 560 p. Wiley and Sons, Hoboken (2005)
2. Branden, C., Tooze, J.: Introduction to Protein Structure, 410 p. Garlang Publishing Inc., New York (1998)
3. Anfinsen, C.B., Haber, E., Sela, M., White Jr., F.H.: Proceedings of the National Academy of Sciences USA. 47, 1309–1314 (1961)
4. Creighton, T.E.: Protein Folding. Biochemical Journal 270, 1–16 (1990)
5. Bujnicki, J.M.: Protein Structure Prediction by Recombination of Fragments. Chembiochem. 7(1), 19–27 (2006)
6. Tramontano, A.: Protein Structure Prediction, 228 p. John Wiley and Sons, Weinheim (2006)
7. Osguthorpe, D.J.: Ab initio Protein Folding. Current Opinion in Structural Biology 10, 146–152 (2000)
8. Moult, J.: A Decade of CASP: Progress, Bottlenecks and Prognosis in Protein Structure Prediction. Current Opinion in Structural Biology 15, 285–289 (2005)
9. Tramontano, A., Morea, V.: Assessment of homology based predictions in CASP5. Proteins: Structure, Function, and Bioinformatics 53, 352–368 (2003)
10. Kolinski, A.: Protein Modeling and Structure Prediction with a Reduced Representation. Acta Biochimica Polonica 51, 349–371 (2004)
11. Jones, D.T., Taylort, W.R., Thornton, J.M.: A New Approach to Protein Fold. Nature 358, 86–89 (1992)

12. Berman, H.M., Westbrook, J., Feng, Z., Gilliland, G., Bhat, T.N., Weissig, H., Shindyalov, I.N., Bourne, P.E.: The Protein Data Bank. Nucleic Acids Research 28(1), 235–242 (2000)

13. Marti-Renom, M.A., Stuart, A., Fiser, A., Sánchez, R., Melo, F., Sali, A.: Comparative Protein Structure Modeling of genes and genomes. Annual Review of Biophysics and Biomolecular Structure 29, 291–325 (2000)

14. Ngo, J.T., Marks, J., Karplus, M.: Computational Complexity, protein structure prediction and the Levinthal Paradox. In: Merz Jr., K., Grand, S.L. (eds.) The Protein Folding Problem and Tertiary Structure Prediction, ch. 14, pp. 435–508. Birkhäuser, Boston (1997)

15. Levinthal, C.: Are there pathways for protein folding? Journal de Chimie Physique et de Physico-Chimie Biologique 65, 44–45 (1968)

16. Altschul, S.F., Madden, T.L., Schäffer, A.A., Zhang, J., Zhang, Z., Miller, W., Lipman, D.J.: Gapped BLAST and PSI-BLAST: a New Generation of Protein Database Search Programs. Nucleic Acids Research 25, 3389–3402 (1997)

17. Chapman, B., Chang, J.: Biopython: Python Tools for Computational Biology. ACM SIGBIO Newsletter 20(2), 15–19 (2002)

18. Ramachandran, G.N., Sasisekharan, V.: Advances in Protein Chemistry 23, 238–437 (1968)

19. Hovmöller, T.Z., Ohlson, T.: Conformation of Amino Acids in Proteins. Acta Crystallographica D58, 768–776 (2002)

20. Witten, I.H., Frank, E.: Data Mining: Practical Machine Learning Tools and Techniques, 2nd edn., 525 p. Elsevier, San Francisco (2005)

21. Case, D.A., Cheatham, T.E., Darden, T., Gohlke, H., Luo, R., Merz, K.M., Onufriev, A., Simmerling, C., Wang, B., Woods, R.J.: The AMBER Biomolecular Simulation Programs. Journal of Computational Chemistry 26(16), 1668–1688 (2005)

22. Cornell, W.D., Cieplak, P., Bayly, C.I., Gould, I.R., Merz Jr., K.M., Ferguson, D.M., Spellmeyer, D.C., Fox, T., Caldwell, J.W., Kollman, P.A.: A Second Generation Force Field for the Simulation of Proteins. Journal of the American Chemical Society 117, 5179–5197 (1995)

23. Starovasnik, M.A., Braisted, A.C., Wells, J.A.: Structural Mimicry of a Native Protein by a Minimized Binding Domain. Proceedings of the National Academy of Sciences USA 94, 10080–10085 (1997)

24. Murzin, A.G., Brenner, S.E., Hubbard, T., Chothia, C.: SCOP: a Structural Classification of Proteins Database for the Investigation of Sequences and Structures. Journal of Molecular Biology 247, 536–540 (1995)

25. Bashford, D., Case, D.A.: Generalized Born Models of Macromolecular Solvation Effects. Annual Review Physical Chemistry 51, 129–152 (2000)

26. Ryckaert, J.P., Ciccotti, G., Berendsen, H.J.C.: Numerical Integration of the Cartesian Equation of Motion of a System with Constraints: Molecular Dynamics of N-alkanes. Journal of Computational Physics 23, 327–341 (1977)

27. Guex, N., Peitsch, M.C.: SWISS-MODEL and The Swiss-PdbViewer: An Environment for Comparative Protein Modeling. Electrophoresis 18, 2714–2723 (1997)

28. DeLano, W.L.: The PyMOL Molecular Graphics System. DeLano Scientific, San Carlos (2002)

29. Laskowski, R.A., MacArthur, M.W., Moss, D.S., Thornton, J.M.: PROCHECK: A Program to Check the Stereochemical Quality of Protein Structures. Journal of Applied Crystallography 26, 283–291 (1993)

30. Kabsch, W., Sander, C.: Dictionary of Protein Secondary Structure: Pattern Recognition of Hydrogen-Bonded and Geometrical Features. Biopolymers 22, 2577–2637 (1983)

31. Clarke, D.T., Doig, A.J., Stapley, B.J., Jones, G.R.: The alpha-helix Folds on the Millisecond Time Scale. Proceedings of the National Academy of Sciences USA 96, 7232–7237 (1999)

# Detecting Statistical Covariations of Sequence Physicochemical Properties

Moshe A. Gadish and David K.Y. Chiu

Department of Computing and Information Science, University of Guelph, Guelph, Ontario, N1G 2W1, Canada

**Abstract.** Sequence analysis often does not take the physicochemical properties into account. On the other hand, some of these properties when identified may be useful in inferring the folding and functional attributes of the molecule when considered with the original sequence information. We evaluated here an analysis using multiple aligned sequences incorporating five physicochemical properties. In addition to site invariance information, we also consider the covariation or interdependence patterns between aligned sites using an information measure. We propose a method based on analyzing the expected mutual information between sites that is statistically significant with a confidence level. When summing the measured information along the aligned sites, we compare the pattern from the measure to the structural and active site of the molecule. In the experiments, the model enzyme molecule lysozyme is chosen. The aligned sequence data are evaluated based on the mapped physicochemical properties of the amino acid residues. Analysis between the original and the transformed sequence data incorporating the physicochemical properties are then compared subtracted and visualized. From the comparisons, the plots show that some of the selected physicochemical properties in the analysis correlate to the locations of active sites and certain folding structure such as helices. The experiments generally support the useful role of incorporating additional physicochemical properties into sequence analysis, when significance of the statistical variations is taken into account.

**Keywords:** Physicochemical, interdependency, lysozyme.

## 1 Introduction

The effect of various physicochemical properties of amino acids on the protein structure and function is well known. For example, by considering the conserved physicochemical properties in addition to the amino acid types of the sequences, a meaningful alignment may be obtained. Thus, the classifier using PHYSEAN (PHYsical Sequence Analysis) adds position-specific physicochemical information for protein classification [1]. PHYSEAN predicts protein classes with highly variable sequences on the basis of their physical, chemical and biological characteristics (such as hydrophobicity). PHYSEAN produces reasonably accurate predictions, indicating the importance of incorporating the physicochemical properties into protein sequence analysis. Hydrophobicity plots have also been used in protein sequence analysis for

A.L.C. Bazzan, M. Craven, and N.F. Martins (Eds.): BSB 2008, LNBI 5167, pp. 57–67, 2008.

the purpose of discovering hydrophobic cores and resolving some of the problems in protein folding. Other successes of incorporating physicochemical properties include the use of amino acid scales and physicochemical properties in predicting secondary structure propensity (alpha helix, beta sheet, turn, etc.) [2]. This paper evaluates further how these physicochemical properties can be used to analyze multiple aligned sequences of a protein family. Many speculations on why physicochemical properties in protein analysis are useful can be made. Proteins have remarkable range of functions from the many distinctive three-dimensional structures given their sequences [3]. Sequence analysis may determine how the amino acids specify the conformations of their structure. An important step in analyzing the sequences then involves finding recurrent patterns in the sequence that may not be obvious. From these patterns, relationship to patterns of the function of the protein can then be analyzed [4]. Information measures such as the Shannon entropy function or mutual information are mathematical measures that are general and may reveal implicit statistical relationships even though the exact properties that are involved may be unknown. Crooks and Brenner [5] have used entropy densities and local inter-sequence mutual information density to study the effect of primary and secondary protein structure. A transformation score is mapped from each amino acid into the three secondary structure classes of extended beta sheets, helices, and loops. Their study supports the view that these information measures may capture the cooperative processes where secondary and tertiary structure can then form.

This paper develops a method by analyzing the statistical significance of expected mutual information based on the physicochemical properties. It further sums all such mutual information at each position and compares it to that without taking the physicochemical properties into account. The plots showing the differences are then evaluated.

In the experiments, the model enzyme molecule lysozyme c is chosen. The aligned sequence data are evaluated based on the mapped physicochemical properties of the amino acid residues. Analysis between the original and the transformed sequence data incorporating the physicochemical properties are then compared and visualized. From the comparisons, the plots show that some of the selected physicochemical properties correlate to the locations of active sites and certain folding structure. The experiments generally support the interesting role of these physicochemical properties when their statistical variations are taken into account.

## 2 Detecting Significant Interactions between Sites

### 2.1 Representation of Aligned Sequence Data

Multiple biological sequences (of a protein family) can be aligned to form a sequence ensemble. For example, each amino acid site in the protein sequence can be considered as a variable where the corresponding amino acid of a sequence is the outcome. This can be represented as $X = (X_1, X_2,..., X_m)$ where $m$ is the number of variables, indicating the length of the alignment. An instance of $X$ is a realization denoted as $x=(x_1,x_2,...,x_m)$. Each $x_j(1 \leq j \leq m)$ can take up an attribute value denoted as $x_j = a_{jq}$. An attribute value $a_{jq}$ is a value taken from an attribute value set $\Gamma_j = \{ a_{jq} \mid q = 1,2, \ldots, L_j \}$ where $L_j$ is the number of possible values for the variable $X_j$, or the cardinality of the set.

## 2.2 Expected Mutual Information

Expected mutual information is a measure of the statistical interdependence between two random variables. The stronger the interdependence between the two variables, the larger is the expected mutual information between them. If the two variables are independent, then the expected mutual information between them is zero [6], [7], [8]. Intuitively, expected mutual information measures the amount of information associated between the two variables. Quantitatively, it can also be considered as the distance between the joint distribution of two variables, and their joint distribution if they were independent.

Formally, the expected mutual information of two discrete random variables $X_i$ and $X_k$ can be defined as,

$$I(X_i, X_k) = \sum_{j=1}^{L_i} \sum_{h=1}^{L_k} p(x_i^j, x_k^h) \log \frac{p(x_i^j, x_k^h)}{p(x_i^j) p(x_k^h)}. \tag{1}$$

where $x_i^j$ and $x_k^h$ are the $j^{th}$ and $h^{th}$ outcome of $X_i$ and $X_k$ respectively.

## 2.3 Testing for Statistical Interdependence

It is important when calculating statistical interdependence to take into consideration their statistical significance, so that their correspondence is not due to chance, otherwise considerable error can be accumulated. This is especially important in case when information from multiple variables is summed. Evidence of statistical interdependence can be evaluated by comparing the two competing hypothesis between the independence and interdependence assumptions.

When comparing the statistical independence between two outcome values of the distinct variables, we use the following method based on evaluating the adjusted residual [8]. Let us denote a joint outcome of the two variables $X_i$ and $X_k$ as $e_{ik}^{jh} = (a_i^j, a_k^h)$, where $e_{ik}^{jh}$ represents the joint observation of $X_i = a_i^j$ and $X_k = a_k^h$. The standard residual is defined as:

$$z(e_{ik}^{jh}) = \frac{obs(e_{ik}^{jh}) - exp(e_{ik}^{jh})}{\sqrt{exp(e_{ik}^{jh})}}. \tag{2}$$

Here, $obs(e_{ik}^{jh})$ is the observed frequency and $exp(e_{ik}^{jh})$ is the expected frequency for the joint observation $e_{ik}^{jh}$ in the sequence ensemble. The adjusted residual is defined as [8]:

$$d(e_{ik}^{jh}) = \frac{z(e_{ik}^{jh})}{\sqrt{v(e_{ik}^{jh})}}. \tag{3}$$

where,

$$v(e_{ik}^{jh}) = (1 - P(X_i = a_i^j))(1 - P(X_k = a_k^h)).$$  (4)

The adjusted residual, $d(e_{ik}^{jh})$, has an asymptotic normal distribution. Hence, by convention, a statistical significance level of either 95% or 99% can be chosen. Using a 2-tailed test, the corresponding tabulated threshold values are 1.96 and 2.58, respectively. We define a statistically significant event as a joint observation, that is, the two values being statistically interdependent as,

$$d(e_{ik}^{jh}) > N_\alpha$$  (5)

where $N_\alpha$ is the threshold value with a statistical significance level α.

## 2.4  Significant Expected Mutual Information

A measure of expected mutual information involving only the significant events in the variable-pair can be denoted as $I*(X_i, X_k)$. Expected mutual information $I*(X_i, X_k)$ as defined in Eq.1 subjected to the selections from the statistical test, as derived in Eq.3, can be denoted as:

$$I.*(X_i, X_k) = I(X_i, X_k) \text{ such that } d(e_{ik}^{jh}) > N_\alpha.$$  (6)

This measure of expected mutual information then calculates the significant expected mutual information of events only if they are selected to be statistically significant, with an adjusted residual value greater then a tabulated threshold with a statistical significance level α. Residual analysis identifies events that deviate from statistical independence. Thus, only those joint observations that are statistical associated will be added to the overall expected mutual information summation. In doing so, those events that are determined as statistically independent will be discarded.

Significant expected mutual information, $I*(X_i, X_k)$, can be normalized to produce values between 0 and 1 by dividing it to Shannon entropy involving only those events. Shannon entropy involving the significant selected events is calculated as follows:

$$H*(X_i, X_k) = -\sum_{j}^{L_i} \sum_{h}^{L_k} p(x_i^j, x_k^h) \log p(x_i^j, x_k^h) \text{ such that } d(e_{ik}^{jh}) > N_\alpha.$$  (7)

The normalized expected mutual information based on the selected significant events, can now be defined as:

$$0 \le R*(X_i, X_k) = \frac{I*(X_i, X_k)}{H*(X_i, X_k)} \le 1.$$  (8)

To evaluate the total amount of interdependency expressed on a given variable $X_i$ (or site on the aligned sequences) induced by the detection of $R*$, it can be calculated as:

$$MR(X_i) = \sum_{k=1}^{m} R*(x_i, x_k) \qquad (9)$$

This measure allows us to determine which aligned locations share large bits of information with others and those which share little.

## 2.5 Detecting Biosequence Interactions Using Significant Expected Mutual Information

To incorporate amino acid properties into protein sequence analysis, we substitute identified physicochemical properties into the corresponding amino acids. The aligned sequences are then transformed, and discretized into different pre-defined intervals for evaluation. The transformed sequences are then analyzed for their statistical interdependency from these discretized physicochemical properties. This method allows analysis on discrete and continuous physicochemical properties. It can also handle patterns due to non-linear and linear dependency. The physicochemical properties of different amino acid types sharing similar characteristics can then be compared and analyzed.

For physicochemical properties that have continuous value (such as molecular weight here), a scheme is developed to discretize the property. After discretization, each amino acid is substituted with its corresponding calculated label for that property. Each continuous physicochemical property is divided into $n$ equal intervals,

$$Interval = \frac{max - min}{n} \qquad (10)$$

where $max$ and $min$ are the maximum and minimum values respectively an amino acid has for that property, and $Interval$ is the interval size. Each property then falls into one of the predefined $n$ intervals. Amino acids that share similar physicochemical values fall into the same interval are assigned identical discrete values. This process is repeated for each physicochemical property, producing a transformed sequence ensemble for each property, with a specified accuracy of discretization.

Significant expected mutual information can be compared between that from the original sequence ensemble and the sequences transformed from the physicochemical properties.

$$R^*_{Difference}(X_i, X_k) = R_{original}(X_i, X_k) - R^*_{physicochemical}(X_i, X_k) \qquad (11)$$

The difference can be visualized along the aligned position of the sequences that reflects the summation from all positions. Each generated plot is visualized in two ways. First, the plot shows the value of significant expected mutual information (normalized) between every pair of sites in the sequence. Second, a plot can be done to visualize the cumulative significant expected mutual information, denoted by the value of $MR(X_i)$ between a variable $X_i$ and the other variables in the alignment.

From the plot, a high score reflects strong interdependencies between sites. Furthermore, clusters (regions with similar characteristics) can also be observed. Because of the transformation and analysis of the differences between the original and the transformed sequences, the strong interactions can be attributed to the physicochemical property being displayed.

# 3  Experiments

## 3.1  Experimental Data

The sequence ensemble consists of 75 complete lysozyme c sequences. The aligned protein sequences have 130 residues. Lysozyme c was chosen because of its qualities as a model protein. It is classified as a monomer (or protein with a single amino acid chain). This simplifies the analysis by eliminating interactions among amino acids of different peptide chains as in more complex polymeric proteins. In addition, lysozyme c lacks any cofactors or prosthetic groups, thus eliminates interactions due to these groups. Lysozyme c has been well studied and its structure and function is reasonably understood [9].

Five physicochemical properties were chosen here: polarity, hydrophobicity [10], molecular weight, molar refractivity [2] and bulkiness [11]. The polarity property is represented as discrete values. It can be broken down into six distinct values [12], [13]. Hydrophobicity, molecular weight, molar refractivity and bulkiness are all continuous values. They are each discretized using different number of intervals, $n=4$, 5, 6, 7, 8, for evaluation.

## 3.2  Experimental Method

Initialy, we calculate the value of significant expected mutual information on the original aligned sequences between sites. Since the alignment has 130 sites, it forms a 130 by 130 matrix of the $R^*(X_i, X_k)$ value. Next, these values calculated from the original sequence are compared to those from each of the five physicochemical properties based on their different discretized labels. The calculated interdependency between all positions is summarized in Table 1. Three classes of patterns were discovered in the analysis, labeled as: gap, peak, and cluster. Gap in the plots refers to a region in the sequence with low cumulative significant value. (In the plot, they are identified as horizontal and vertical white color coded bands.) The positions that are located within the gaps are often conserved with respect to the property considered. A peak in the plots reflects positions that have high cumulative significant values (indicative of strong interdependency.) A cluster is an area in the plot that represents at least one position having strong value with another region (with a length of more than one site).

## 3.3  Experimental Results

A comparison of different physicochemical effects on the sequence can be visualized (Fig.1, Table 1). Bulkiness and hydrophobicity have the weakest effect; while polarity has the clearest, peaked at position P76. Hydrophobicity and to a lesser extent bulkiness, display clear gaps across the sequence. Gaps are indicative of lack of the effect due to the physicochemical property. Some gaps overlap between plots (Table 2). Overlapping indicates a combined effect of the physicochemical properties

**Table 1.** Patterns from the plots after subtracting the values of $R^*$ from the original sequences (extracted from Fig.1)

| Site | Pol | Hydro | Bulk | MW | MR |
|------|-----|-------|------|-----|-----|
| P10-12 | | | | | Cluster |
| P25 | Peak | | Peak | Peak, Cluster | Peak |
| P26 | Peak | | | Peak, Cluster | |
| P27 | | | | Peak, Cluster | |
| P28 | | | Gap | Peak | |
| P29-31 | | | Gap | | |
| P41 | | | Peak | Cluster | |
| P42 | | Peak | Peak | Peak, Cluster | Peak |
| P43 | | | | Peak, Cluster | |
| P44 | | | Peak | Cluster | |
| P45-47 | | | | Cluster | |
| P53-56 | | | Gap | Gap | Gap |
| P57 | | | Gap | | Gap |
| P58-60 | | | Gap | Gap | Gap |
| P61 | Peak | | Peak | | |
| P62 | Peak | | | | |
| P65-67 | | | | Peak, Cluster | |
| P69 | | | | | Peak |
| P76 | Peak | | | | |
| P86-87 | | | | | Peak, Cluster |
| P95-97 | | | | Gap | Gap |
| P98-99 | | | | | Gap |
| P100 | | Peak | | | |
| P101-4 | | | | | Gap |
| P105 | Peak | | Peak | | Peak |
| P121 | | | | | Peak |
| P124 | | | Peak | | |

*Pol* polarity, *Hydro* hydrophobicity, *Bulk* bulkiness, *MW* molecular weight, *MR* molar refractivity.

at these positions. Gaps that overlap among properties correspond to regions in the aligned sequences that are not affected by the physicochemical properties (e.g. hydrophobicity and bulkiness).

Some of the gaps include amino acids that are located in the secondary structural regions. The gap at positions P53 – P59 includes amino acids that line up with the active site cleft, in positions P57 – P59 [9]. The gap at positions P79 – P81 includes amino acids that form part of a $3_{10}$ helix (a helix structure that is characterized by shorter turns then found in an α-helix) [14]. Molecular weight, molar refractivity and polarity are more irregular than hydrophobicity and bulkiness in terms of distribution of peaks and gaps in their cumulative plots. Additionally, many peaks overlap between bulkiness, molecular weight and molar refractivity. These overlapping positions show strong interactions with respect to the property being displayed. There

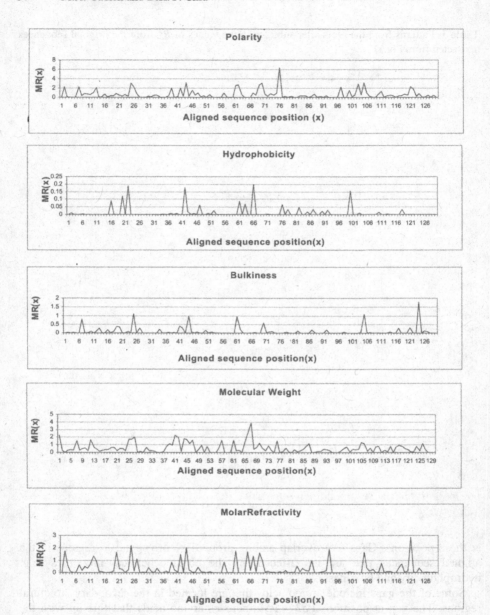

**Fig. 1.** Plots of $MR(X)$ calculated as the differences from that of the original sequences among the 5 physicochemical properties. Interval size for molecular weight and hydrophobicity is 8; bulkiness is 5; and refractivity is 4.

are two possible explanations. It is possible that at these positions all three properties interact together, in synergy. Alternatively, the similarity between these plots can be possibly attributed to the close relationship between these three properties. For

**Table 2.** Consistent patterns observed from the selected physicochemical properties

| Physicochemical Properties | Pattern Type | Site | Characteristics of the molecule |
|---|---|---|---|
| Hydrophobicity, Bulkiness | Gap | P26 – P33 | Inside α-helix at positions P25 – P36. |
| Hydrophobicity, Bulkiness | Gap | P53 – P59 | Inside the active site cleft P57 – P59. |
| Hydrophobicity, Bulkiness | Gap | P79 – P81 | Part of a single-turn $3_{10}$ helix P80 – P83, and half of the disulfine bridge between P64-P80. |
| Hydrophobicity, Bulkiness | Gap | P95 – P97 | Positions are inside α-helix in P89 – P100. |
| Hydrophobicity, Bulkiness | Gap | P104 – P109 | Overlap P104, P108 – P109 active site cleft. |
| Bulkiness, Molecular weight, molar refractivity | Peak | P25 | Inside and start of α-helix P25 – P36. |
| Bulkiness, Molecular weight, molar refractivity | Peak | P41, P44 | P44 is in the active site. |
| Molecular weight, molar refractivity | Peak | P65 – P67 | Near positions P63 – P64 that are in the active site. Also next to P64 which is part of a disulfide bridge (P64-P80). Possible stability role. |
| Bulkiness, Molecular weight, molar refractivity | Peak | P105 | In the active site. |

instance, molecular weight, bulkiness and molar refractivity are all alternate measures of amino acid size. The peak at position P44 is the active site, while peaks at positions P41, P65 – P67 are close to it [9]. Locations that are close to active site may be accounted from the shape of the catalytic site. Positions P105 is observed to interact with several other positions in the sequence (P25, P41) with respect to bulkiness and molecular weight. Positions P105 and P41 are located in the active site, while positions P105 and P25 are spatial neighbors in the 3-Dimensional model.

### 3.3.1 Physicochemically Invariant Patterns
It is generally agreed that the amino acid sequence of protein when considering the physicochemical properties hold important information about the protein [15].

Lysozyme, when considering all the occurrences by a wide variety of organisms, provides a unique opportunity to examine the common relationship between its sequences and the other relevant information of the molecule such as structure, folding characteristics and evolutionary relationships. Lysozyme c sequences highly vary with respect to sequence similarity. For example, human and chicken lysozyme, show differences in 51 sites. However, they are structurally similar [16]. Although they exhibit differences in their amino acid values, many of the variant sites are actually invariant with respect to some physicochemical properties. Many of these invariant patterns are identified by the gaps in this study.

## 4  Conclusion

The experiments showed that the selected physicochemical properties have an effect on the biosequence and can be measured using the proposed significant expected mutual information. This information measure reflects an underlying pattern of interactions. Some of these patterns are located at the active sites while others are located in the secondary structural elements like helices. Many of the identified patterns are spatial neighbors that congregate sequentially. The research shows the importance of eliminating statistical variations that are not significant and focusing on events that are, thus resulting in a more accurate calculation in very noisy sequence data.

**Acknowledgements.** The research is supported by the Discovery Grant of the National Science and Engineering Research Council of Canada and the Korea Research Foundation Grant (KRF-2004-042-C00020).

## References

1. Ladunga, I.: PHYSEAN: PHYsical Sequence Analysis for the identification of protein domains on the basis of physical and chemical properties of amino acids. Bioinformatics 15(12), 1028–1038 (1999)
2. Jones, D.D.: Amino acid properties and side-chain orientation in proteins: a cross correlation approach. J. Theor. Biol. 50(1), 167–183 (1975)
3. Branden, C., Toolze, J.: Introduction to Protein Structure, 2nd edn. Garland Publishing (1999)
4. Stolorz, P., Lapedes, A., Xia, Y.: Predicting protein secondary structure using neural net and statistical methods. J. Mol. Biol. 225(2), 363–377 (1992)
5. Crooks, G.E., Brenner, S.E.: Protein secondary structure: entropy, correlations and prediction. Bioinformatics 20(10), 1603–1611 (2004)
6. Haberman, S.J.: The analysis of residuals in cross-classified tables. Biometrics 29, 205–220 (1990)
7. Li, W.: Mutual Information Functions Versus Correlation Functions. Journal of Statistical Physics 60(5-6), 823–837 (1990)
8. Wong, A.K.C., Wang, Y.: High-order pattern discovery from discrete-valued data. IEEE Trans. Knowledge and Data Eng. 9(6), 877–893 (1997)
9. Jolles, P.: Lysozymes: Model Enzymes in Biochemistry and Biology (1996)

10. Eisenberg, D., Schwarz, E., Komarony, M., Wall, R.: Analysis of membrane and surface protein sequences with the hydrophobic moment plot. J. Mol. Biol. 179(1), 125–142 (1984)
11. Zimmerman, J.M., Eliezer, N., Simha, R.: The characterization of amino acid sequences in proteins by statistical methods. J.Theor. Biol. 21(2), 170–201 (1968)
12. Darnell, J., Lodish, H., Baltimore, D.: Molecular Cell Biology. Scientific American Books
13. Lesk, M.A.: Introduction to Protein Architecture: The Structural Biology of Proteins. Garland Publishing (1999); 2nd edition(1990)
14. Iyer, L.K., Qasba, P.K.: Molecular dynamics simulation of a-Lactalbumin and calcium binding c-type lysozyme. Protein Engineering 12(2), 129–139 (1999)
15. Phillips, D.: The Hen-White Lysozyme Molecule. Proceedings of the National Academy of Sciences of the United States of America 57, 483–495 (1967)
16. Hooke, S.D., Radford, S.E., Dobson, C.M.: The Refolding of Human Lysozyme: A Comparison with the Structurally Homologous Hen. Biochemistry 33(19), 5867–5876 (1994)

# Molecular Models to Emulate Confinement Effects on the Internal Dynamics of Organophosphorous Hydrolase

Diego E.B. Gomes[1], Roberto D. Lins[2], Pedro G. Pascutti[1], Tjerk P. Straatsma[2], and Thereza A. Soares[2]

[1] Instituto de Biofísica Carlos Chagas Filho, Universidade Federal do Rio de Janeiro,
RJ 21949-900, Brazil
[2] Computational Science and Mathematics Division, Pacific Northwest National Laboratory
P.O. Box 999, MSIN K7-90, Richland, WA 99352
tasoares@pnl.gov

**Abstract.** The confinement of the metalloenzyme organophosphorous hydrolase in functionalized mesoporous silica (FMS) enhances the stability and increases catalytic specific activity by 200% compared to the enzyme in solution. The mechanism by which these processes take place is not well understood. We have developed macroscopic and coarse-grain models of confinement to provide insights into how the nanocage environment steers enzyme conformational dynamics towards enhanced stability and enzymatic activity. The structural dynamics of organophosphorous hydrolase under the two confinement models are very distinct from each other. Comparisons of the present simulations show that only one model leads to an accurate depiction of the internal dynamics of the enzyme.

**Keywords:** phosphotriesterase, functionalized nanoporous support, enzyme immobilization, atomistic molecular dynamics, enhanced catalytic activity.

## 1 Introduction

Organophosphorous compounds are potent synthetic substances used exclusively as pesticides and chemical warfare agents (*e.g.* sarin, soman, VX). Due to the high toxicity and widespread use of these compounds, there is an increasing interest to develop strategies for their detection and detoxification.[1] Recent breakthroughs in sensory technology have enabled the development of recyclable enzyme-based biosensors, through their confinement within nanomaterials [1, 2]. The bacterial enzyme organophosphorous hydrolase (OPH; EC 3.1.8.1) is an excellent candidate to be immobilized within biosensors due to their unique ability to catalytically detoxify organophosphorous compounds. OPH is a homodimeric $(\alpha/\beta)_8$-barrel containing an active site with two divalent metal ions which are bridged by a water molecule and a carbomoylated lysine residue Figure 1). $Zn^{+2}$ is the apparent native metal, but substantial activity is observed after substitution of the binuclear metal center by $Co^{2+}$, $Cd^{2+}$, $Mn^{2+}$, or $Ni^{2+}$ [3, 4]. Both metals ions are required for full catalytic

A.L.C. Bazzan, M. Craven, and N.F. Martins (Eds.): BSB 2008, LNBI 5167, pp. 68–78, 2008.

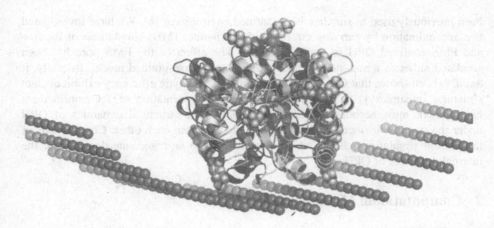

**Fig. 1.** Representation of two confinement models for organophosphorous hydrolaśe (OPH). In the positional constraint model, the $N_\zeta$ atoms of lysine residues (in CPK) are harmonically constrained (except for the carbamylated Lys169 in the active site). In the coarse-grain model functional groups COO⁻ of the FMS pore are represented by van deer Waals spheres in red. The substrate soman is shown in ball-and-stick and $Zn^{2+}$ ions in van deer Waals spheres in blue.

activity, and the kinetic constants, $k_{cat}$ and $k_{cat}/K_M$, are dependent upon the identity of the specific metal cations within the active site. OPH catalyzes the cleavage of P-O, P-F, and P-S bonds in a variety of organophosphate triesters and related phosphonates with a high catalytic turnover and broad substrate specificity [5]. Remarkably, the immobilization of OPH in functionalized mesoporous silica (FMS) was shown to enhance stability and increase enzyme catalytic activity by 200% compared to OPH free in solution [2].

The stabilization of proteins through confinement has been extensively studied through experimental and computational techniques [2, 6-16]. Based on concepts of statistical mechanics and polymer physics, confinement-induced stabilization of proteins has been attributed to a restriction of the configurational space for denatured states, *i.e.*, reduction of the entropy of the unfolded state[12, 14]. Yet, the effect of confinement on the catalytic activity of enzymes remains less understood. In part, this is because a detailed investigation of chemical reactions requires the knowledge of its electronic structure, *i.e.*, a quantum mechanical description. This finer level of description demands a much larger computational cost than the minimalist models traditionally used to study the effect of confinement on folding and stability of proteins [15-18]. Therefore, it imposes severe restrictions on the length and time scale of the systems to be simulated.

In order to calculate enzymatic rates for FMS-confined OPH in explicit solvent, it is desirable to emulate pore properties relevant for enzymatic activity while increasing only minimally the size of the system. Since the FMS pore is a rigid and mostly inert scaffold, it is assumed that these properties can be adequately described by a macroscopic and/or coarse representation of the pore. Indeed, a macroscopic model has been previously used to simulate in a confined environment [6]. We have investigated this approximation by carrying out molecular dynamics (MD) simulations of the free and FMS-confined OPH in explicit solvent. The effect of the FMS pore has been emulated either as a non-atomic model [6] or as a coarse-grained model. Recently, it has also been shown that OPH mutants with distinct catalytic efficiency exhibit distinct structural dynamics [19]. Therefore, a realistic representation of the confinement environment must account for these differences. The structural dynamics of OPH under the two confinement models are very distinct from each other. Comparisons of the present simulations show that one model leads to an inaccurate depiction of the internal dynamics of OPH.

## 2   Computational Methodology

### 2.1   OPH Model

The molecular model of the enzyme OPH was built from crystallographic coordinates of the structure determined at 1.9 Å resolution (PDB code 1EZ2) [20]. Atoms are represented by a van der Waals atomic model containing atom-centered point charges to mimic the partial charge of atoms in the system. The AMBER force field was used to treat bonded and non-bonded interactions. The co-crystallized diisopropylmethyl phosphonate analog in the X-ray structure was replaced by the *SpSc*-soman enantiomer. Amino acid protonation states were assigned accordingly to a pH of 7.0. Zinc ions in the active site of the enzyme were treated using a non-bonded model with a formal charge of +2. Partial atomic charges and parameters for soman and the carbamylated Lys169 were calculated as described by Soares et al. 2007.

### 2.2   FMS Model

The interactions between OPH and the FMS have two components: steric due to the inert nature of the silica material, and electrostatic due to functionalization of the mesopore. We assume that i. steric interactions can be approximated by a non-atomic model where the positions of atoms $N_\zeta$ lysine residues are harmonically constrained (except for the carbamylated Lys169). Lysine side-chains were chose because these residues are the linkage sites in covalently linked OPH-FMS complexes [9]. Furthermore, this model was successfully used to study the confinement of beta-galactosidases by Bismuto and coworkers [6]; ii. electrostatic interactions can be modeled as a cylindrical, uniform array of atoms, each atom corresponding to a given functional group. This coarse-grain model incorporates the atomic attributes (van der Waals and coulomb parameters) characteristic of the functional group in consideration [10] derived from the AMBER force field [21]. Hence, in the case of the functional group $COO^-(CH_2)_n$ experimentally used to functionalize the mesoporous silica, the pore surface was represented by point charged particles with the charge number of -1 and van der Waals parameters corresponding to a carboxylate anion. These particles can be spaced apart to reproduce the percentage of functional group coverage (1 nm for 20% coverage) [2]. The OPH structure was docked to the FMS pore wall based on the complementarity of their electrostatic potential surfaces calculated with the program APBS [22].

## 2.3  MD Simulations Setup

MD simulations were carried out for OPH free in solution ($OPH_{free}$), OPH confined through atom positional constraints ($OPH_{fix}$) and through the coarse-grain representation of the FMS pore ($OPH_{fms}$). For the sake of conciseness, a brief description of computational methods is presented here. For more details see [19, 23, 24]. Runs were performed under a NPT ensemble with a time step of 1fs during the equilibration and 2 fs during the production runs. The temperatures of solute and solvent were controlled by separately coupling them to a Berendsen thermostat with a relaxation time of 0.1 ps. The pressure was maintained at $1.025 \times 10^5$ Pa by means of isotropic coordinate scaling with a relaxation time t = 0.4 ps. A time step of 2 fs was used to integrate the equations of motion based on the leapfrog algorithm. The bond lengths between hydrogen and heavy atoms were constrained by using the SHAKE algorithm with a tolerance of $10^{-3}$ nm. A short-range cutoff of 1.0 nm was used for all non-bonded interactions, and long-range electrostatic interactions were treated by the smooth Particle Mesh Ewald method. The equilibration procedure consisted of thermalization of the solvent, with the solute atoms fixed, for 20 ps at 298.15 K, followed by minimization of all solute atoms, keeping the solvent coordinates fixed, and then simulation of the complete system by raising the temperature from 0 to 298.15 K in 20 ps increments of 50 K each of MD simulation. Data production was carried out for 5 ns and configurations of the trajectory were recorded every 0.2 ps. Within modest simulation times of 5 ns, several structural properties, including backbone RMSD, have reached convergence. All simulations were performed with the NWChem program [25] and the analyses of molecular trajectories were carried out with the Gromacs program [26].

# 3  Results

## 3.1  Structural Stability

Atom-positional root-mean-square deviations (RMSD) were determined for backbone atoms in the MD trajectories with respect to their positions in the X-ray structure (Figure 2). The RMSD profiles of $OPH_{free}$ and $OPH_{fms}$ are comparable but significantly distinct from that of $OPH_{fix}$. The RMSD for the $OPH_{fix}$ simulation displays values of 0.07-0.08 nm (+/- 0.005 nm) early after the equilibration phase and remains as such throughout the entire trajectory. In contrast, the RMSD for both $OPH_{free}$ and $OPH_{fms}$ converged after ca. 4 ns to values between 0.12-0.15 nm (+/- 0.013 nm).

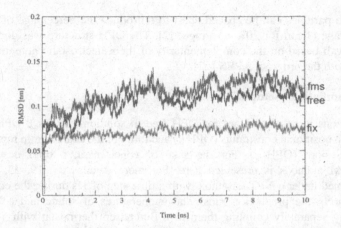

**Fig. 2.** Root-mean-square deviation of backbone atoms of OPHfree (free), OPHfix (fix) and OPHfms (FMS) with respect to the X-ray structures 1EZ2[20]

## 3.2  Structural Dynamics

The effect of the confinement models on internal dynamics of OPH can be inferred by comparisons of the atom-positional RMS fluctuations (RMSF) and essential dynamics (ED) for $OPH_{free}$, $OPH_{fix}$ and $OPH_{fms}$. The RMSF of backbone atoms were calculated for $OPH_{free}$, $OPH_{fix}$ and $OPH_{fms}$ with respect to the X-ray structure (Figure 3). The three simulations exhibit average atomic fluctuations below 0.03 nm, with average RMSF values of 0.06 nm ± 0.02 for $OPH_{free}$ and $OPH_{fms}$, and 0.05 ± 0.02 for $OPH_{fix}$. The RMSF profiles are equivalent for the three systems except for the region corresponding to residues 165 to 180, which have much lower flexibility in $OPH_{fix}$.

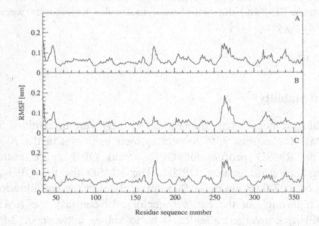

**Fig. 3.** Root-mean-square fluctuations of backbone atoms of A) OPHfree, B) OPHfix and C) OPHfms with respect to the X-ray structures 1EZ2

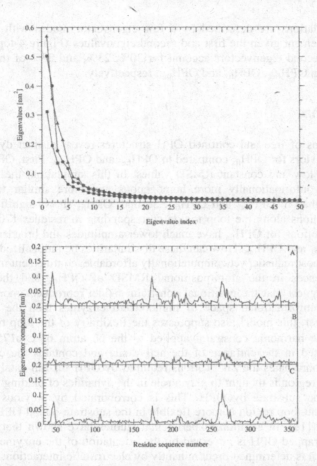

**Fig. 4.** Top panel: Magnitudes of eigenvalues calculated from the covariance matrix of backbone atom coordinates corresponding to the MD simulations of OPHfree, (circle) OPHfix (square) and OPHfms (triangle). Bottom panel: Eigenvector components for atomic displacement along the first eigenvector for the MD-generated ensembles of A) OPHfree, B) OPHfix and C) OPHfms.

ED analysis techniques were applied to the MD trajectories to separate internal motions into orthogonal motions [27]. Large-amplitude motions of the protein are described by a few eigenvector modes and separated from a much larger number of remaining small-scale motions. The technique is based on the diagonalization of the covariance matrix of atomic fluctuations obtained from the MD trajectories, after removal of overall translation and rotation [27]. The eigenvalues are the average square displacements and, consequently, a measure of the amplitude of the motions along the corresponding eigenvectors.

The contributions of the backbone atoms to the first and second eigenvectors are displayed in Figure 4. They represent the relative displacement of each residue due to the motion described by a given eigenvector. The anharmonic motions of OPH in the all three simulations are described by a few eigenvector modes with most of the atomic displacement given the first and second eigenvalues (Figure 4-top). Together, the first and second eigenvectors account for 30%, 23%, and 28% of the total atom displacement in OPH$_{free}$, OPH$_{fix}$ and OPH$_{fms}$, respectively.

# 4  Discussion

MD simulations of free and confined OPH structures reveal distinct dynamical and structural behaviors for OPH$_{fix}$ compared to OPH$_{free}$ and OPH$_{fms}$. First, OPH$_{fix}$ exhibits comparatively low and constant RMSD values. In this simulation, the ensemble of structures is conformationally more homogenous and more similar to the X-ray conformation than in OPH$_{free}$ and OPH$_{fms}$. Second, OPH$_{fix}$ shows significantly lower atomic fluctuations along the loop region corresponding to residues 170-180. Third, anharmonic motions for OPH$_{fix}$ have much lower amplitudes and broader distribution than for OPH$_{free}$ and OPH$_{fms}$. How can these dissimilarities be rationalized to allow the choice of the most realistic, yet computationally affordable, confinement model?

The differences in the atom-positional RMSD of OPH$_{fix}$ and the other two simulations suggest that the positional constraint model reproduces more accurately the reduced conformational space of immobilized enzymes than the coarse-grain model. However, this model also suppresses the flexibility of the loop residues 170-180 due to the harmonic constraint applied to the N$_f$ atom of Lys175. This loop region is located in the entrance of the active site and contains the carbamylated Lys169 that coordinates the Zn$^{2+}$ cations required by OPH for full catalytic activity. Therefore, the region is thought to play a role in the dynamics of binding and possibly catalysis of the substrate by OPH. This is corroborated by previous simulations showing that the loop region is more flexible in the substrate-bound OPH than in the unbound form [19]. In addition, experimental studies have shown that the specific activity of entrapped OPH is governed by the orientation of the enzyme in the FMS pore that in turn is determined predominantly by electrostatic interactions between the positively-charged enzyme and the negatively-charged FMS [10]. OPH shows a positive electrostatic potential spread over the surface opposed to the active site (Figure 5). The most favorable binding orientation of OPH to the electronegative pore-wall surface is via this "back" region. In such orientation the active site and residues 170-180 faces the center of the pore and are away from the functionalized groups of the pore wall. Therefore, Lys175 and neighboring residues should be under minimal steric influence of the FMS pore wall. These findings strongly suggest that the lower atomic fluctuations of residues 170-180 are an artifact introduced by the atom positional constraints.

ED analyses of MD trajectories provide insight into the persistent motions of the protein in the equilibrated state as sampled in the computer simulation. These motions need not correspond to the relevant motions required for the function of the protein, but offer a quantitative means to compare large-scale motions from different simulations. The highest-amplitude anharmonic atomic displacement represented by the eigenvalues is considerably lower for OPH$_{fix}$ (0.31 nm$^2$) compared to OPH$_{free}$ (0.50 nm$^2$) and OPH$_{fms}$ (0.57 nm$^2$) (Figure 4-top). The regions of the protein chiefly contributing to these motions are evident for OPH$_{free}$ and OPH$_{fms}$ (Figure 4-bottom).

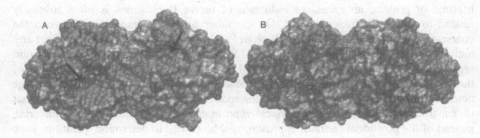

**Fig. 5.** Representation of the electrostatic potential distribution on the molecular surface of OPH. A) Front. View (black arrows highlight the two active sites. B) Back view (which faces the FMS pore wall). Blue color represents a positive potential, red color represents a negative potential and the white color indicates areas of a neutral potential. The scale of the surface potential is given in kBT and in the range between -5 to 5 kBT.

In contrast, the same regions are nearly indistinguishable from regions contributing only marginally to anharmonic motions in OPH$_{fix}$. Thus, it indicates that the positional constraint model suppresses the conformational fluctuations of the whole enzyme in a non-selective fashion. This is clearly not a realistic representation of confined OPH. Enzymatic reactions intrinsically involve multiple kinetic steps, complex protein-substrate interactions, and substantial protein conformational changes [28]. Rate fluctuations among the individual molecules has been attributed to protein conformational fluctuations [29]. Different conformations of the active site of enzymes are primarily responsible for the differences in enzymatic reactivity. Furthermore, OPH mutants with distinct catalytic efficiency were shown to exhibit distinct structural dynamics [19]. The residues contributing more significantly to the conformational difference between these mutants are confined to well-defined regions of the protein. Therefore the general suppression of atomic fluctuations irrespective of the their location in the protein structure is expected to decrease catalytic efficiency.

## 5  Conclusion

Comparisons of the RMSD curves and fluctuation amplitudes for the three simulations showed that the positional constraint model limits the phase space of the enzyme, reducing the number of conformations accessible to the catalytically competent form. Thus, the dynamics of OPH$_{fix}$ is restricted to a region of the configurational space different from that sampled by the OPH$_{free}$ and OPH$_{fms}$. If only the RMSD analysis is taken into account, the OPH$_{fix}$ simulation seems to better describe the pool of configurations around the X-ray structure. However, analyses of the fluctuations and persistent motions in the three systems reveal that the lower flexibility exhibited by the OPH$_{fix}$ is an artifact induced by the positional constraint model. The indiscriminate suppression of internal motions along the entire protein is likely to translate into decrease of catalytic efficiency. While restriction of denatured states can extend the lifetime of protein, an excessive reduction of native fluctuations is often inversely related to catalytic efficiency [28]. On the other hand, the interaction between the coarse-grained FMS model and the all-atom OPH enzyme was shown not to affect any native state motions presented by the free enzyme. Although a coarse-grain representation of the functional groups will yield a more homogenous description of the charge distribution along the silica mesoporous material, the resulting average potential of mean force associated with the model is expected to be equivalent to that of an atomistic model. Yet, a physical representation of the mesoporous material, instead of the positional restraint approach, will be crucial to determine quantities such as diffusion coefficients and collision rates in the confined environment. These results point to the multiscale approach as a viable model for more tangible simulations of confined proteins.

The interactions of proteins with FMS are key to the understanding of molecular confinement and interactive effects. This understanding is essential to direct the design and engineering of enzyme-FMS complexes with a higher protein load capacity and improved biosensor performance.

## Acknowledgments

The authors acknowledge the William R. Wiley Environmental Molecular Sciences Laboratory for the computational resources required for this work (project gc20896). TAS acknowledges Dr. Chenghong Lei for fruitful discussions. D.E.B.G and P.G.P. acknowledge the financial support of the Brazilian National Council for Scientific and Technological Development (CNPq). The research was performed at the Pacific Northwest National Laboratory as part of the 2006 Summer Research Institute in Interfacial and Condensed Phase Chemical Physics. This is a program of the Office of Basic Energy Sciences of the U.S Department of Energy (DOE). Pacific Northwest National Laboratory is operated for the Department of Energy by Battelle.

## References

1. Cao, L.: Immobilized Enzymes: science or art. Current Opinion in Chemical Biology 9, 217–226 (2005)
2. Lei, C., Shin, Y., Liu, J., Ackerman, E.J.: Entrapping enzyme in a functionalized nanoporous support. Journal of the American Chemical Society 124, 11242–11243 (2002)
3. Omburo, G.A., Kuo, J.M., Mullins, L.S., Raushel, F.M.: Characterization of the zinc binding site of bacterial phosphotriesterase. Journal of Biological Chemistry 267, 13278–13283 (1992)
4. Rochu, D., Renault, F., Viguille, N., Crouzier, D., Froment, M.T., Masson, P.: Contribution of the active-site metal cation to the catalytic activity and to the conformational stability of phosphotriesterase: temperature- and pH-dependence. Biochemical Journal 380, 627–633 (2004)
5. Raushel, F.M.: Bacterial detoxification of organophosphate nerve agents. Current Opinion in Microbiology 5, 288–295 (2002)

6. Bismuto, E., Martelli, P.L., Maio, A.D., Mita, D.G., Irace, G., Casadio, R.: Effect of molecular confinement on internal enzyme dynamics: Frequency domain fluorometry and molecular dynamics simulation studies. Biopolymers 67, 85–95 (2002)
7. Bolis, D., Politou, A.S., Kelly, G., Pastore, A., Temussi, P.A.: Protein stability in nanocages: a novel approach for influencing protein stability by molecular confinement. Journal of Molecular Biology 336, 203–212 (2004)
8. Eggers, D.K., Valentine, J.S.: Molecular confinement influences protein structure and enhances thermal stability. Protein Science 10, 250–261 (2001)
9. Lei, C., Shin, Y., Liu, J., Ackerman, E.J.: Synergetic effects of nanoporous support and urea on enzyme activity. Nano Letters 7, 1050–1053 (2007)
10. Lei, C., Soares, T.A., Shin, Y., Liu, J., Ackerman, E.J.: Enzyme specific activity in functionalized nanoporous supports Nanotechnology, vol. 19, pp. 125102–125111 (2008)
11. Lucent, D., Vishal, V., Pande, V.S.: Protein folding under confinement: A role for solvent. Proceedings of the National Academy of Sciences USA 104, 10430–10434 (2007)
12. Minton, A.P.: The influence of macromolecular crowding on HIV-1 protease internal dynamics. Proceedings of the National Academy of Sciences USA 276, 10577–10580 (2001)
13. Thurmalai, D., Klimov, D.K., Lorimer, G.H.: Caging helps proteins fold. Proceedings of the National Academy of Sciences USA 100, 11195–11197 (2003)
14. Zhou, H.X., Dill, K.A.: Stabilization of proteins in confined spaces. Biochemistry 40, 11289–11293 (2001)
15. Klimov, D.K., Newfield, D., Thirumalai, D.: Simulations of beta-hairpin folding spherical pores using distributed computing. Proceedings of the National Academy of Sciences USA 99, 8019–8024 (2002)
16. Takagi, F., Koga, N., Takada, S.: How protein thermodynamics and folding mechanisms are altered by the chaperonin cage: Molecular simulations. Proceedings of the National Academy of Sciences USA 100, 11367–11372 (2003)
17. Lu, D., Liu, Z., Wu, J.: Structural transitions of confined model proteins: molecular dynamics simulation and experimental validation. Biophysical Journal 90, 3224–3238 (2006)
18. Rathore, N., Knotts-IV, T.A., dePablo, J.J.: Confinement effects on the thermodynamics of protein folding: Monte Carlo simulations. Biophysical Journal 90, 1767–1773 (2006)
19. Soares, T.A., Osman, M., Straatsma, T.P.: Molecular dynamics of organophosphorous hydrolases bound to the nerve agent soman. Journal of Chemical Theory and Computation 3, 1569–1579 (2007)
20. Benning, M.M., Hong, S.B., Raushel, F.M., Holden, H.M.: The binding of substrate analogs to phosphotriesterase. Journal of Biological Chemistry 275, 30556–30560 (2000)
21. Cornell, W.D., Cieplak, P., Bayly, C.I., Gould, I.R., Merz, K.M., Ferguson, D.M., Spellmeyer, D.C., Fox, T., Caldwell, W., Kollman, P.A.: A second generation force field for the simulation of proteins and nucleic acids. Journal of the American Chemical Society 117, 5179–5197 (1995)
22. Baker, N.A., Sept, D., Joseph, S., Holst, M.J., McCammon, J.A.: Electrostatics of nanosystems: application to microtubules and the ribosome. Proceedings of the National Academy of Sciences USA 98, 10037–10041 (2001)
23. Mustata, G.I., Soares, T.A., Briggs, J.M.: Molecular dynamics studies of alanine racemase: A structural model for drug design. Biopolymers 70, 186–200 (2003)
24. Soares, T.A., Lins, R.D., Straatsma, T.P., Briggs, J.M.: Internal dynamics and ionization states of the macrophage migration inhibitory factor: Comparison between wild-type and mutant forms. Biopolymers 65, 313–323 (2002)

25. Bylaska, E.J., Jong, W.A.d., Kowalski, K., Straatsma, T.P., Valiev, M., Wang, D., Aprà, E., Windus, T.L., Hirata, S., Hackler, M.T., Zhao, Y., Fan, P.-D., Harrison, R.J., Dupuis, M., Smith, D.M.A., Nieplocha, J., Tipparaju, V., Krishnan, M., Auer, A.A., Nooijen, M., Brown, E., Cisneros, G., Fann, G.I., Frücht, H., Garza, J., Hirao, K., Kendall, R., Nichols, J.A., Tsemekhman, K., Wolinsk, K., Anchell, J., Bernholdt, D., Borowski, P., Clark, T., Clerc, D., Dachsel, H., Deegan, M., Dyall, K., Elwood, D., Glendening, E., Gutowski, M., Hess, A., Jaffe, J., Johnson, B., Ju, J., Kobayashi, R., Kutteh, R., Lin, Z., Littlefield, R., Long, X., Meng, B., Nakajima, T., Niu, S., Pollack, L., Rosing, M., Sandrone, G., Stave, M., Taylor, H., Thomas, G., Lenthe, J.v., Wong, A., Zhang, Z.: NWChem, A Computational Chemistry Package for Parallel Computers, Version 5.0. Pacific Northwest National Laboratory, Richland, Washington 99352-0999, USA (A modified version) (2006)
26. Lindahl, E., Hess, B., Spoel, D.v.d.: GROMACS 3.0: A package for molecular simulation and trajectory analysis. Journal of Molecular Modeling 7, 306–317 (2001)
27. García, A.E.: Large-amplitude nonlinear motions in proteins. Physical Review Letters 68, 2696–2699 (1992)
28. Boehr, D.D., Dyson, H.J., Wright, P.E.: An NMR Perspective on Enzyme Dynamics. Chemical Reviews 106, 3055–3079 (2006)
29. Whitten, S.T., Garcia-Moreno, E.B., Hilser, V.J.: Local conformational fluctuations can modulate the coupling between proton binding and global structural transitions in proteins. Proceedings of the National Academy of Sciences USA 102, 4282–4287 (2005)

# On the Toric Graph as a Tool to Handle the Problem of Sorting by Transpositions

Rodrigo de A. Hausen[1,*], Luerbio Faria[2], Celina M.H. de Figueiredo[1], and Luis Antonio B. Kowada[3]

[1] Universidade Federal do Rio de Janeiro
hausen@cos.ufrj.br
[2] Universidade do Estado do Rio de Janeiro
[3] Universidade Federal Fluminense

**Abstract.** To this date, neither a polynomial algorithm to sort a permutation by transpositions has been found, nor a proof that it is an NP-hard problem has been given. Therefore, determining the exact transposition distance $d_t(\pi)$ of a generic permutation $\pi$, relative to the identity, is generally done by an exhaustive search on the space $S_n$ of all permutations of $n$ elements. In a 2001 paper, Eriksson *et al.* [1] made a breakthrough by proposing a structure named by them as *toric graph*, which allowed the reduction of the search space, speeding-up the process, such that greater instances could be solved. Surprisingly, Eriksson *et al.* were able to exhibit a counterexample to a conjecture by Meidanis *et al.* [2] that the transposition diameter would be equal to the distance of the reverse permutation $\lfloor n/2 \rfloor + 1$. The goal of the present paper is to further study the toric graph, focusing on the case when $n+1$ is prime. We observe that the transposition diameter problem for $n = 16$ is still open. We determine that there are exactly $\frac{n!-n}{n+1} + n$ vertices in the toric graph and find a lower bound $d_t(\pi) \geq \lfloor n/2 \rfloor$ on the transposition distance for every permutation $\pi$ in a unitary toric class that is not the identity permutation. We provide experimental data on the exact distance of those permutations to back our conjecture that $d_t(\pi) \leq \lfloor n/2 \rfloor + 1$, where $\pi$ belongs to a unitary toric class, and that $\lfloor n/2 \rfloor + 1$ is equal to the transposition diameter when $n + 1$ is prime.

## 1 Introduction

In the last few years, we have witnessed formidable advances in our understanding of genome rearrangements — for background on this topic, the reader is referred to the introductory text [3]. Bafna and Pevzner [4] analyzed the problem with respect to transpositions, presenting approximation algorithms and leaving a number of open questions; among them, the complexity of the problem, the determination of the transposition distance of the reverse permutation and the determination of the diameter (largest possible distance between two permutations of $n$ elements). Meidanis, Walter and Dias [2] answered one of those

* Corresponding author.

A.L.C. Bazzan, M. Craven, and N.F. Martins (Eds.): BSB 2008, LNBI 5167, pp. 79–91, 2008.
© Springer-Verlag Berlin Heidelberg 2008

questions: they found that $\lfloor n/2 \rfloor + 1$ is the minimum number of transpositions needed to transform a permutation $[\pi_1 \pi_2 \ldots \pi_n]$ into its reverse $[\pi_n \pi_{n-1} \ldots \pi_1]$. Besides that, they showed a sequence that transformed a permutation into its reverse with exactly $\lfloor n/2 \rfloor + 1$ transpositions, which implied that the transposition distance between a permutation and its reverse is indeed $\lfloor n/2 \rfloor + 1$. Meidanis, Walter and Dias conjectured that the reverse permutation $[n\, n-1 \ldots 1]$ was the most difficult case to sort by transpositions, which would set the transposition diameter to $\lfloor n/2 \rfloor + 1$ for $n \geq 3$.

Eriksson *et al.* [1] showed that Meidanis, Walter and Dias' conjecture on the transposition diameter was not valid in general, since they found permutations of $n = 13$ elements (the so-called bridge player case) and also of $n = 15$ elements that needed $\lfloor \frac{n+1}{2} \rfloor + 1$ transpositions to be sorted. Still, they hoped that, apart from $n = 13$ and $n = 15$, the conjecture remained valid. More recently, Elias and Hartman [5] managed to extend the counter-examples from Eriksson *et al.* to all odd values of $n$, $n \geq 13$, improving the lower bound on the transposition diameter to $D_t(n) \geq \lfloor \frac{n+1}{2} \rfloor + 1$.

Our goal in this paper is to merge two successful strategies: we further investigate the toric graph proposed by Eriksson *et al.* [1] and determine the structure of the reality and desire diagram [3,4] for a number of toric classes, thus obtaining a lower bound on their transposition distance.

This article is organized as follows. In this first section, we provide the basic background on the problem of determining the transposition distance between two given permutations. Section 2 shows the toric graph, an approach used in [1] that allowed the study of larger permutations. In Sect. 3, we determine the size of the toric graph $Tor(n)$, for $n + 1$ prime and show that the reality and desire diagram can be used to devise a lower bound of $n/2$ on the transposition distance for a family of permutations, namely those that belong to unitary toric classes. This lower bound seems to be tight, as discussed in the concluding remarks of Sect. 4, which also examines how our results seem to confirm Meidanis, Walter and Dias' conjecture [2] on the transposition diameter in the case $n = 16$, and more generally when $n + 1$ is prime.

## 1.1   Basic Definitions

**Definition 1.** *A permutation is a bijective function of a finite set $X$ onto itself.*

Since we are dealing, for the most part, with permutations of the set $[n] = \{1, 2, \ldots, n\}$ onto itself, we use the term permutation to denote a permutation of $[n]$ onto itself, except where explicitly stated otherwise.

The notation

$$\pi = [\pi_1 \, \pi_2 \, \ldots \, \pi_i \, \ldots \, \pi_n]$$

denotes a permutation of $n$ elements that maps 1 to $\pi_1$, 2 to $\pi_2$, ..., $i$ to $\pi_i$, ..., $n$ to $\pi_n$. Since $\pi$ is bijective, $\pi_i \neq \pi_j$ if $i \neq j$.

If we define the product $\pi\sigma$ of two permutations $\pi$, $\sigma$ to be the composition of functions $\sigma \circ \pi$, then the set of all permutations of $n$ elements along with the product operation forms a symmetric group, which we denote as $S_n$.

**Definition 2.** *The* identity permutation *of n elements is defined as*

$$\iota_{[n]} := [1\,2\,\ldots\,i\,\ldots\,n].$$

**Definition 3.** *[4] A* transposition[1], *denoted by* $t(i,j,k)$, *where* $1 \leq i < j < k \leq n+1$, *"cuts" the elements between the positions* $j$ *and* $k-1$ *(both inclusive) and "pastes" them immediately before the i-th position. Let*

$$\pi = [\pi_1\pi_2\ldots\pi_{i-1}\pi_i\ldots\pi_{j-1}\boxed{\pi_j\ldots\pi_{k-1}}\pi_k\ldots\pi_n],$$

*so*

$$\pi \cdot t(i,j,k) = [\pi_1\pi_2\ldots\pi_{i-1}\boxed{\pi_j\ldots\pi_{k-1}}\pi_i\ldots\pi_{j-1}\pi_k\ldots\pi_n].$$

**Definition 4.** *[4] The* transposition distance $d_t(\pi,\sigma)$ *of two different permutations* $\pi,\sigma$ *is the length* $q$ *of the shortest sequence of transpositions* $t_1, t_2, \ldots, t_q$ *such that* $\pi t_1 t_2 \ldots t_q = \sigma$. *If we have* $\pi = \sigma$, *then we define* $d_t(\pi,\sigma) = 0$.

It follows easily from the definition that, given permutations $\pi,\sigma$ and $\gamma$ in $S_n$, the transposition distance satisfies: i) $d_t(\pi,\sigma) = 0$ if, and only if, $\pi = \sigma$; ii) $d_t(\pi,\sigma) = d_t(\sigma,\pi)$; and iii) $d_t(\pi,\gamma) \leq d_t(\pi,\sigma) + d_t(\sigma,\gamma)$. Therefore, $d_t$ is a metric in $S_n$.

It is also true that, if we relabel the elements of $\sigma$ and $\pi$ in the same manner, then the transposition distance is preserved, i. e., $d_t(\gamma\sigma, \gamma\pi) = d_t(\sigma,\pi)$, for any permutation $\gamma$. More specifically, if we choose $\gamma = \sigma^{-1}$, then the equality becomes $d_t(\sigma,\pi) = d_t(\iota, \sigma^{-1}\pi)$.

Given a permutation $\sigma$, the problem of finding a smallest sequence of transpositions $t_1, \ldots, t_q$ such that $\iota\, t_1 t_2 \ldots t_q = \sigma$ is called *sorting by transpositions*. In this case we write $d_t(\sigma) = q$ as a shorthand for $d_t(\iota, \sigma) = q$.

Since $d_t(\pi,\sigma)$ is a metric on $S_n$, the following question arises: what pair(s) of permutations maximizes the transposition distance? Or, more formally:

**Definition 5.** *[4] The* transposition diameter $D_t(n)$ *of the symmetric group* $S_n$ *is the maximum attainable value for* $d_t(\sigma,\pi)$, *where* $\sigma$ *and* $\pi$ *are permutations of n elements.*

Since $d_t(\sigma,\pi) = d_t(\iota, \sigma^{-1}\pi) = d_t(\sigma^{-1}\pi)$, we may give an alternate definition for the transposition diameter: $D_t(n) = \max\{d_t(\sigma)\,|\,\sigma$ is in $S_n\}$. Therefore, the problem of determining the transposition diameter becomes the problem of finding the maximum number of transpositions needed to sort any permutation of $n$ elements.

In an attempt to solve another related problem on genome rearrangements, Bafna and Pevzner [6] introduced a graph that captures the structure of the permutations being compared: the *reality and desire diagram*, or *breakpoint graph*.

---

[1] Nomenclature note: to the reader used to Group Theory, it may seem strange that the name "transposition" is used to define a different concept in this text. We have chosen to adopt the nomenclature more commonly used for the study of genome rearrangement problems.

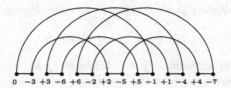

**Fig. 1.** Reality and desire diagram $RD([3\,6\,2\,5\,1\,4], \iota)$

**Definition 6.** *[3,4,6] Given two permutations $\pi, \sigma$ in $S_n$, the* reality and desire diagram $RD(\pi, \sigma)$ *is a graph on the following set of vertices:*

$$V(RD(\pi, \sigma)) = \{0, -1, +1, -2, +2, \ldots, -n, +n, -(n+1)\},$$

*and whose set of edges is partitioned into two sets $R$ and $D$, respectively* reality *and* desire *edges, defined as*

$$R = \big\{(+\pi_\ell, -\pi_{\ell+1}) \,|\, \ell = 1, \ldots, n-1\big\} \cup \big\{(0, -\pi_1), \, (+\pi_n, -(n+1))\big\},$$
$$D = \big\{(+\sigma_\ell, -\sigma_{\ell+1}) \,|\, \ell = 1, \ldots, n-1\big\} \cup \big\{(0, -\sigma_1), \, (+\sigma_n, -(n+1))\big\}.$$

Figure 1 depicts a reality and desire diagram; the reality edges are drawn as straight horizontal lines, whereas the desire edges are drawn as arcs. By definition, every vertex of the reality and desire diagram has degree 2. As a consequence, the diagram can be partitioned into disjoint cycles. A cycle in the diagram has the same number of reality and desire edges; those reality and desire edges alternate along the cycle. The length of a cycle is the number of reality (or desire) edges it has. A cycle is said to be an *odd* (*even*) *cycle* if it has an odd (resp. even) length. The number $c_{odd}(\pi, \sigma)$ of odd cycles in $RD(\pi, \sigma)$ is an important parameter, since the best known estimates for the transposition distance are a function of it.

**Theorem 1.** *[4] Let $\pi, \sigma$ be two permutations of $n$ elements. The transposition distance between $\pi$ and $\sigma$ satisfies the inequality*

$$d_t(\pi, \sigma) \geq \frac{n + 1 - c_{odd}(\pi, \sigma)}{2}.$$

## 2   The Toric Graph

The relations between the permutations in $S_n$, relative to transpositions, can be expressed as a graph.

**Definition 7.** *The* transposition rearrangement graph, *denoted as $TRG(n)$, is a graph whose vertices are the permutations in $S_n$ and whose edges are $\pi\sigma$, such that $\pi = \sigma t$ and $t$ is a transposition (or, equivalently, $\sigma = \pi t'$ for another transposition $t'$).*

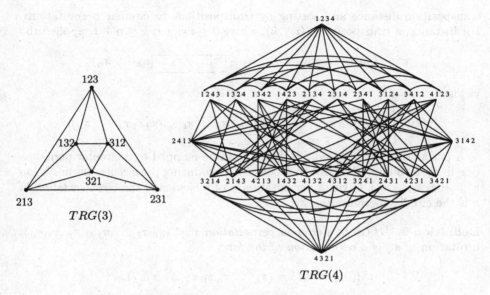

**Fig. 2.** The graphs $TRG(3)$ and $TRG(4)$

Most concepts from the classical study of rearrangements by transpositions can be translated in terms of the transposition rearrangement graph $TRG(n)$. In particular, a shortest path between two vertices $\pi$ and $\sigma$ can be identified with a sequence of transpositions that transforms $\pi$ into $\sigma$, and the length of a shortest path (the number of edges it contains) is the same as the distance $d_t(\pi, \sigma)$.

By construction, $TRG(n)$ is a regular graph with $n!$ vertices. The degree of each vertex $\pi$ is the number of distinct transpositions that can be applied to the permutation, which is $(n^3 - n)/6$ for any permutation of $n$ elements.

Figure 2 depicts the transposition rearrangement graphs $TRG(n)$ for $n = 3$ and $n = 4$.

Since $TRG(n)$ grows at a factorial rate as $n$ increases, a more compact representation of it becomes necessary. In the remainder of this section, we describe the approach of Eriksson *et al.* [1] as a means to this end.

**Definition 8.** *A circular permutation $\pi^c$ is a permutation of $[n] \cup \{0\}$.*

The notation

$$\pi^c = (\pi_0 \, \pi_1 \, \ldots \, \pi_n)$$

is used to mean that $\pi^c$ maps 0 to $\pi_0$, 1 to $\pi_1$, ..., $n$ to $\pi_n$, where each $\pi_i$ is an integer such that $0 \leq \pi_i \leq n$. Notice that, to avoid confusion, we are using square brackets for ordinary permutations and parentheses for circular permutations.

The group of circular permutations is denoted by $S_n^c$. Since it is easy to find an isomorphism between $S_n^c$ and $S_{n+1}$, we can extend the concepts of transposition,

transposition distance and sorting by transpositions to circular permutations. For instance, a transposition $t(i, j, k)$, where $0 \leq i < j < k \leq n + 1$, applied to

$$\pi^c = (\pi_0 \, \pi_1 \, \ldots \, \pi_{i-1} \, \pi_i \, \ldots \, \pi_{j-1} \, \boxed{\pi_j \, \ldots \, \pi_{k-1}} \, \pi_k \, \ldots \, \pi_n)$$

yields

$$\pi^c t(i, j, k) = (\pi_0 \, \pi_1 \, \ldots \, \pi_{i-1} \, \boxed{\pi_j \, \ldots \, \pi_{k-1}} \, \pi_i \, \ldots \, \pi_{j-1} \, \pi_k \, \ldots \, \pi_n).$$

A permutation $\pi = [\pi_1 \pi_2 \ldots \pi_n]$ in $S_n$ can be mapped to a circular permutation in $S_n^c$ by adding the element 0 before $\pi_1$, producing the circular permutation $\pi^c = (0\pi_1\pi_2 \ldots \pi_n)$. Given a permutation $\pi$ of $n$ elements, the *circularization* of $\pi$ is the circular permutation $\pi^c$.

**Definition 9.** *[1] Given a circular permutation $\pi^c = (\pi_0 \, \pi_1 \, \ldots \, \pi_{j-1} \, \pi_j \, \ldots \, \pi_n)$, a rotation of $\pi^c$ is a permutation of the form*

$$\pi^c \, t(0, j, n+1) = (\pi_j \, \ldots \, \pi_n \, \pi_0 \, \pi_1 \, \ldots \, \pi_{j-1}),$$

*for some value $0 < j < n + 1$.*

We say that two circular permutations $\pi^c$ and $\sigma^c$ are *circularly equivalent*, denoted as $\pi^c \equiv^c \sigma^c$, if $\sigma^c = \pi^c$ or if $\sigma^c$ is a rotation of $\pi^c$, that is $\pi^c \, t(0, j, n+1) = \sigma^c$ for some $j$ (or, equivalently, $\sigma^c \, t(0, j', n+1) = \pi^c$ for some $j'$).

For instance, the following circular permutations are all circularly equivalent: $(0\,3\,4\,1\,2) \equiv^c (3\,4\,1\,2\,0) \equiv^c (4\,1\,2\,0\,3) \equiv^c (1\,2\,0\,3\,4) \equiv^c (2\,0\,3\,4\,1)$.

**Definition 10.** *[1] Let $\pi$ be a permutation in $S_n$ and $m$ an integer. An $m$-step cyclic value shift of $\pi$ is the circular permutation*

$$m + \pi^c := (\overline{m} \, \overline{m + \pi_1} \ldots \overline{m + \pi_n}),$$

*where $\overline{k}$ is the remainder of the division of $k$ by $n + 1$.*

*Example 1.* Let $\pi = [3\,4\,1\,2]$. The only circular permutations that result from a cyclic value shift of $\pi$ are:

$$1 + \pi^c = (1\,4\,0\,2\,3) \equiv^c (0\,2\,3\,1\,4), \qquad 2 + \pi^c = (2\,0\,1\,3\,4) \equiv^c (0\,1\,3\,4\,2),$$
$$3 + \pi^c = (3\,1\,2\,4\,0) \equiv^c (0\,3\,1\,2\,4), \text{ and } 4 + \pi^c = (4\,2\,3\,0\,1) \equiv^c (0\,1\,4\,2\,3).$$

Any cyclic value shift of the identity permutation $[1\,2 \ldots n]$ generates a circular permutation that is circularly equivalent to $(0\,1\,2 \ldots n)$. In a similar manner, a cyclic value shift of the reverse permutation $[n\,n-1 \ldots 1]$ yields a circular permutation that is circularly equivalent to $(0\,n\,n-1 \ldots 1)$.

**Definition 11.** *[1] Two permutations $\pi, \sigma$ are torically equivalent, $\pi \equiv_\circ^\circ \sigma$, if $\pi^c \equiv^c m + \sigma^c$ for some integer $m$.*

From example 1, we can infer that $[3\,4\,1\,2]$, $[2\,3\,1\,4]$, $[1\,3\,4\,2]$, $[3\,1\,2\,4]$ and $[1\,4\,2\,3]$ belong to the same equivalence class under the toric equivalence relation. We use $\pi_\circ^\circ$ to denote the toric equivalence class of $\pi$.

As we can see in Theorem 2 and Corollary 1, it is possible to group vertices in $TRG(n)$ according to their toric equivalence.

**Theorem 2.** *[1] Let $\pi\sigma$ be an edge of $TRG(n)$. For every permutation $\pi'$ such that $\pi' \equiv_\circ^\circ \pi$, there is a permutation $\sigma'$ torically equivalent to $\sigma$ such that $\pi'\sigma'$ is also an edge of $TRG(n)$.*

**Corollary 1.** *[1] If two permutations $\pi, \pi'$ are torically equivalent, then $d_t(\pi) = d_t(\pi')$.*

**Definition 12.** *[1] The toric graph of order $n$, $Tor(n) = (V, E)$, is a graph where each vertex in $V$ corresponds to an equivalence class under the toric equivalence of the permutations of $n$ elements, and the set of edges is:*

$$E = \{\pi_\circ^\circ \sigma_\circ^\circ \mid \pi\sigma \text{ is an edge of } TRG(n)\}.$$

The toric graphs $Tor(3)$ and $Tor(4)$ are depicted in Fig. 3.

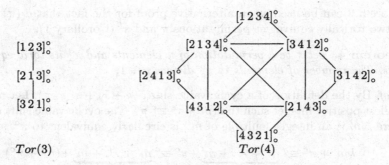

**Fig. 3.** The toric graphs $Tor(3)$ and $Tor(4)$

## 3 New Results

We start this section with a connection between the classic approach using the reality and desire diagram and the less used approach by toric classes. Afterwards, we characterize the toric equivalence classes that have only 1 element — the unitary classes — in the case $n + 1$ prime. This characterization is used to calculate the size of the toric graph $Tor(n)$. We also estimate the transposition distance between two unitary classes, an interesting result given the difficulty of finding bounds on the transposition distance.

**Theorem 3.** *The reality and desire diagrams $RD(\pi, \iota)$ and $RD(\pi', \iota)$ of two torically equivalent permutations $\pi, \pi'$, respectively, are isomorphic graphs.*

*Proof.* Let $\pi, \pi'$ be two torically equivalent permutations. By the definition of toric equivalence, there exists an integer $m$ such that $\pi^c \equiv^c m + \pi'^c$. Comparing the elements of $\pi^c$ and $\pi'^c$, we have $\pi_i \equiv \pi'_{\overline{i+\ell}} + m \pmod{n+1}$ for $i = 0, \ldots, n$, where $\ell$ is such that $\pi'_\ell + m \equiv 0 \pmod{n+1}$.

Let us now turn our attention to the reality and desire diagrams $RD(\pi, \iota)$ and $RD(\pi', \iota)$. Both graphs are on the same set of vertices, and have the same set of desire edges $\left( +i, -(i+1) \right)$, $i = 0, \ldots, n$. In the remainder of this proof, we will demonstrate that there is an isomorphism on that preserves the adjacency of the vertices joined by reality edges.

In $RD(\pi, \iota)$, there exists a reality edge between $+\pi_i$ and $-\pi_j$ if, and only if, $|\pi_i - \pi_j| = 1$, where $0 \leq i, j \leq n$. The equivalence

$$\pi_i \equiv \pi'_{\overline{i+\ell}} + m \pmod{n+1}$$

allows us to state that

$$|\pi_i - \pi_j| \equiv \left| \pi'_{\overline{i+\ell}} + m - (\pi'_{\overline{j+\ell}} + m) \right| \equiv \left| \pi'_{\overline{i+\ell}} - \pi'_{\overline{j+\ell}} \right| \pmod{n+1}.$$

Therefore, a function $\Phi : V(RD(\pi, \iota)) \rightarrow V(RD(\pi', \iota))$, such that $\Phi(\pm\pi_i) = \pm\pi'_{\overline{i+\ell}}$, preserves adjacencies and is, consequently, an isomorphism. ∎

Theorem 3 can be used as an alternative proof for the fact that $d_t(\pi) = d_t(\pi')$ for two torically equivalent permutations $\pi$ and $\pi'$ (Corollary 1).

**Theorem 4.** *Let $\pi$ be a permutation of $n$ elements and $\pi_\circ^\circ$ its toric equivalence class. The number of elements in $\pi_\circ^\circ$ divides $n + 1$.*

*Proof.* By the definition of a cyclic value shift, $(n+1) + \pi^c = \pi^c$. Let $m'$ be the smallest positive integer such that $m' + \pi^c \equiv^c \pi^c$. The cyclic value shift $km' + \pi^c$, where $km'$ is an integer multiple of $m'$, is circularly equivalent to $\pi^c$, since that

$$km' + \pi^c \equiv^c \underbrace{m' + \ldots + m'}_{k} + \pi^c \equiv^c \underbrace{m' + \ldots + m'}_{k-1} + (m' + \pi^c)$$

$$\equiv^c \underbrace{m' + \ldots + m'}_{k-1} + \pi^c \equiv^c \ldots$$

$$\equiv^c \pi^c.$$

Suppose that $m'$ does not divide $n+1$; it means that $n+1 = km' + r$, for integers $k, r$, where $0 < r < m'$. It follows that,

$$\pi^c = (n+1) + \pi^c \equiv^c (r + km') + \pi^c = r + (km' + \pi^c) \equiv^c r + \pi^c.$$

Or, more concisely, $r + \pi \equiv^c \pi$; but this equivalence contradicts the fact that $m'$ is the smallest positive integer such that $m' + \pi \equiv^c \pi$. We conclude that $m'$ is indeed a divisor of $n + 1$. ∎

**Corollary 2.** *If $n+1$ is prime, each toric equivalence class contains either 1 or $n + 1$ elements.*

In the case $n + 1$ is prime, it is also possible to characterize the classes that contain just 1 element. A toric equivalence class is said to be *unitary* if only 1 element belongs to it. For instance, for $n = 4$ there are exactly 4 unitary classes, namely: $[1234]_\circ^\circ$, $[2413]_\circ^\circ$, $[3142]_\circ^\circ$ e $[4321]_\circ^\circ$.

**Theorem 5.** *If $n + 1$ is prime, a toric equivalence class is unitary if, and only if, it is of the form*

$$\left[\, \overline{k}\ \overline{2k}\ \overline{3k}\ \ldots\ \overline{\ell k}\ \ldots\ \overline{nk}\,\right]_\circ^\circ,$$

*where $k$ is an integer, $1 \le k \le n$.*

*Proof.* For any integer $k$ in the range $1 \le k \le n$, if $n + 1$ is prime, then $\ell k \not\equiv 0 \,(\mathrm{mod}\ n + 1)$ for $\ell = 1, \ldots, n$. We will show that a toric equivalence class that contains the permutation $[\, \overline{k}\ \overline{2k}\ \overline{3k}\ \ldots\ \overline{nk}\,]$ is unitary. Consider the permutation $1 + (\, \overline{0}\ \overline{k}\ \overline{2k}\ \overline{3k}\ \ldots\ \overline{nk}\,)$, and choose an integer $\ell$, $1 \le \ell \le n$, such that $\overline{\ell k + 1} = 0$:

$$
\begin{aligned}
1 + (\, \overline{0}\ \overline{k}\ \overline{2k}\ \ldots\ \overline{nk}\,) &= \\
&= (\, \overline{0+1}\ \overline{k+1}\ \overline{2k+1}\ \ldots\ \overline{\ell k+1}\ \overline{(\ell+1)k+1}\ \ldots\ \overline{nk+1}\,) \\
&\equiv^c (\, \overline{\ell k+1}\ \overline{(\ell+1)k+1}\ \ldots\ \overline{nk+1}\ \overline{0+1}\ \overline{k+1}\ \overline{2k+1}\ \ldots\ \overline{(\ell-1)k+1}\,) \\
&= (\, \overline{0}\ \overline{\ell k+k+1}\ \ldots\ \overline{nk+1}\ \overline{0+1}\ \overline{k+1}\ \overline{2k+1}\ \ldots\ \overline{\ell k-k+1}\,) \\
&= (\, \overline{0}\ \overline{k}\ \overline{2k}\ \ldots\ \overline{nk}\,).
\end{aligned}
$$

By induction, $m + (\overline{0}\ \overline{k}\ \overline{2k}\ \ldots\ \overline{nk}) = \underbrace{1 + \ldots + 1}_{m-1} + 1 + (\overline{0}\ \overline{k}\ \overline{2k}\ \ldots\ \overline{nk}) = \underbrace{1 + \ldots + 1}_{m-1} + (\overline{0}\ \overline{k}\ \overline{2k}\ \ldots\ \overline{nk}) = \ldots = (\overline{0}\ \overline{k}\ \overline{2k}\ \ldots\ \overline{nk})$, so the toric equivalence class of $[\overline{k}\ \overline{2k}\ \ldots\ \overline{nk}]$ is unitary.

On the other hand, consider that $\pi = [\pi_1 \pi_2 \ldots \pi_n]$ is the only permutation that belongs to a unitary class; this implies that $m + \pi^c$ is circularly equivalent to $\pi^c$ for any integer $m$, in particular for $m = 1$. That is,

$$(0\pi_1\pi_2\ldots\pi_n) \equiv^c (\overline{1}\ \overline{\pi_1+1}\ \overline{\pi_2+1}\ \ldots\ \overline{\pi_n+1}).$$

Let $\ell$ be such that $\overline{\pi_\ell + 1} = 0$. So,

$$
\begin{aligned}
\overline{\pi_{\ell+1} + 1} &= \pi_1, \\
\overline{\pi_{\ell+2} + 1} &= \pi_2, \\
&\ \ \vdots \\
\overline{\pi_{\ell+n} + 1} &= \pi_n,
\end{aligned}
$$

that is, $\overline{\pi_{\ell+i}} + 1 \equiv \pi_i \pmod{n+1}$ for every integer $i$ between 1 and $n$. Since $\pi_i \ne \pi_j$ if $i \ne j$, and $1 \le \pi_1 \le n$ for every $i$ between 1 e $n$, the system of modular equations is satisfiable if $\pi_i = ik$ where $k = \overline{\pi_{\ell+1} + 1}$. ∎

Theorem 5 allows us to precisely determine the number of vertices of $Tor(n)$, where $n + 1$ is prime. According to the theorem, if $n + 1$ is prime, there are exactly $n$ unitary toric equivalence classes. It follows that the remaining $n! - n$ vertices of $TRG(n)$ are distributed among classes of size $n + 1$, that is, there are exactly $\frac{n!-n}{n+1}$ classes of size $n + 1$. Theorem 6 summarizes this result.

**Theorem 6.** *If $n + 1$ is prime, $Tor(n)$ has exactly $\frac{n!-n}{n+1} + n$ vertices.*

We will now adopt a more compact representation for the unitary classes, in the form of $U_{n,k}$, meaning the unitary toric equivalence class that contains the permutation of $n$ elements that starts with the element $k$, that is,

$$U_{n,k} := \left[\, \overline{k} \ \ \overline{2k} \ \ \overline{3k} \ \ \ldots \ \ \overline{\ell k} \ \ \ldots \ \ \overline{nk} \,\right]^{\circ}_{\circ}.$$

**Theorem 7.** *Let $\pi$ be a permutation that belongs to a unitary class $U_{n,k}$, where $n + 1$ is prime and $k > 1$. Then $RD(\pi, \iota)$ has only one cycle.*

*Proof.* Let $C = 0, -\pi_1, +\overline{\pi_1 - 1}, \ldots, -1, 0$ be the cycle in $RD(\pi, \iota)$, starting from vertex 0 and following the reality edge incident to it. Given a vertex $+i$ in the diagram, let $s(+i)$ be the first successor of $+i$ in cycle $C$, according to the order, that is non-negative, i. e., $s(+i)$ appears in $C$ after following a reality edge and subsequently a desire edge. For instance, $s(0) = +\overline{\pi_1 - 1}$ in every diagram, and in Fig. 1, $s(0) = +2$, $s(+2) = +4$, $s(+4) = +6$, $s(+6) = +1$, $s(+1) = +3$, $s(+3) = +5$, $s(+5) = 0$.

Since $\pi$ belongs to a unitary class, we know that $\pi_1 = k$ — note that, as a consequence, we have $s(0) = +\overline{\pi_1 - 1} = +\overline{k - 1}$ — and we can write any element $\pi_\ell$ as $\overline{\ell k}$, so the sequence $\{0, s(0), s(s(0)), \ldots\}$ is equal to $\{0, +\overline{\ell_1 k}, +\overline{\ell_2 k}, \ldots, +\overline{\ell_x k}\}$, for integers $\ell_1, \ell_2, \ldots, \ell_x$ (where $x$, for now, is unknown). This means that

$$s(0) = +\overline{\ell_1 k}.$$

Since $s(0)$ is also equal to $+\overline{k-1}$, we have the identity

$$+\overline{\ell_1 k} = +\overline{k-1}. \tag{1}$$

Generalizing the above identity, we have

$$s(+\overline{\ell_p k}) = +\overline{\ell_{p+1} k},$$

and also $s(+\overline{\ell_p k}) = +\overline{(\ell_p + 1)k - 1}$, which gives us

$$+\overline{\ell_{p+1} k} = +\overline{(\ell_p + 1)k - 1}. \tag{2}$$

We summarize identities 1 and 2 in the following recurrence relation:

$$\begin{cases} \ell_1 k \equiv k - 1 \ (\mathrm{mod} \ n + 1) \\ \ell_p k \equiv \ell_p k + k - 1, \text{ for } p > 1, \end{cases}$$

which has the following equivalence as a solution

$$\ell_p k \equiv (p + 1)(k - 1) \pmod{n + 1}.$$

Hence the sequence $\{0, +\overline{\ell_1 k}, +\overline{\ell_2 k}, \ldots, +\overline{\ell_x k}\}$ becomes

$$\{0, +\overline{k-1}, +\overline{2(k-1)}, \ldots, +\overline{x(k-1)}\}.$$

As we must have that $s(+\overline{x(k-1)}) = 0$, the only value of $x$ that satisfies the equation $(x+1)(k-1) = 0$ is $x = n$. That is, the sequence contains every element of $\pi$ and, consequently, there is only one cycle in $RD(\pi, \iota)$.

As a byproduct of our proof, we immediately notice that the sequence of successive elements $\{+\overline{k-1}, +\overline{2(k-1)}, \ldots, +\overline{n(k-1)}\}$ in the cycle corresponds to the same sequence of elements $\{\sigma_1, \sigma_2, \ldots, \sigma_n\}$ in a permutation $\sigma$ that belongs to the unitary class $U_{n,k-1}$. ■

**Corollary 3.** *If $n+1$ is prime, a permutation $\pi \neq \iota$ that belongs to a unitary class satisfies $d_t(\pi, \iota) \geq n/2$.*

Corollary 3 hints us there is some symmetry in the toric graph when $n+1$ is prime. It also tells us that the transposition distance from the identity to the unitary classes is close to the known bounds for the transposition diameter [1,2], which indicates they are good samples for studying the behavior of $D_t(n)$.

## 4 Conclusion

Corollary 3 is an interesting development of the approach advocated in this paper. We have found the lower bound $d_t(\pi, \sigma) \geq n/2$ is very close to the exact transposition distance between the two permutations $\pi$, $\sigma$ belonging to two different unitary classes, never differing by more than 1 transposition, as it can be seen in Table 1. We have used a Dias' implementation [7] of a branch-and-bound algorithm, modified to take advantage of the equivalence classes, to exactly determine the transposition distance of the unitary classes $d_t(U_{n,k}, \iota)$, for values of $n$ up to 18 such that $n+1$ is prime. In a future paper, we hope to formally demonstrate Conjecture 1 — related to Meidanis, Walter and Dias' [2] result for the reverse permutation.

*Conjecture 1.* If $n+1$ is prime and $\pi$ belongs to a unitary class $U_{n,k}$, then $n/2 \leq d(\pi) \leq n/2+1$.

**Table 1.** Transposition distances $d_t(U_{n,k}, \iota)$ and the diameter $D_t(n)$

| $d_t(U_{n,k}, \iota)$ | | $k$ | | | | | | | | | | | | | | | | | $D_t(n)$ |
|---|---|---|---|---|---|---|---|---|---|---|---|---|---|---|---|---|---|---|---|
| | | 2 | 3 | 4 | 5 | 6 | 7 | 8 | 9 | 10 | 11 | 12 | 13 | 14 | 15 | 16 | 17 | 18 | |
| $n$ | 4 | 2 | 2 | 3 | — | — | — | — | — | — | — | — | — | — | — | — | — | — | 3 |
| | 6 | 3 | 4 | 3 | 4 | 4 | — | — | — | — | — | — | — | — | — | — | — | — | 4 |
| | 10 | 5 | 6 | 6 | 6 | 5 | 6 | 6 | 6 | 6 | — | — | — | — | — | — | — | — | 6 |
| | 12 | 6 | 7 | 7 | 7 | 6 | 6 | 7 | 7 | 7 | 6 | 7 | — | — | — | — | — | — | 7 |
| | 16 | 8 | 9 | 8 | 9 | 9 | 9 | 8 | 8 | 9 | 9 | 9 | 8 | 9 | 8 | 9 | — | — | 9 or 10 |
| | 18 | 9 | 9 | 10 | 10 | 10 | 10 | 9 | 10 | 9 | 10 | 9 | 9 | 9 | 9 | 10 | 10 | 10 | 10 or 11 |

We have noted by looking at the reality and desire diagram that the most distant permutations, with respect to the identity, always have either 0, 1 or 2 odd cycles in every example we could conceive. For $3 \le n \le 12$ and $n = 14$, the diameter is attained by the reverse permutation, which always has less than 3 odd cycles. For $n = 13$ and $n = 15$, the most distant permutations found by Eriksson et al. [1] have 2 odd cycles. For $n$ odd, $n > 15$, Elias and Hartman [5] described permutations that are more distant to the identity than the reverse permutation — requiring more than $\lfloor n/2 \rfloor + 1$ transpositions — and those permutations have also 2 odd cycles. We hope that the combined use of the reality and desire diagram and the toric graph may provide an answer as to why this happens. For even values of $n$ where $n + 1$ is prime, the permutations having the smallest number of odd cycles are those that have 1 odd cycle, and we believe those permutations are good candidates to investigate the transposition diameter $D_t(n)$, as it can be seen in the following conjecture.

*Conjecture 2.* Let $\Omega$ be the set of permutations with just one odd cycle in the reality and desire diagram, and $\Delta$ be the set of permutations whose transposition distance is equal to $D_t(n)$. If $n + 1$ is prime, then $\Omega \cap \Delta \ne \emptyset$.

Another interesting result that seems to be close to achievement is the determination of the transposition diameter $D_t(16)$. All the values of $D_t(n)$, for $n < 16$ have been exactly determined but, to this day, $D_t(16)$ is still undetermined, lying within $9 \le D_t(16) \le 10$. Notice that $16 + 1$ is prime, so it is one of the cases where more information can be derived from the toric graph, as shown in Sect. 3 of this paper. Given the symmetry of the toric graph for $n + 1$ prime, we hope that $D_t(16)$ is equal to the distance $d_t(\pi, \iota)$ for some $\pi$ in a unitary class. If this scenario turns out to be true, then $D_t(16)$ would be 9. Actually, a bolder conjecture is: for even $n$ such that $n + 1$ is prime, $D_t(n) = n/2 + 1$, a result that would determine an infinite family of even values of $n$ for which Meidanis, Walter and Dias' conjecture [2] holds.

**Acknowledgment.** The authors wish to thank André Korenchendler (UFRJ) for modifying Dias' implementation to speed-up the process of finding the transposition distances.

# References

1. Eriksson, H., Eriksson, K., Karlander, J., Svensson, L., Wästlund, J.: Sorting a bridge hand. Discrete Math. 241(1), 289–300 (2001)
2. Meidanis, J., Walter, M.E.M.T., Dias, Z.: Transposition distance between a permutation and its reverse. In: Baeza-Yates, R. (ed.) Proceedings of the 4th South American Workshop on String Processing, Valparaíso, Chile, pp. 70–79. Carleton University Press (1997)
3. Setubal, C., Meidanis, J.: Introduction to Computational Molecular Biology. PWS Publishing (January 1997)

4. Bafna, V., Pevzner, P.A.: Sorting by transpositions. SIAM J. Discrete Math. 11(2), 224–240 (1998)
5. Elias, I., Hartman, T.: A 1.375-approximation algorithm for sorting by transpositions. IEEE/ACM T. Comput. Bi. 3(4), 369–379 (2006)
6. Bafna, V., Pevzner, P.A.: Genome rearrangements and sorting by reversals. SIAM J. Comput. 25(2), 272–289 (1996)
7. Dias, Z.: Rearranjo de genomas: uma coletânea de artigos. PhD thesis, Unicamp, Campinas, São Paulo (2002)

# A Customized Class of Functions for Modeling and Clustering Gene Expression Profiles in Embryonic Stem Cells

Shenggang Li[1], Miguel Andrade-Navarro[2], and David Sankoff[1]

[1] Department of Mathematics and Statistics, University of Ottawa, Canada
[2] Max Delbrück Center for Molecular Medicine, Berlin-Buch, Germany

**Abstract.** Based on the trajectories of individual genes, we address the problem of clustering time course gene expression data for embryonic stem cells (ESC) differentiation. We propose a class of functions determined by only two parameters but flexible enough to model realistic time courses. This serves as a basis for a mixed model clustering method. This method takes into account (1) genetic function profile induced or controlled by other regulators, (2) unobservable random effects producing heterogeneity within gene clusters, and (3) autoregressive components defining the stochastic and autocorrelation structures. We employ an EM algorithm to fit the mixture model and clustering follows monitoring via Bayesian posterior probabilities. Our method is applied to a mouse ESC line during the first 24 hours of differentiation period. We assess the biological credibility of the results by detecting significantly associated FatiGO Gene Ontology terms for each cluster.

## 1   Introduction

Cluster analysis of gene expression profiles over a time course often treat each sampling time as one of the dimensions of a multivariate variable, reducing the problem of clustering the gene trajectories to one of clustering multivariate observations. Since the object of gene expression clustering is to detect common trajectories, however, this "static" multivariate characterization loses power and precision, since the temporal order plays no role in the analysis; indeed the times can be permuted in any order without changing the results of the cluster analysis.

Gene expression profiles during cell growth, differentation, tissue activation of various kinds, and during cyclical changes tend to follow well-defined patterns and are often highly autocorrelated. These facts lead to the incorporation of more "dynamic" considerations into clustering procedures. Model-based clustering techniques [9] incorporate dynamical features by implementing formal statistical modeling and parametric models in preference to pure data mining.

A number of model-based clustering methods for dynamical gene expression data have been proposed [1,5,14,17]. Here a group of genes following the same probability model fall into the same cluster, taking into account autoregressive and other random effects. For example, [19] discusses autoregressive models for clustering time course gene expression data. [2,11] apply cubic spline and B-spline mixture models to analyze gene expression time series data.

A.L.C. Bazzan, M. Craven, and N.F. Martins (Eds.): BSB 2008, LNBI 5167, pp. 92–103, 2008.
© Springer-Verlag Berlin Heidelberg 2008

Purely autoregressive models, however, only consider autocorrelative structure without explicitly taking account of other properties of functional interactions among genes. Although a p-order autoregressive model may explain a p-order polynomial time trend effect, it fails to match exponential time growth effects such as $\exp(\lambda t)$ or periodic effects such as $\sin(\omega t)$. Spline techniques can represent data trends but still remain essentially black boxes [8] with respect to genetic functions. [8] suggests a novel clustering technique based on gene functional curves, making use of plausible biological models for gene expression dynamics.

## 1.1 The Proposed Model

Here we treat a gene profile over a time course as composed of the following components

1. impact of related genes or other regulation mechanisms (modeled as a dynamical system of differential equations),
2. autoregressive factors representing autocorrelation structure and feedback or loop effects,
3. random components allowing for heterogeneity among the individual genes in each cluster.

This method is flexible in assigning both dynamic and fixed functional components into an integrated time series model with random mixtures. We note that by appropriately incorporating randomness into the model we can avoid the tendency to generate clusters based purely on chance properties of the data.

## 2 The Mixture Time Series Model for Functional Curve Clustering

We denote an expression profile (or observation vector over time course) of an individual gene $g_i$ as $Y_i = (y_{i1}, y_{i2}, \ldots, y_{iT})$. In this notation $T$ refers to the total number of time points sampled over a time course. Our objective is to cluster target genes into distinct clusters in terms of the similarities of gene functional behavior. Genes are grouped together on the basis of the form of their expression profiles (curve shapes) rather than similarity in Euclidean distance. The model-based clustering analysis assumes that the genes in every cluster will perfectly fit an underlying mixture time series model, whereany gene profile $Y_i$ is considered as an observation of a functional curve following the probability model:

$$Y_{it} = \text{Gene Network Interactions} + \text{Auto Effects}$$
$$+ \text{Time–dependent Random Effect} + \text{Noise} \tag{1}$$

If all target genes $g_i, i = 1, 2, \ldots, N$ satisfy the model above, then the $Y_{it}, i = 1, 2 \ldots, N$ are generated by the following model:

$$Y_{it} = f^{(c)}(t|\Phi^{(c)}) + \sum_{j=t-p}^{t-1} \alpha_{jc} Y_{ij} + \gamma_c + \varepsilon \quad (t = 1, 2 \ldots, T \text{ and } i = 1, 2, \ldots, N), \tag{2}$$

where the "within" random effect $\gamma_c \sim$ normal$(0, \tau_c^2)$ $(c = 1, 2, \ldots, C)$ are independent of each other, indicating that genes in the same cluster have a unified correlation structure, $\varepsilon$ is the i.i.d. white noise $\sim$ normal$(0, \sigma^2)$, the trend curve $f^{(c)}(t|\Phi^{(c)})$ contains the internal function effect of $g_i$, combined with the other network interactions (or regulatory effect on $g_i$), and $\Phi^{(c)}$ is the parameter set for the fixed mean curve in cluster $c$ $(c = 1, 2, \ldots, C)$. We have included autoregressive items in the model because we wish to capture feedback or loop effects in genetic pathways.

The key problem here is to determine the form of function $f^{(c)}(t|\Phi^{(c)})$. We will estimate it with the trend deduced from a genetic transcription model. The B spline techniques previously employed to deal with this problem [11] have no direct biological functional interpretation. Instead we are inspired Chen's linear transcription model [7] to elaborate a function $f^{(c)}(t|\Phi^{(c)})$. Chen's model is a nonlinear dynamic system with the following form:

$$\frac{dr}{dt} = Cp - Vr \qquad \frac{dp}{dt} = Lr - Up \tag{3}$$

where $r$ is the mRNA concentration, $p$ is the protein concentration, $L$ contains the translational constants, $V$ is the degradation rate of mRNA and $U$ is the degradation rate of proteins. According to Theorem 1 in [7], the solution to model (3) has form:

$$x(t) = Q(t)e^{t\lambda} \tag{4}$$

where $Q(t) = \{q_{ij}\}$ is a $2n \times 2n$ matrix whose elements are polynomial functions of $t$. In [7] it is stated that a gene system should be stable system and its expression should not have an exponential or a polynomial growth rate, which implies that $Q(t)$ is a constant and $x(t)$ is actually an ordinary exponential function. However, an exponential function is monotonic and cannot fully reflect the wave-like shapes that characterize many gene functional curves. Consequently we do not adopt (4) directly, though we will utilize features of (3) and (4) to develop a more effective functional curve.

To do so so, we have studied the functional gene curves of mouse embryonic stem cells (mESC) in the first 24 hours of differentiation (for experimental details and the data bank, see [10]) and found that gene expression of these genes can be well described by the following hyperbolic function:

$$f(t) = \frac{1}{\exp[b(t-a) + \sqrt{1 + (t-a)^2}]} \tag{5}$$

To see the connection between (5) on one hand and (3) and (4) on the other, we note that the gene's growth rate satisfies:

$$\frac{df(t)}{dt} = -[b + \frac{t-a}{\sqrt{1 + (t-a)^2}}]f(t), \tag{6}$$

where the expression (6) indicates that this gene system also remains stable, but is more flexible than the one in (3). Here $\frac{t-a}{\sqrt{1+(t-a)^2}}$ is restricted to the

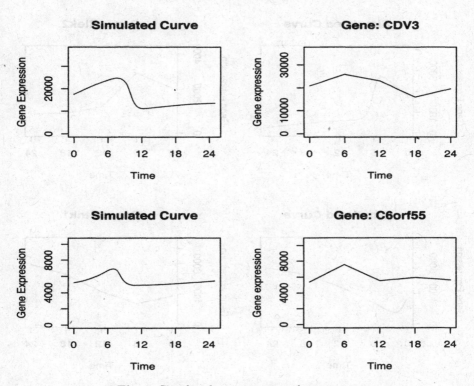

**Fig. 1.** Simulated curve *vs.* actual gene curve

range [-1,1], but can model behaviours more varied than a the constant growth rate. In Figure 1, the gene profiles (over the time course 0 to 24 hours) of Cdv3(CDV3 homolog (mouse)) and C6orf55 (chromosome 6 open reading frame 55) are plotted against the corresponding simulated hyperbolic functional curves. In the same way, Figure 2 presents the plots for genes Riok2 (RIO kinase 2) and Etnk1(Ethanolamine kinase 1). These genes are highly active over the time course in the early period of stem cell differentiation. These figures illustrate how parameter settings are available to produce functional curve shapes similar to those of actual gene profiles.

For curve fitting purposes, we can include linear and quadratic parts without affecting system stability. Thus, we define gene functional curves as follows:

$$f(t|\beta_l) = \beta^{(1)} + \beta^{(2)} \exp\{-\beta^{(3)}(t - \beta^{(4)}) - \sqrt{1 + (t - \beta^{(4)})^2}\} + \beta^{(5)}t + \beta^{(6)}t^2 \quad (7)$$

From (2) and (7), by setting different curve parameters $\beta_c = (\beta_c^{(1)}, \beta_c^{(2)}, \beta_c^{(3)}, \beta_c^{(4)}, \beta_c^{(5)})$, random effects $\gamma_c$ and auto regression coefficients $\alpha_{jc}$ $(c = 1, 2, \ldots, C)$ we can determine different gene clusters.

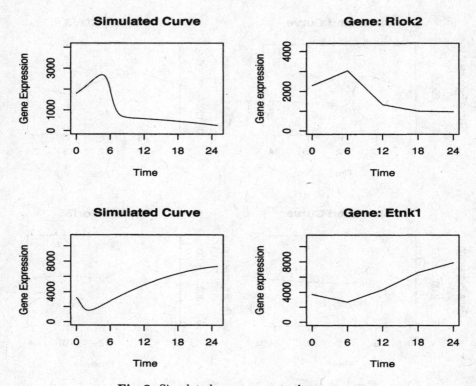

**Fig. 2.** Simulated curve *vs.* actual gene curve

To implement cluster recognition, we assume the following mixture-density model:

$$P(Y|\Theta, \Omega) = \sum_{c=1}^{C} \omega_c p_c(Y|\theta_c), \qquad (8)$$

where the parameter set $\Theta = (\beta_1, \ldots, \beta_C, \alpha_{j1}, \ldots, \alpha_{jC}, \gamma_1, \ldots, \gamma_C)$ (j=1,2...,p) and $\Omega = (\omega_1, \ldots, \omega_C)$ such that $\sum_{c=1}^{C} \omega_c = 1$ and $p_c(Y|\theta_c)$ is the density function generated by the model (2) defined previously. Given observed samples $Y = (Y_1, Y_2, \ldots, Y_N)$, the log-likelihood expression for the above mixture density is:

$$\log(P(Y|\Theta, \Omega)) = \log(\sum_{c=1}^{C} \omega_c p_c(Y|\theta_c)) = \sum_{i=1}^{N} \log(\sum_{c=1}^{C} \omega_c p_c(Y_i|\theta_c)), \qquad (9)$$

where $Y_i = (y_{i1}, y_{i2}, \ldots, y_{iT})$ ($i = 1, 2, \ldots, N$) represents the profile of gene $g_i$ over the time course $t = 1, 2, \ldots, T$. Since it is hard to optimize (9) by ordinary analytical methods, we will apply the well known expectation maximization(EM) algorithm [13] to estimate these parameters. The details of the EM algorithm approach and the corresponding inference technique is given in the Appendix.

# 3    Numerical Tests

## 3.1    Clustering Results

In this section we illustrate the result of clustering gene profiles for V6.5 mouse embryonic stem cells over the time course [0h, 6h, 12h, 18h, 24h],which represents the early period of mESC differentiation. At the first stage, we select as target genes 419 with high differential expression as detected by the SAM method [18]. A standardization procedure is first applied to all gene profiles before running the clustering program. We arbitrarily choose a small number of clusters, namely $C = 3$, in order to facilitate the evaluation of the method, and set the initial cluster proportion to be $\frac{1}{3}$. Thus, we will optimize (9) with respect to $\Theta = (\theta_1, \theta_2, \theta_3)$ , $\Omega = (\omega_1, \omega_2, \omega_3)$ and $\sigma^2$.

Figure 3 presents the results of clustering the 419 genes. The three clusters clearly have different patterns over the time course. Briefly, cluster one is basically up-regulated compared to cluster three which has a distinct down-regulated pattern. Cluster two contains the largest number of genes. Note that that these clusters have different "compactness" levels. For instance, cluster three is characterized by the fact that the gene functional curves are more closely intertwined while cluster two is more loosely arranged, indicating a larger intra-cluster variation. This effect is captured by the different random gene effect within the three clusters, a feature of the mixture model. In visually assessing the clusters, we must recall that the curves are not clustered by the overall proximity to each other, but by the similarities of their patterns.

We choose the order of autoregressive component to be 1 (i.e. $p = 1$) to avoid the increased noise effect associated with larger order components demonstrated in numerical experiments [11].

To validate the clustering, we characterized the genes in each cluster by compiling Gene Ontology (GO) terms. We also searched the FatiGO server to compare the three clusters. Table 1 displays the distribution of genes featured by different biological processes.

**Table 1.** Distribution (%) of genes according to biological process

| Biological Functions | Cluster one | Cluster two | Cluster three |
|---|---|---|---|
| RNA metabolic | 17.14 | 40.57 | 42.65 |
| Cellular lipid metabolic | 13.33 | 2.83 | 1.47 |
| Cellular protein metabolic | 45.71 | 29.25 | 35.29 |
| Nucleoside, nucleic metabolic metabolic | 25.64 | 50.91 | 52.94 |
| Regulation of cellular process | 23.29 | 43.64 | 27.42 |
| Cellular macromolecule metabolic | 43.84 | 28.18 | 35.59 |
| Protein metabolic | 43.84 | 30.02 | 38.24 |
| Transcription | 18.57 | 33.33 | 20.97 |
| Cellular biosynthetic process | 21.92 | 13.76 | 27.42 |
| Biosynthetic process | 24.66 | 14.16 | 28.97 |
| N | 94 | 153 | 85 |

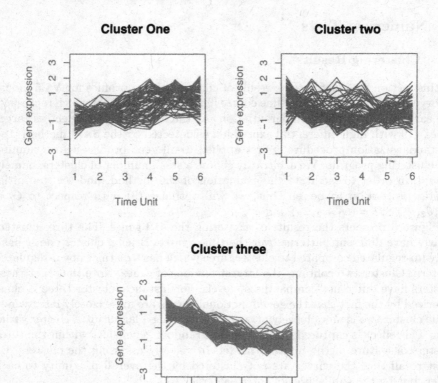

**Fig. 3.** Clustering result for gene profiles of V6.5 embryonic stem cells

## 3.2   Biological Analysis

Cluster one includes 119 genes, of which 94 had associated GO terms, largely with protein metabolism, processing of macromolecules and catalytic functions, such as Sc4mol, the Rpl and Rps family (Rpl4 Rpl13 Rpl14 Rpl23 Rpl41 Rps2 Rps6 Rps12 Rps17 Rpl22 Rps27 Rps28 Rps27l), Uba52, Csnk1e, Otx2, Igfbp2 and Gpi1. These genes follow a generally up-regulated trend during ESC differentiation and participate in ESC metabolism or protein synthesis processes. For example, Otx2 is an early stage murine ESC marker playing a cental role in gastrulation, essential for the early specification of the neuroectoderm destined to become fore midbrain [15]. Csnk1e, which undergoes a persistent up-regulation pattern over the time course, performs a catalytic function for serine/threonine kinase activity. The Rpl/Rps family is involved in ribosomal structure and hence protein biosynthesis. Note that there was some evidence, discounted by the authors as well as our results here, that Rpl4 and Rps24 are among the genes constituting a unique molecular signature in human ESC [3].

There are 198 genes in cluster two, 153 with GO annotations. These genes are involved in RNA metabolism, regulation of cellular process and DNA-dependent transcription. Many key ESC markers such as Nanog, Sox21, Zfp57, Cbx7, Vcl, Dnajb6, Msi2h and Cggbp1 fall into this cluster. They generally usually down-regulated for the first 18 or 24 hours and are up-regulated later. By checking the correlation distance, we found these gene profiles are remarkably similar to the expression patterns of undifferentiated ESC markers such as OCT4, Sox2 and Foxd3. From the point of view of stem cell differentiation, these genes are crucial for stem cell self-renewal and maintenance of the inner cell mass (ICM) of the blastocyst. With the loss of cell proliferation and pluripotency, they undergo a significant and persistent down-regulation pattern [6,16].

Many members of cluster two are also related to the cell cycle, cell proliferation or growth. For example, C2ORF29, Cdv3 and Rbbp7 are involved in cell proliferation. Socs3 and Ltbp4 function in the regulation of cell growth. Nmyc1, Cdk2ap1, Nipbl, Cdc34, Mcm5, Nipbl, BC068171 and Ccne1 are cell-cycle related genes. They mediate the progression through the cell cycle, particularly the G1/S transition of the mitotic cell. That these genes are in cluster two agrees with theories [12], whereby the cells initially derived from a population of stem cells undergo rapid cell division during early differentiation; throughout this period, expression of genes keeping control of the cell cycle or proliferation should be attenuated.

Another 102 genes are found in cluster three, 85 with GO annotations. Compared with cluster one, cluster three is enriched for genes in charge of nucleobase, nucleoside, nucleotide and nucleic acid metabolic process, such as Ctbp2, Cdk2ap1, Apex1, Hmgb2, Mybbp1a Ran, Gars, H2afz, Sod2, Nola2, Mki67ip, Etv4, Atp5l, Bzw1, Nr0b1, Klf5, Rbm14, Polr2f, Ankrd17, Lsm3, Zfp36l1, Ddx5, Sfrs1, Rbm3, Cars and Psmc5. This cluster is also associated with microtubule-based movement, signal transduction and biosynthetic processes. These include Arpc4, Lefty1, Ptprf, Stmn1, Cfl1, Trh and Eif4ebp1. Lefty1 is an important "stemness" marker expressed in the left half of gastrulating mouse embryos and involved in the TGF-beta signaling pathway. Ptprf has an intrinsic protein tyrosine phosphatase activity (PTPase) and plays a role in cell adhesion receptor and the insulin signaling pathway. Ptprf has also been identified in human ESC studies. Stmn1 is involved in signal transducing, participates in the regulation of the microtubule (MT) filament and promotes disassembly of microtubules. Trh plays a role in cell-cell signaling and neuroactive ligand-receptor interaction. Arpc4 is related to cytoskeleton and actin filament polymerization.

Since clusters two and three have a similar down-regulated pattern, especially in the first 12 hour period, it is not surprising that some of their members have similar gene functions in signalling, ATP/GTP binding, actin binding and microtubules. For example, the genes Pfn1, Wdr1, Efna2, Lefty2, Ak7, Ptch1, Riok2, Arf6 and Actg1 are classified into cluster two. This is not surprising; maintenance of the pluripotent state of ESC requires intrinsic signalling as well as extrinsic environmental elements, involving microtubules. It is known that environmental factors such as cell-surface receptors and cytokines play an important

**Table 2.** Over-represented GO terms for each cluster from GOstat

| Cluster | Biological Function | In cluster | In genome | P-value |
|---------|---------------------|------------|-----------|---------|
| I | primary metabolic process | 60 | 5694 | 0.000107 |
| | cellular protein metabolic process | 34 | 2421 | 7.44E-05 |
| | structural constituent of ribosome | 14 | 147 | 4.41E-10 |
| Total | | 94 | 14456 | |
| II | gene expression | 57 | 2452 | 4.21E-08 |
| | RNA metabolic process | 46 | 2082 | 1.59E-05 |
| | transcription, DNA-dependent | 35 | 1704 | 0.00215 |
| | ribonucleoprotein complex biogenesis | 11 | 174 | 0.000302 |
| | translational initiation | 5 | 40 | 0.00266 |
| | glycolysis | 5 | 42 | 0.00326 |
| Total | | 153 | 14456 | |
| III | gene expression | 33 | 2452 | 2.02E-05 |
| | translation | 13 | 369 | 2.50E-05 |
| | amino acid,derivative metabolic process | 9 | 264 | 0.00111 |
| | ribonucleoprotein complex | 10 | 382 | 0.00267 |
| Total | | 85 | 14456 | |

role in the maintenance of stem cell functions [12]. Transcription profiles of this type generally take a persistent down-regulated pattern during differentiation. Examples include the actin binding related gene Ptprf and receptor activity-associated gene Tagln, which decrease sharply throughout the first 24 hours in ESC differentiation.

Table 2 uses a t-test to evaluate the over-representation of various kinds of GO terms in each cluster. The analysis in Table 2 confirms and deepens that of Table 1. For example, the high value for RNA metabolism in cluster 2 possibly results from the selection of genes involved in transcriptional regulation. The higher proportion of cellular protein metabolic process in cluster 1, amino acid derivative metabolic processes and ribonucleoprotein complex, in cluster 3, are all closely related to protein biosynthesis. This similarity possibly originates from genes involved in translation process(cluster 3). We also found interesting to see five glycolitic enzymes in cluster 2, and a number of genes involved in the formation of RNA-protein complexes in clusters 2 and 3. In the case of cluster 2, this includes five genes involved in translation initiation.

# References

1. Aach, J., Church, G.M.: Aligning gene expression time series with time warping algorithms. Bioinformatics 17, 495–508 (2001)
2. Bar-Joseph, Z., Gerber, G., Gifford, D., Jaakkola, T., Simon, I.: Continuous representations of time-series gene expression data. Journal of Computational Biology 10, 341–356 (2003)

3. Bhattacharya, B., Miura, T., Brandenberger, R., Mejido, J., Luo, Y., Yang, A.X., Joshi, B.H., Ginis, I., Thies, R.S., Amit, M., Lyons, I., Condie, B.G., Itskovitz-Eldor, J., Rao, M.S., Puri, R.K.: Gene expression in human embryonic stem cell lines: unique molecular signature. Blood 103, 2956–2964 (2004)
4. Bilmes, J.A.: A Gentle Tutorial of the EM Algorithm and its Application to Parameter Estimation for Gaussian Mixture and Hidden Markov Models. Technical Report 97-021. International Computer Science Institute, Berkeley, CA (1997)
5. Brumback, B.A., Rice, J.: Smoothing spline models for the analysis of nested and crossed samples of curves. Journal of the American Statististical Association 93, 961–976 (1998)
6. Chambers, I., Colby, D., Robertson, M., Nichols, J., Lee, S., Tweedie, S., Smith, A.: Functional expression cloning of Nanog, a pluripotency sustaining factor in embryonic stem cells. Cell 113, 643–655 (2003)
7. Chen, T., He, H.L., Church, G.M.: Modeling gene expression with differential equations. In: Pacific Symposium on Biocomputing, pp. 29–40 (1999)
8. Chudova, D., Hart, C., Mjolsness, E., Smyth, P.: Gene expression clustering with functional mixture models. In: Advances in Neural Information Processing, vol. 16. MIT Press, Cambridge (2004)
9. Fraley, C., Raftery, A.E.: How many clusters? Which clustering method? Answers via model-based cluster analysis. Computer Journal 41, 578–588 (1998)
10. Hailesellasse Sene, K., Porter, C.J., Palidwor, G., Perez- Iratxeta, C., Muro, E.M., Campbell, P.A., Rudnicki, M.A., Andrade-Navarro, M.A.: Gene function in mouse embryonic stem cell differentiation. BMC Genomics 8, 85 (2007)
11. Luan, Y., Li, H.: Clustering of time-course gene expression data using a mixed-effects model with B-splines. Bioinformatics 19, 474–482 (2003)
12. Martinez Arias, A., Stewart, A.: Molecular Principles of Animal Development. Oxford University Press, NY (2002)
13. McLachlan, G.J., Krishnan, T.: The EM Algorithm and Extensions. John Wiley and Sons, New York (1997)
14. Medvedovic, M., Yeung, K.Y., Bumgarner, R.E.: Bayesian mixture model based clustering of replicated microarray data. Bioinformatics 20, 1222–1232 (2004)
15. Morsli, H., Tuorto, F., Choo, D., Postiglione, M.P., Simeone, A., Wu, D.K.: Otx1 and Otx2 activities are required for the normal development of the mouse inner ear. Development 126, 2335–2343 (1999)
16. Niwa, H., Burdon, T., Chambers, I., Smith, A.: Self-renewal of pluripotent embryonic stem cells is mediated via activation of STAT3. Genes and Development 12, 2048–2060 (1998)
17. Ramoni, M.F., Sebastiani, P., Kohane, I.S.: Cluster analysis of gene expression dynamics. Proceedings of the National Academy of Sciences USA 99, 9121–9126 (2002)
18. Tusher, V.G., Tibshirani, R., Chu, G.: Significance analysis of microarrays applied to the ionizing radiation response. Proceedings of the National Academy of Sciences USA 98, 5116–5121 (2001)
19. Wu, F., Zhang, W.J., Kusalik, A.J.: Dynamic model-based clustering for time-course gene expression data. Journal of Bioinformatics and Computational Biology 3, 821–836 (2005)

# A  Appendix: EM Algorithm of Mixture Model

## A.1  Inference of the Log-Likelihood Function for the Mixture Model

For convenience, we only consider the first order autoregressive item (i.e. $p = 1$ in model (2)). According to model (2), we infer that if the gene $g_i$ belongs to cluster c then its expression profile $Y_i = (y_{i1}, \ldots, y_{iT})$ at time point t satisfies the following conditional probability model:

$$P(y_{it}|\theta_c, Y_{i(t-1)})) = \text{Normal}(f^{(c)}(t|\Phi^{(c)}) + \alpha_c y_{i(t-1)}), \gamma_c{}^2 + \varepsilon^2) \quad (10)$$

Thus, the log-likelihood for $Y_i$ over time course $t = 1, 2, \ldots, T$ is

$$L_c(Y_i|\theta_c) = \log[P(y_{i1}|\theta_c) \prod_{j=2}^{T} P(y_{ij}|\theta_c, y_{i(j-1)})] \quad (11)$$

From expression (10), (11) can be finally expressed as

$$L_c(Y_i|\theta_c) = C_0 - TLog(\sigma_i) - \frac{1}{2\sigma_i}[(y_{i1} - f(1|\beta_c) - \mu_0)^2 + \sum_{j=2}^{T}(y_{ij} - f(j|\beta_c) - \alpha_{(c)}y_{i(j-1)})^2]$$
$$(12)$$

where the variance of $Y_i$, $\sigma_i = \sqrt{\gamma_c^2 + \varepsilon^2}$, $C_0$ is a constant and $\mu_0$ represents the mean at the initial time point. The log-likelihood of the mixture model of total observed samples can be expressed as

$$L(Y|\Theta, \Omega) = \sum_{i=1}^{N} \log(\sum_{j=1}^{C} \omega_j P_j(Y_i|\theta_j)) \quad (13)$$

where $P_j(Y_i|\theta_j)$ is identified by $\exp(L_j(Y_i|\theta_j))$, and $\omega_j, (j = 1, \ldots, C)$ are the unknown cluster membership parameters such that $\sum_{j=1}^{C} \omega_j = 1$.

## A.2  EM Algorithm Approach

The optimization for (12) can be carried out by using an EM algorithm. To see the specific computational steps, the reader can refer to [4].

1. Set initial parameters $\Theta^{(0)} = (\theta_1^{(0)}, \ldots, \theta_C^{(0)})$ for the given number of clusters $C$ and cluster proportion $\Omega^{(0)} = (\omega_1^{(0)}, \ldots, \omega_C^{(0)})$.
2. Define cluster membership (a random variable) $l$, where $l \in \{1, 2, \ldots, C\}$ and $l = c$ if gene $g_i$ belongs to cluster $c$. For $k = 0, 1, 2, \ldots$ repeat the following iterative steps until a given threshold is reached.
3. E-step: Calculate the posterior of the cluster membership $l$ given $Y_i$, $\Theta^{(k)}$ and $\Omega^{(k)}$ at the $k^{th}$ iterative step from the following procedure:

$$P(l|Y_i, \Theta^{(k)}, \Omega^{(k)}) = \frac{\omega_l^{(k)} P_l(Y_i|\theta_l^{(k)})}{\sum_{j=1}^{C} \omega_j^{(k)} P_j(Y_i|\theta_j^{(k)})} \quad (14)$$

4. M-step: Maximize the expected posterior log-likelihood with respect to cluster membership parameters $\Omega$ and model parameters $\Theta$ given observed $Y$ and current parameter estimates:

$$\omega_l^{(k+1)} = \frac{1}{N} \sum_{i=1}^{N} P(l|Y_i, \Theta^{(k)}, \Omega^{(k)}) \tag{15}$$

and

$$\text{Maximize } F = \sum_{l=1}^{C} \sum_{i=1}^{N} [L_l(Y_i|\theta_l^{(k+1)}) P(l|Y_i, \Theta^{(k)}, \Omega^{(k)})] \tag{16}$$

where (16) can be maximized by non-linear optimization techniques such as BFGS or the conjugate gradients method. Note that solving (16) is much easier than directly optimizing (9).

# Extracting Information from Flexible Receptor-Flexible Ligand Docking Experiments

Karinà S. Machado, Evelyn K. Schroeder, Duncan D. Ruiz, Ana Wink,
and Osmar Norberto de Souza

Laboratório de Bioinformática, Modelagem e Simulação de Biossistemas – LABIO
Programa de Pós-Graduação em Ciência da Computação, Faculdade de Informática,
PUCRS, Av. Ipiranga, 6681 – Prédio 32, sala 602, 90619-900, Porto Alegre, RS, Brazil
{karina.machado,duncan.ruiz,ana.wink,osmar,norberto}@pucrs.br

**Abstract.** Recent progress in structural biology and bioinformatics contributed to the increased amount of data that need to be stored and analyzed. Advances in data mining research have allowed the development of efficient methods to find interesting patterns in large databases. In this context, this work proposes a method to automatically extract detailed information from molecular docking experiments. Completely flexible molecular docking studies (including ligand and receptor explicit flexibilities) of the InhA enzyme from *Mycobacterium tuberculosis* in complex with NADH were performed with AutoDock3.05 using receptor snapshots generated by nanosecond molecular dynamics simulations. To analyze the results we applied our data mining method which was capable of identifying important information about intermolecular interactions and association rules. The method allowed a fast and concise analysis which led to identification of relevant residues and conformations essential to ligand binding.

**Keywords:** Data Mining, Molecular Docking, Molecular Dynamics Simulation, AutoDock, WEKA.

## 1 Introduction

According to Wang *et al.* [1], bioinformatics is the science responsible for managing, integrating and interpreting biological data in different levels such as genomic, proteomic, metabolic, phylogenetic and cellular levels. Actually, bioinformatics projects such as those involving DNA sequences, gene interactions and phylogenetic trees have to deal with a vast amount of data. One example is the GenBank [2] repository of nucleic acids fragments and genomes which in February 2008 had over 100 billion nucleotide bases from nearly 83 million individual sequences.

Recent progress in data mining has allowed the development of efficient and scalable methods to find interesting patterns in large databases through the application of different techniques, for example, association, classification and clustering [3]. Thus, applying data mining techniques in bioinformatics allows the extraction of important information, helping to solve problems like finding patterns in single protein sequences, resuming cluster rules for multiple DNA or protein sequences, etc.

A.L.C. Bazzan, M. Craven, and N.F. Martins (Eds.): BSB 2008, LNBI 5167, pp. 104–114, 2008.

Computational molecular docking is a valuable tool to explore interactions between a target molecule (called receptor, usually a protein) and a ligand (a small molecule). As molecular geometries can change upon ligand binding both (receptor and ligand) flexibility should be explicitly considered in the molecular docking experiment. However, this is not a simple task and most current docking algorithms are only able to explicitly include the ligand flexibility. The receptor is treated as a rigid body with a partially flexible active site [4]. To overcome this problem, we consider an ensemble of receptor snapshots produced by molecular dynamics simulations [5] as an alternative to the explicit treatment of full receptor flexibility in docking experiments. As receptor and ligand were considered in many different conformations, a large number of information had to be computed and organized for the flexible molecular docking data analysis. Hence, a data mining methodology was developed to automatically analyze and extract important information from the docking results such as which receptor and ligand conformations and interactions lead to better receptor-ligand affinities or how a protein conformation affects its interaction with the ligand.

In this work we report the development of a method to automatically extract detailed information from molecular docking experiments that consider the receptor flexibility in an explicit manner. In this method we employed the WEKA [6] data mining tools with the purpose of recognizing some energetic and conformational characteristics of the molecular docked system. We discuss the association rules obtained from the analysis and how useful they can be when searching for new ligands. To the best of our knowledge, there is no previous related work describing the application of data mining algorithms to analysis of flexible receptor-flexible ligand docking experiments.

This article is organized as follows: Sections 2 and 3 present background concepts about data mining techniques, molecular docking, molecular dynamics (MD) simulation, and the target receptor. Section 4 explains the developed methodology. More specifically we list the tools employed in this work, describe the molecular system and the database model, as well as each step of our methodology, and present the initial results. In section 5 we conclude with final considerations and future work.

## 2   Data Mining in Bioinformatics

Piatetsky-Shapiro [7] defines data mining as a process of nontrivial extraction of implicit, previously unknown and potentially useful information from data in databases. For Tan *et al.* [8], the data mining techniques can be applied to discover valuable and previously unknown patterns in large databases. The data mining procedure is part of the field known as Knowledge Discovery in Databases (KDD) which comprises the whole process of converting raw data into functional information. KDD is described by Fayyad *et al.* [9] as an interactive and iterative process that follows some steps: the first step, using the input data, is the data preprocessing which prepares (e.g., remove noise or outliers) and integrates data from several sources. Subsequently, it is necessary to choose and apply a data mining technique to extract knowledge. The last step is the analysis of the results obtained in the previous steps using some type of data visualization techniques [9].

Data mining may help bioinformatics to solve problems such as [3]:

- Comparison and similarity search among biosequences and structures;
- Identification of co-occurring biosequences or other correlated patterns;
- Discovery of pairwise frequent patterns in biological databases and cluster these data based on such frequent patterns;
- Facilitate pattern understanding, knowledge discovery and interactive data exploration using data visualization tools.

## 3   Molecular Docking, Molecular Dynamics and the *M. tuberculosis* InhA Enzyme

Developments in molecular biology and computer simulation tools over the past years made possible a more accurate rational drug design (RDD) [10], based on the theoretical analysis of the interactions between small molecules and proteins [11]. RDD basically involves a set of four steps [12] where:

1. The target protein (receptor) structure is analyzed to identify possible binding sites, e. g., regions where another molecule (ligand) can be bound;
2. Based on the identified binding site, a set of probable ligands is selected and the protein-ligand interactions can be computationally evaluated by a simulation or docking software;
3. The ligands that theoretically had the best interaction scores to the protein are then experimentally tested;
4. Based on these experimental results, a possible ligand is detected, or the process returns to step 1.

In molecular docking experiments, the receptor-ligand interaction is calculated in *silico* and analyzed by an algorithm. In this process, the ligand molecule is tested in different orientations and conformations and its interaction with the receptor is systematically evaluated (Figure 1a). A large number of iterations are performed in order to identify the best ligand orientation inside the binding pocket. This information is computed in terms of the free energy of binding (FEB – the more negative, the more effective is the receptor-ligand association [13]).

As ligands are usually small molecules, the different conformations they can assume inside the binding pocket are easily simulated by docking software [13]. However, limitations generally occur when one wants to consider the receptor flexibility which consists in one of the major hurdles in molecular docking. According to Huang and Zou [14] this is specially challenging because of the large number of degrees of freedom a receptor can have. To overcome this problem, some alternatives to incorporate receptor mobility should be considered. There are a number of alternatives to incorporate at least part of the receptor mobility (reviewed in [14] and [4]). Among them, there is the use of MD simulation trajectories to mimic the explicit flexibility of the receptor [4].

Accordingly to Sali [15], the investigation of biological systems was initially limited to experimental data observation and interpretation. Experimental techniques could only make an analysis of the macroscopic features that correspond to the

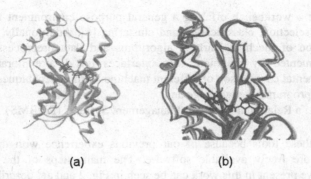

(a)                                                (b)

**Fig. 1.** A molecular docking experiment. (a) The ligand molecule (in cyan and magenta) in two different orientations inside its InhA receptor (gray) binding pocket. (b) Flexibility of the *Mycobacterium tuberculosis* enzyme InhA bound to its ligand NADH (blue). Superposition of four different InhA backbone conformations (cyan, yellow, magenta and green) generated by MD simulations (Adapted from Machado et al. [18]).

characteristic of an ensemble of atoms and molecules. However, the development of experimental techniques allowed a more precise view of biological processes by accessing the atomic properties of biological macromolecules. This made possible a more detailed study - by MD simulation - which simulates a molecule natural movement in atomic level [16].

The InhA (or trans-2-enoyl ACP reductase) enzyme from *M. tuberculosis* (Fig. 1a and 1b) is the bonafide target for isoniazid (INH), a first line drug used in the treatment of tuberculosis [17]. It was demonstrated that the activated drug covalently binds to NADH inside the binding pocket to inhibit the enzymatic activity, leading to mycobacterial death. It is also known that mutations in the NADH binding pocket restores the enzymatic activity by lowering the enzyme affinity for the coenzyme molecule (and therefore for the inhibitor INH-NADH). To understand the differences in affinities, in an earlier study [5] we performed MD simulations to identify the characteristics of the InhA-NADH association. Since the InhA enzyme proved to be highly flexible (Figure 1b), snapshots from its dynamic trajectory [5] were later used to simulate the receptor (InhA) flexibility in a fully flexible molecular docking study, considering the NADH coenzyme as the ligand [18].

## 4   The Developed Methodology

The developed methodology is aimed at finding patterns in the flexible receptor-flexible ligand docking experiment results. As different NADH and InhA conformations are used, one of the key information to address is the InhA amino acid residues that interact with the ligand, independent of its conformation.

For this work we employed the following tools:

- AutoDock3.05: a set of computer programs capable of an automatic prediction of the interaction between receptor molecules (usually proteins) and ligands. It considers the protein static and analyses its interaction with static or flexible ligands [19];

- WEKA: a workbench offering a general purpose environment for automatic feature selection, classification and clustering [6]. Additionally, it contains a collection of machine learning algorithms and data preprocessing methods complemented by graphical user interfaces for data exploration and the experimental comparison of different machine learning techniques [20];
- PHP: a programming language and;
- MySQL: a Relational Database Management Systems (RDBMS).

We chose these tools because of our previous experience with them and also because they are freely available software. The main steps of the data mining methodology we present in this work can be seen in Fig. 2 and are described below.

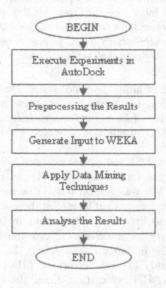

**Fig. 2.** The data mining methodology developed to analyze the results of fully flexible receptor-flexible ligand docking experiments

## 4.1 Docking Experiments Using AutoDock

The first step consists of executing the docking experiments considering the receptor flexibility using the scientific workflow described in [18]. This workflow was developed to automatically execute molecular docking experiments considering the receptor's flexibility in an explicit manner using different conformations generated by a MD simulation. In this work the NADH molecule was flexibly docked into every InhA 2.0 ps instantaneous conformation generated in a previous MD simulation study [5, 18]. About 4,000 docking experiments were performed. For each experiment one result file was obtained. These files were used in the next step.

## 4.2 Pre-processing the Docking Results

Initially, the results of 40 docking experiment were processed, a number good enough to test the viability of the proposed methodology in capturing the relevant information for our work. An example of an AutoDock3.05 docking output file can be seen in Fig. 3a. For this work, only the information about the best docking results were stored: the Final Docked Energy (the docking run with the most negative Final Docked Energy corresponds to the best docking result), the run number of the best docking result, and the *Ki* (inhibition constant) value. This information was stored in a database table called *Docking*. A table called *Ligand_atoms* saved the numbers and names of the atoms. The atomic coordinates were stored in a table called *Coord_ligand_atoms_docking* that links each atom to its coordinates. These information (number, name and coordinates) were stored in different files because an atom can appear more than once in a docking experiment. In this way, even though an atom can be used many times, it is only stored once. After storing the docking information and the ligand coordinates, it is necessary to store information about the InhA receptor (a sample of this file is shown in Fig. 3b).

As done for the ligand, the receptor instantaneous coordinates are stored in a table called *Coord_protein_atoms_docking*. The numbers and names of the atoms, as well as the numbers and names of the amino acid residues, are then stored in a table called *Protein_atoms*. Fig. 4 illustrates the final database model.

However, not all the protein atoms must be stored. In this work, it is important to know which receptor atoms are within a cut-off radius of 4.0 Å from any ligand atom. If any of the atoms of one residue is within this distance, all the atoms from that residue are stored, independent of their distance to the ligand. This is a residue-based analysis. A SwissPdbViewer [21] compatible output file is generated listing all the amino acid residues in the binding site. Then, the important records for data mining are recovered in a WEKA compatible format so the next steps can be executed.

```
USER     RMSD from reference structure          = 6.078 A
USER
USER     Estimated Free Energy of Binding       =  -9.91 kcal/mol   [=(1)+(3)]
USER     Estimated Inhibition Constant, Ki      =  +5.46e-08        [Temperature = 298.15
USER
USER     Final Docked Energy                    =  -9.91 kcal/mol   [=(1)+(2)]
USER
USER     (1) Final Intermolecular Energy        =  -9.91 kcal/mol
USER     (2) Final Internal Energy of Ligand    =  +0.00e+00 kcal/mol
USER     (3) Torsional Free Energy              =  +0.00e+00 kcal/mol
USER
USER                Rank          x        y        z       vdW     Elec      q      RMS
ATOM     1   A6N  ***    1     -5.508   1.228   -0.426   -0.45   -0.07   -0.133   6.078
ATOM     2   A5N  ***    1     -5.315  -0.184   -0.408   -0.56   -0.01   -0.047   6.078
ATOM     3   A4N  ***    1     -5.443  -0.870    0.830   -0.48   +0.03   +0.175   6.078
ATOM     4   A3N  ***    1     -5.672  -0.339    2.067   -0.43   -0.05   -0.223   6.078
ATOM     5   C7N  ***    1     -5.625  -1.137    3.304   -0.37   +0.19   +0.829   6.078
ATOM     6   O7N  ***    1     -5.742  -2.471    3.332   +0.48   -0.10   -0.610   6.078
                                        (a)
ATOM     1   N    ALA    1     19.051  -16.907   10.352   0.00   0.00    0.141   9.00
ATOM     2   H1   ALA    1     19.114  -17.156   11.329   0.00   0.00    0.200   0.00
ATOM     3   H2   ALA    1     19.864  -17.299    9.900   0.00   0.00    0.200   0.00
ATOM     4   H3   ALA    1     19.007  -15.941   10.063   0.00   0.00    0.200   0.00
ATOM     5   CA   ALA    1     17.915  -17.581    9.720   0.00   0.00    0.096   9.40
ATOM     6   HA   ALA    1     18.058  -17.735    8.651   0.00   0.00    0.089   0.00
ATOM     7   CB   ALA    1     17.512  -18.995   10.243   0.00   0.00   -0.060   16.15
ATOM     8   HB 1 ALA    1     16.950  -18.915   11.174   0.00   0.00    0.030   0.00
ATOM     9   HB 2 ALA    1     17.002  -19.595    9.488   0.00   0.00    0.030   0.00
ATOM    10   HB 3 ALA    1     18.442  -19.537   10.413   0.00   0.00    0.030   0.00
ATOM    11   C    ALA    1     16.629  -16.764    9.698   0.00   0.00    0.616   9.82
                                        (b)
```

**Fig. 3.** Example of an AutoDock3.05 docking output used in the developed data mining methodology. (a) Information about the receptor-ligand final docked energy and final ligand conformation. (b) A sample of the InhA receptor coordinates.

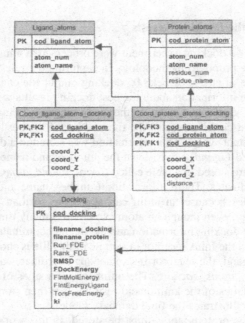

**Fig. 4.** Final database model

### 4.3 Generating the WEKA Inputs, Applying Data Mining Techniques and Analyzing the Results

In this step, we generated a WEKA compatible output. We performed some tests, but the most important were the experiments whose WEKA output is shown in Fig. 5. The first line shows all the 20 possible natural amino acids found in proteins in a three-letter code. For each docking experiment (that corresponds to one full line in the output) saved in the database, we analyzed the occurrence of protein amino acid residues within the 4.0 Å cut-off radius. If the cut-off is satisfied, a "Y" (for yes) is printed, otherwise, "N" (for not) is printed. Thus, it is possible to discover which protein amino acid residues interact with the ligand in each different protein conformation (for each saved docking result). This knowledge is very important to identify the amino acids–ligand interactions that are determining for receptor-ligand binding and affinity. With this information it is possible, for instance, to discover other ligands that interact with this protein in a similar manner. When this generated output is opened in WEKA, without applying any data mining technique, it is possible to identify the total number of experiments in which each of the residues appears.

This result can be seen in Fig. 6. From the graphics we can conclude, for example, that the amino acid residues PHE, LEU, ILE, GLY, and ALA are present in the binding site in all the stored docking experiments.

After this initial analysis, we decided to apply the association technique offered by WEKA to find association rules linking the amino acids in the protein. We

```
ALA,GLY,VAL,ILE,LEU,MET,PRO,PHE,TRP,TYR,ASN,GLN,CYS,THR,SER,ASP,GLU,LYS,ARG,HIE
Y,Y,Y,Y,Y,Y,N,Y,N,Y,N,N,N,Y,Y,Y,N,Y,N,N
Y,Y,Y,Y,Y,Y,Y,Y,N,Y,N,Y,N,Y,Y,Y,Y,N,Y,Y
Y,Y,Y,Y,Y,N,N,N,N,N,N,N,N,Y,Y,Y,N,N,Y,N
Y,Y,Y,Y,Y,Y,Y,Y,N,N,Y,N,Y,Y,Y,Y,N,N,N,N
Y,Y,Y,Y,Y,Y,Y,Y,N,N,N,N,Y,Y,Y,N,N,N,N,N
Y,Y,N,Y,Y,Y,Y,Y,N,Y,N,N,N,Y,Y,Y,N,N,N,N
Y,Y,N,Y,Y,Y,Y,Y,N,N,N,N,Y,N,Y,Y,N,N,N,Y
Y,Y,N,Y,Y,Y,Y,Y,N,M,N,Y,N,Y,Y,Y,N,N,Y,Y,N
Y,Y,Y,Y,Y,Y,Y,Y,N,N,Y,N,Y,N,Y,Y,Y,Y,N,N,N
Y,Y,N,Y,Y,Y,Y,Y,N,N,N,N,Y,N,N,N,N,Y,Y,N
```

**Fig. 5.** Output from WEKA showing, in the first line, the 20 natural amino acid residues in a three-letter code. The following lines, each corresponding to a different docking experiment, show which of the 20 types of amino acid residues are present in each different docked conformation. For simplicity, only 10 conformations (docking experiments) are illustrated.

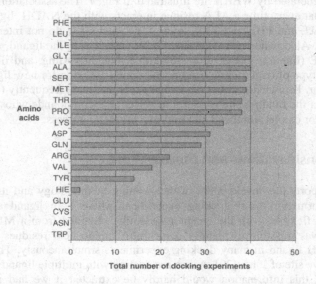

**Fig. 6.** Initial results of our data mining methodology for 40 docking experiments. PHE, LEU, ILE, GLY, and ALA amino acid residues from InhA are interacting with the NADH ligand in all experiments.

**Table 1.** Association rules' parameters used in WEKA

| Option | Function | Value |
|--------|----------|-------|
| -N | Define the maximum number of rules to be found | 50 |
| -C | Minimum metric score. Consider only rules with scores higher than this threshold | 0.75 |
| -D | Iteratively decrease support | 0.05 |
| -U | Upper bound for minimum support | 1.0 |
| -M | Lower bound for minimum support | 0.1 |
| -T | Name of training set | 0 |

have chosen to use association rules for it is a convenient technique to verify co-occurrences of objects (amino acids) [8]. The initial parameters are described in Table 1. In particular, the minimum threshold was 10% (0.1).

```
ALA=Y 40 ==> GLY=Y ILE=Y LEU=Y PHE=Y TRP=N ASN=N CYS=N GLU=N 40    conf:(1)
ALA=Y GLY=Y 40 ==> ILE=Y LEU=Y PHE=Y TRP=N ASN=N CYS=N GLU=N 40    conf:(1)
GLY=Y TRP=N 40 ==> ALA=Y ILE=Y LEU=Y PHE=Y ASN=N CYS=N GLU=N 40    conf:(1)
ALA=Y GLY=Y ILE=Y 40 ==> LEU=Y PHE=Y TRP=N ASN=N CYS=N GLU=N 40    conf:(1)
PHE=Y TRP=N CYS=N 40 ==> ALA=Y GLY=Y ILE=Y LEU=Y ASN=N GLU=N 40    conf:(1)
ILE=Y TRP=N ASN=N CYS=N 40 ==> ALA=Y GLY=Y LEU=Y PHE=Y GLU=N 40    conf:(1)
ALA=Y PHE=Y TRP=N GLU=N 40 ==> GLY=Y ILE=Y LEU=Y ASN=N CYS=N 40    conf:(1)
ALA=Y ILE=Y LEU=Y TRP=N ASN=N 40 ==> GLY=Y PHE=Y CYS=N GLU=N 40    conf:(1)
```

**Fig. 7.** Examples of association rules generated by WEKA, for the experiment in Fig. 5, using the parameters in Table 1, and with 100 % confidence

The rules generated by WEKA are illustrated in Fig. 7. The association rules show, for instance, that every time a ALA residue interacts with the NADH ligand, so does GLY, ILE, LEU, and PHE and TRP, ASN, CYS, and GLU do not interact with the ligand (line 1). Also, whenever ALA and GLY interact with the ligand, so does ILE, LEU, and PHE (line 2). These rules are simple, but interesting, and illustrate how important this type of data mining can be when one is looking for new ligands for the studied receptor. Knowledge about the amino acids that most frequently (based on the rules) appear in the binding site is useful to select new compounds whose interaction with the receptor can be simulated and improve the RDD process.

## 5   Final Considerations and Future Work

This article reports the development of data mining methodology and its application to extract information from docking experiment where both ligand and receptor are considered flexible, with the receptor flexibility obtained from a MD simulation trajectory. It was possible to identify some InhA amino acid residues that interact with the NADH ligand in many docking experiments simultaneously. These residues define the active site of InhA [22]. As we are dealing with multiple ligand and receptor conformations, this information would hardly be extracted if we had not used the developed methodology. Further analysis should give more detail on the dynamics of the binding site, showing residues than can not possibly be seen in experimental structures [22, 23].

As part of future work we shall refine and improve the database described here to use all the stored data, and appropriate data mining techniques, in order to select the most representative snapshots from a MD simulation trajectory for particular classes of ligands. In special, we intend to treat the following data: catalogued compounds from ZINC [24], snapshots from MD simulations, and molecular docking results. Indeed, we can apply data preparation techniques [8] to obtain better qualified data to be used by data mining algorithms. It is expected this data preparation can improve data mining results. Using selected snapshots is expected to speed up molecular docking experiments with a fully flexible receptor model derived from a MD simulation trajectory.

**Acknowledgements.** We thank the reviewers for their useful comments and suggestions to improve the original manuscript. This project was supported by grants from CNPq to ONS. KSM is supported by a CAPES PhD. scholarship. ATW is supported by a CT-INFO/CNPq PhD. scholarship.

# References

1. Wang, J., Zaki, M., Toivonen, H., Shasha, D.: Data Mining in Bioinformatics. In: Advanced Information and Knowledge Processing. Springer, Heidelberg (2005)
2. Benson, D.A., Karsch-Mizrachi, I., Lipman, D.J., Ostell, J., Wheeler, D.L.: GenBank. Nucl. Acids Res. 33, 34–38 (2005)
3. Han, J.: How can Data Mining help Bio-Data Analysis? In: Workshop on Data Mining in Bioinformatics (with SIGKDD 2002 Conference) (2002)
4. Alonso, H., Bliznyuk, A.A., Gready, J.E.: Combining Docking and Molecular Dynamic Simulations in Drug Design. Med. Res. Rev. 26, 531–568 (2006)
5. Schroeder, E.K., Basso, L.A., Santos, D.S., Norberto de Souza, O.: Molecular Dynamics Simulation Studies of the Wild-Type, I21V, and I16T Mutants of Isoniazid-Resistant Mycobacterium tuberculosis Enoyl Reductase (InhA) in Complex with NADH: Toward the Understanding of NADH-InhA Different Affinities. Biophys. J. 89, 876–884 (2005)
6. Waikato Environment for Knowledge, Analysis (accessed, March 2008), http://www.cs.waikato.ac.nz/ml/weka
7. Piatetsky-Shapiro, G., Frawley, W.J.: Knowledge Discovery in Databases. AAAI/MIT Press (1991)
8. Tan, P., Steinbach, M., Kumar, V.: Introduction to Data Mining. Person Addison Wesley (2006)
9. Fayyad, U.M., Piatetsky-Shapiro, G., Smyth, P.: The KDD Process for Extracting Useful Knowledge from Volumes of Data. Communications of the ACM 39, 27–34 (1996)
10. Drews, J.: Drug discovery: A historical perspective computational methods for biomolecular docking. Curr. Opin. Struct. Biol. 6, 402–406 (1996)
11. Lybrand, T.P.: Ligand-protein docking and rational drug design. Curr. Opin. Struct. Biol. 5, 224–228 (1995)
12. Kuntz, I.D.: Structure-based strategies for drug design and discovery. Science 257, 1078–1082 (1992)
13. Goodsell, D.S., Olson, A.J.: Automated docking of substrates to proteins by simulated annealing. Proteins 8, 195–202 (1990)
14. Huang, S., Zou, X.: Ensemble Docking of Multiple Protein Structures: Considering Protein Structural Variations in Molecular Docking. Proteins 66, 399–421 (2007)
15. Sali, A.: 100.000 Protein Structures for the Biologist. Nat. Struct. Biol. 5, 1029–1032 (1998)
16. van Gunsteren, W.F., Berendsen, H.J.C.: Computer Simulation of Molecular Dynamics Methodology, Applications and Perspectives in Chemistry. Angew. Chem. Int. Engl. Ed. 29, 992–1023 (1990)
17. Schroeder, E.K., Norberto de Souza, O., Santos, D.S., Blanchard, J.S., Basso, L.A.: Drugs that inhibit mycolic acids biosynthesis in Mycobacterium tuberculosis. Curr. Pharm. Biotech. 3, 197–225 (2002)
18. Machado, K.S., Schroeder, E.K., Ruiz, D.D., Norberto de Souza, O.: Automating Molecular Docking with Explicit Receptor Flexibility Using Scientific Workflows. In: Sagot, M.-F., Walter, M.E.M.T. (eds.) BSB 2007. LNCS (LNBI), vol. 4643, pp. 1–11. Springer, Heidelberg (2007)
19. Morris, G.M., Goodsell, D.S., Halliday, R.S., Huey, R., Hart, W.E., Belew, R.K., Olson, A.J.: Automated Docking Using a Lamarckian Genetic Algorithm and Empirical Binding Free Energy Function. J. Comput. Chem. 19, 1639–1662 (1998)
20. Frank, E., Hall, M., Trigg, L., Holmes, G., Witten, I.H.: Data Mining in Bioinformatics using Weka. Bioinformatics 20, 2479–2481 (2004)

21. Guex, N., Peitsch, M.C.: SWISS-MODEL and the Swiss-PdbViewer: An environment for comparative protein modeling. Electrophoresis 18, 2714–2723 (1997)
22. Dessen, A., Quémard, A., Blanchard, J.S., Jacobs Jr., W.R., Sacchettini, J.C.: Crystal structure and function of the isoniazid target of Mycobacterium tuberculosis. Science 267, 1638–1641 (1995)
23. Berman, H.M., Westbrook, J., Feng, Z., Gilliland, G., Bhat, T.N., Weissig, H., Shindyalov, I.N., Bourne, P.E.: PDB - Protein Data Bank. Nucl. Acids Res. 28, 235–242 (2000)
24. Irwin, J.J., Shoichet, B.K.: ZINC - A Free Database of Commercially Available Compounds for Virtual Screening. J. Chem. Inf. Model. 45, 177–182 (2005)

# Transposition Distance Based on the Algebraic Formalism

Cleber V.G. Mira[1], Zanoni Dias[1], Hederson P. Santos[2], Guilherme A. Pinto[2], and Maria Emilia M.T. Walter[2]

[1]Institute of Computing, University of Campinas (UNICAMP), Campinas, Brasil
cleber@ic.unicamp.br, zanoni@ic.unicamp.br
[2]Department of Computer Science, University of Brasília (UnB), Brasília, Brasil
hpsantos@cic.unb.br, gap@cic.unb.br, mariaemilia@unb.br

**Abstract.** In computational biology, genome rearrangements is a field in which we study mutational events affecting large portions of a genome. One such event is the *transposition*, that changes the position of contiguous blocks of genes inside a chromosome. This event generates the problem of *transposition distance*, that is to find the minimal number of transpositions transforming one chromosome into another. It is not known whether this problem is $\mathcal{NP}$-hard or has a polynomial time algorithm. Some approximation algorithms have been proposed in the literature, whose proofs are based on exhaustive analysis of graphical properties of suitable *cycle graphs*. In this paper, we follow a different, more formal approach to the problem, and present a 1.5-approximation algorithm using an algebraic formalism. Besides showing the feasibility of the approach, the presented algorithm exhibits good results, as our experiments show.

## 1 Introduction

Genome rearrangements analysis focus on the relative positions of the same blocks of genes on two or more distinct genomic sequences, and investigates mutational events affecting blocks of genes of these genomes that possibly transformed an organism into another. In this work, we study the *transposition*, a mutational event that moves gene blocks from its original position to the position immediately before another gene block (Figure 1).

Assigning to each gene block a value that uniquely identifies it, a chromosome is modeled as a permutation built with these values, following the order of the gene blocks in the chromosome. The *problem of transposition distance* is to find a minimal sequence of transpositions that transforms a chromosome (linear or circular) into another.

Several approximation algorithms for this problem have been proposed. The known approximation algorithm of Bafna and Pevzner [2] has a $O(n^2)$ theoretical time complexity and a 1.5 ratio. Christie [6] proposed a different algorithm with the same approximation ratio, but introducing some improvements, with $O(n^4)$ run time complexity. A simpler sub-quadratic 1.5-approximation algorithm was

A.L.C. Bazzan, M. Craven, and N.F. Martins (Eds.): BSB 2008, LNBI 5167, pp. 115–126, 2008.
© Springer-Verlag Berlin Heidelberg 2008

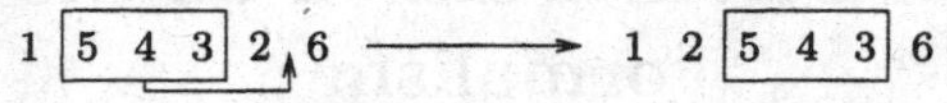

$$1 \boxed{5 \quad 4 \quad 3} \; 2 \, 6 \longrightarrow 1 \quad 2 \boxed{5 \quad 4 \quad 3} \; 6$$

**Fig. 1.** A *transposition* changes the position of a whole sequence of blocks of genes

proposed by Hartman and Shamir [10]. Elias and Hartman [7] devised a 1.375-approximation algorithm, whose proof was assisted by a computer program. Christie and Irving [5,6] proposed a polynomial time algorithm to solve the block-interchange distance problem, a generalization of the transposition event, in which two non-adjacent blocks are changed inside a chromosome. Despite all the recently success in solving other rearrangement problems, such as the problem of sorting signed permutations by reversals [8,1], the time complexity characterization of the transposition distance problem is unknown so far, that is, it is not known whether $\mathcal{NP}$ there is a polynomial time algorithm that solves the problem or if it is $\mathcal{NP}$-hard. All these works are based on the *cycle graph* structure, created to represent the relationships between the gene blocks of a chromosome relative to the gene blocks of the other chromosome. Properties of this cycle graph are used to devise the algorithms and the proofs are essentially graphic, sometimes very complex and requiring the assistance of computer verification programs [7]. Recently, a different approach was proposed by Benoît-Gagné and Hamel [4] whose resulting algorithm is much simpler than these. It performs well in practice, but has an approximation ratio of 3.

Trying to introduce a more formal approach to the algorithms solving genome rearrangement problems, Meidanis and Dias [12] proposed the *algebraic formalism* based on the theory of permutation groups. In this context, we present a simpler new approximation algorithm for the the problem of transposition distance with 1.5 ratio, inspired on the Bafna and Pevzner theory [2], but using the algebraic formalism of [12]. In Section 2 we formalize the problem of transposition distance and present the algebraic formalism. The 1.5-approximation algorithm is described on Section 3 (some proofs are omitted due to the limited space). Experiments and analysis are made in Section 4. Finally, we conclude and suggest future work in Section 5.

## 2   Definitions

A chromosome is described as a permutation over a set $E$, a bijection $\pi : E \rightarrow E$. Each block of genes in a chromosome is assigned to an element of $E = \{1, 2, 3, \ldots, n\}$. Given a permutation $\pi = [x_1, \ldots, x_{i-1}, x_i, \ldots, x_{j-1}, x_j, \ldots, x_{k-1}, x_k, \ldots, x_n]$ over $E$ representing a chromosome, a **transposition** $\tau(i, j, k)$, $1 \leq i < j < k \leq n + 1$ acting on $\pi$ is defined as: $\tau(i, j, k)\pi = [x_1, \ldots, x_{i-1}, x_j, \ldots, x_{k-1}, x_i, \ldots, x_{j-1}, x_k, \ldots, x_n]$.

The **transposition distance problem** consists in finding the minimum number of transpositions transforming a genome $\pi$ into a genome $\sigma$, that is, we want to find a sequence of transpositions $\tau_1, \ldots, \tau_t$ such that $\sigma = \tau_t \tau_{t-1} \ldots \tau_1 \pi$ and $t$ is minimum. The number $t$ is the transposition distance $d_\tau(\pi, \sigma)$ between two genomes $\pi$ and $\sigma$. A particular case arises when we want to compute the transposition distance between a genome $\pi$ and the genome $\sigma = [1, 2, \ldots, n]$. In this case, we have the equivalent problem of **sorting by transpositions**. For example, considering the following sequence of transpositions that sorts the permutation $\pi = [4, 3, 2, 1, 5]$, we obtain $d_r(\pi, \sigma) = 3$: $\tau(1,4,5)\pi = [1, 4, 3, 2, 5]$, $\tau(2,4,5)\tau(1,4,5)\pi = [1, 2, 4, 3, 5]$, $\tau(3,4,5)\tau(2,4,5)\tau(1,4,5)\pi = [1, 2, 3, 4, 5]$.

## 2.1 Permutations

The **identity permutation** $\iota$ is defined by $\iota(x) = x$ for any $x \in E$. For a permutation $\pi$ over $E$, element $x$ is called a **fixed element** when $\pi(x) = x$. The **support**, $Supp(\pi)$, of a permutation $\pi$ is the subset of elements not fixed in $\pi$. For example, in the permutation $\pi = [0, 3, 1, 5, 4, 2]$ over $E = \{0, 1, 2, 3, 4, 5\}$, elements 0 and 4 are fixed and $Supp(\pi) = \{1, 2, 3, 5\}$.

Given a permutation $\pi$ over $E$, the **orbit** of an element $x \in E$ in $\pi$ is the set $orb(x, \pi) = \{y \mid y = \pi^k(x) \text{ for some integer } k\}$. For example, the orbit of 2 in the above $\pi$ is $\{1, 2, 3, 5\}$. The number of orbits of $\pi$ over $E$ is $o(\pi, E)$. An orbit is called **trivial** when it contains only one element, otherwise it is called **nontrivial**. A **cycle** is a permutation with at most one nontrivial orbit. A $k$-**cycle**, $k > 1$, is a cycle such that its nontrivial orbit has size $k$. We denote a $k$-cycle $\alpha$ as a sequence of numbers enclosed under parenthesis $(x_1\ x_2\ \ldots\ x_k)$, such that $\alpha(x_i) = x_{i+1}$, for $1 \le i \le k - 1$, and $\alpha(x_k) = x_1$. For example, permutation $\pi$ above is a 4-cycle that can be represented by $(1\ 3\ 5\ 2)$.

Given permutations $\pi$ and $\sigma$ over $E$, the product $\pi\sigma$ is obtained as follows: for each element $x \in E$, $(\pi\sigma)(x) = \pi(\sigma(x))$. For instance, given $\pi = (3\ 2\ 5\ 1)$, $\sigma = (6\ 4\ 2)$, and $E = \{0, 1, 2, 3, 4, 5, 6\}$, then $\pi\sigma = (1\ 3\ 2\ 6\ 4\ 5)$. The **inverse permutation**, $\pi^{-1}$, is the one such that $\pi\pi^{-1} = \iota$. For example, $\pi^{-1} = (1\ 5\ 2\ 3)$ is the inverse of $\pi = (3\ 2\ 5\ 1)$.

It is a well known result that a permutation has a unique decomposition as a product of cycles with disjoint orbits. Fixed elements are omitted in the cycle decomposition representation. Two cycles are **disjoint** when both have disjoint non-trivial orbits or when one of the cycles is the identity. For a permutation $\pi$, the **cycle decomposition** is a product of disjoint orbits that equals $\pi$. For example, the product $(1)(2\ 5\ 3)(4\ 6)$ is the cycle decomposition of $[1, 5, 2, 6, 3, 4]$. A $k$-cycle is **odd** if $k$ is odd, otherwise it is an **even** cycle. Denote by $o_{odd}(\pi, E)$ $(o_{even}(\pi, E))$ the number of orbits whose size is odd (even) in the cycle decomposition of $\pi$.

## 2.2 Algebraic Formalism

In this section, we present the algebraic formalism to model genomes and transpositions. Bafna and Pevzner [2] represented the initial and target permutations using a representation called *cycle graph* [2]. Analysis made on this graph allowed the discovery of the proper transposition to apply next. So, their arguments and proofs were based on graphics. The algebraic formalism [12,14] introduced a more formal way to solve the problem of transposition distance, in which transpositions are formalized as permutations.

Let $[x_1, x_2, \ldots, x_n]$ be a permutation over $\{1, 2 \ldots, n\}$ modeling a linear, unichromosomal genome. Taking $E = \{0, 1, \ldots, n\}$, this genome in the algebraic formalism is represented as $\pi = (0 \ x_1 \ x_2 \ \ldots \ x_n)$. Observe that a "dummy block" zero is used in order to represent the linear genome, and that the $n!$ circular orderings of $E$ can be mapped to the $n!$ permutations in the traditional representation. We will consider only unichromosomal genomes in this paper.

In the algebraic formalism, a **transposition** is a 3-cycle $\tau = (u \ v \ w)$, with $u, v, w \in E$. We say that this transposition is **applicable** to a permutation $\pi$ over $E$ if $u, v$ and $w$ are all in the same cycle of the cycle decomposition of $\pi$ and appear in this cycle in this order $u, v, w$. Formally, we say that $w$ *follows* $v$ for the pair $(u, \pi)$, denoted by $v \rightarrow_{u,\pi} w$, when $v = \pi^{k_1}(u)$, $w = \pi^{k_2}(u)$, and $0 < k_1 < k_2 < |orb(u, \pi)|$. A transposition is then related to the elements of the permutation $\pi$, instead of to the positions of these elements in $\pi$ as proposed by Bafna and Pevzner [2]. In the algebraic approach, to apply a transposition $\tau$ to the genome $\pi$ is to perform the product $\tau\pi$.

The **problem of transposition distance** then consists of, given the source $\pi$ and the target $\sigma$ chromosomes, finding a sequence of transpositions $\tau_1, \ldots, \tau_t$ such that $\tau_t \tau_{t-1} \ldots \tau_1 \pi = \sigma$, $\tau_i$ is applicable to $\tau_{i-1} \ldots \tau_1 \pi$, $1 \le i \le t$, and $t$ is minimum.

The product $\sigma\pi^{-1}$, in the algebraic formalism, produces orbits corresponding to the cycles of the cycle decomposition of the cycle graph, as proposed by Bafna and Pevzner. The idea of Bafna and Pevzner was to transform $\pi$ into $\sigma$ applying transpositions, by creating $(n+1)$ cycles from the cycles already existing in the first cycle graph. We used the same idea in the sense that "transforming $\pi$ into $\sigma$" means "to create $(n + 1)$ cycles from the cycles existing in $\sigma\pi^{-1}$". In the algebraic formalism, when $\pi = \sigma$, $\sigma\pi^{-1} = \sigma\sigma^{-1} = \iota$ that is composed of $(n + 1)$ trivial orbits: $(0)(1)(2)(3)(4)(5)(6)$.

Following this idea, Meidanis, Dias and Mira [12,14] proved the next two results. The first one says that we can create or destroy exactly 2 odd cycles when we apply transposition $\tau$ to permutation $\pi$. The second result proves a lower bound for the transposition distance.

**Lemma 1.** $o_{odd}(\sigma\pi^{-1}\tau^{-1}, E) = o_{odd}(\sigma\pi^{-1}, E) + x$, $x \in \{0, -2, +2\}$.

**Theorem 1.** $d_\tau(\pi, \sigma) \ge \frac{1}{2}((n + 1) - o_{odd}(\sigma\pi^{-1}, E))$.

## 3    A 1.5-Approximation Algorithm

In this section we first present some definitions and results that allowed us to devise an upper bound for the transposition distance, such that the constructive proofs were used to show the correctness of a 1.5-approximation algorithm for this problem.

From here on, permutations $\pi$ and $\sigma$ formalize two chromosomes over $E$, and this will be denoted only by $\pi$ and $\sigma$ over $E$. Besides, cycle $\alpha$ on the cycle decomposition of $\sigma\pi^{-1}$ will be referred only by cycle $\alpha$ on $\sigma\pi^{-1}$. Given $\pi$ and $\sigma$ over $E$, a transposition $\tau$ applicable to $\pi$ is a $x$-**move** when $o(\sigma\pi^{-1}\tau^{-1}) =$

$o(\sigma\pi^{-1}) + x$. A $x$-move is a **valid** $x$-**move** if $o_{odd}(\sigma\pi^{-1}\tau^{-1}) = o_{odd}(\sigma\pi^{-1}) + x$. Given $\pi$ and $\sigma$ over $E$, two cycles $\alpha$, $|\alpha| = k_1$, $k_1 \geq 2$, and $\beta$, $|\beta| = k_2$, $k_2 \geq 2$, on $\sigma\pi^{-1}$ are **linked** on the cycle decomposition of $\sigma\pi^{-1}$ if $x \rightarrow_{u,\pi} \pi\sigma^{-1}u \rightarrow_{u,\pi} \sigma\pi^{-1}x$, $u \in orb(\alpha, \sigma\pi^{-1})$ and $x \in orb(\beta, \sigma\pi^{-1})$.

Given $\pi$ and $\sigma$ over $E$, $u, v, w \in \alpha$, $|\alpha| = k$, $k \geq 3$, $v \rightarrow_{u,\pi} w$, then if there is at least one 3-cycle $\beta = (u\ v\ w)$ such that $o(\sigma\pi^{-1}\beta^{-1}, E) = o(\sigma\pi^{-1}, E) + 2$ then $\alpha$ is an **oriented cycle**. If for all 3-cycle $\beta = (u\ v\ w)$, $o(\sigma\pi^{-1}\beta^{-1}, E) = o(\sigma\pi^{-1}, E)$, then $\alpha$ is a **non-oriented cycle**. Given $\pi$ and $\sigma$ over $E$, let $\alpha = (u\ \cdots)$ a $k$-cycle, $k \geq 3$, and $\beta = (x\ \cdots)$ a $l$-cycle, $l \geq 3$ and $l \leq k$, be cycles on $\sigma\pi^{-1}$; the cycles $\alpha$ and $\beta$ are **crossing cycles** when there are integers $f_1, f_2, \ldots, f_l$ such that $\pi^{i_j}(u) \rightarrow_{u,\pi} \pi^{f_j}(u) \rightarrow_{u,\pi} \pi^{i_{j+1}}(u)$, $\pi^{i_j}(u) \in orb(\alpha, u)$, and $\pi^{f_j}(u) \in orb(\beta, x)$ for $1 \leq j \leq l < n$.

**Lemma 2.** *Given $\pi$ and $\sigma$ over $E$ and a non-oriented cycle $C = (x \cdots y \cdots z \cdots)$ on $\sigma\pi^{-1}$. For all $x$, $y$ and $z \in C$, the 3-cycle $\tau = (z\ y\ x)$ with $y \rightarrow_{z,\pi} x$ transforms $C$ on a non-oriented cycle on $\sigma\pi^{-1}\tau^{-1}$.*

Given $\pi$ and $\sigma$ over $E$ and two oriented cycles $C$ and $C'$ on $\sigma\pi^{-1}$, then $C$ and $C'$ are **non-interfering cycles** if $C$ and $C'$ are not crossing.

**Lemma 3.** *Given $\pi$ and $\sigma$ over $E$, cycles $C = (x \cdots y \cdots)$ and $D = (x' \cdots y' \cdots)$ on $\sigma\pi^{-1}$, $\tau$ a transposition applicable to $\pi$ formed by three among the four elements $x$, $y$, $x'$ and $y'$, then:*

1. *If cycles $C$ and $D$ are not linked then $\tau$ creates a non-oriented cycle on $\sigma\pi^{-1}\tau^{-1}$.*
2. *If cycles $C$ and $D$ are linked then $\tau$ creates an oriented cycle on $\sigma\pi^{-1}\tau^{-1}$.*

Given a cycle $C = (\cdots\ i\ \cdots\ j\ \cdots)$ on $\sigma\pi^{-1}$, the **distance between two elements** $i, j \in C$, denoted by $d(i, j)$, is the least positive integer $k$ such that $j = (\sigma\pi^{-1})^k(i)$. The following lemma has a constructive proof, and indicates the valid moves to be applied when the cycle decomposition of $\sigma\pi^{-1}$ has at least one oriented cycle.

**Lemma 4.** *Given $\pi$ and $\sigma$ over $E$, if there is an oriented cycle on $\sigma\pi^{-1}$ then there is a transposition $\tau$ applicable to $\pi$ such that $\tau$ is a valid 2-move or there are $\tau_1$, $\tau_2$, $\tau_3$ transpositions applied to $\pi$, $\tau_1\pi$, $\tau_2\tau_1\pi$, that are respectively a valid 0-move, and two consecutive valid 2-moves.*

*Proof.* If there is a valid 2-move on an oriented cycle of $\sigma\pi^{-1}$, then we are done. Now suppose that there is no valid 2-moves on $\sigma\pi^{-1}$ with $z \rightarrow_{y,\pi} x$. The intuitive idea of this proof is to test all possibilities for applying transpositions on an oriented cycle, and to show that there is only one case where an oriented cycle does not allow a valid 2-move, the last case. So, take an oriented cycle $C$ on $\sigma\pi^{-1}$. Let us build a set $S = \{(x\ y\ z)|x, y, z \in C, d(x, y)\ odd\}$, that is, $S$ is a set of transpositions applicable to $\pi$, $\tau = (x\ y\ z)$, $y \rightarrow_{x,\pi} z$, $x, y, z \in C$, such that $o(\sigma\pi^{-1}\tau^{-1}) = o(\sigma\pi^{-1}) + 2$ and $y = (\sigma\pi^{-1})^k(x)$, $k$ odd. This is possible, because $C = (x \cdots y \cdots z \cdots)$ is an oriented cycle.

As $x, y, z \in C$ then $\tau = (y \; z \; x)$ is applicable to $\pi$, acting only on $C$, then $\pi' = \tau\pi$ is such that cycle $C$ on $\sigma\pi^{-1}$ is transformed on three cycles $C_1$, $C_2$ and $C_3$ on $\sigma\pi^{-1}\tau^{-1}$, that is, $\sigma\pi^{-1}\tau^{-1} = \cdots(\cdots x \cdots y \cdots z)\cdots(x \; z \; y)\cdots(x \cdots)(y \cdots)(\dot{z} \cdots)$, with $C_1 = (x \cdots)$, $C_2 = (y \cdots)$ and $C_3 = (z \cdots)$.

As $\tau \in S$ and $d(x,y)$ is odd then $C_2$ is odd, due to the construction of $S$. If $C_1$ or $C_3$ is odd then $o_{odd}(\sigma\pi^{-1}\tau^{-1}) = o_{odd}(\sigma\pi^{-1}) + 2$ and so $\tau$ is a valid 2-move, which contradicts the hypothesis that there are no valid 2-moves on $\pi$. Then $C_1$ and $C_3$ are even and $C_1$ and $C_3$ has length at least 2, that is, $x = (\sigma\pi^{-1})^k(z)$, $k \geq 2$ and $z = (\sigma\pi^{-1})^l(y)$, $l \geq 2$.

If there are $a$ and $b$ on $C \in \sigma\pi^{-1}$ such that $a$ is between $x$ and $z$, $a = (\sigma\pi^{-1})^{-i_1}(z)$, $a = (\sigma\pi^{-1})^{-i_2}(x)$, or $b$ is between $z$ and $x$, $b = (\sigma\pi^{-1})^{k_1}(z)$, $b = (\sigma\pi^{-1})^{-k_2}(x)$, for least positive integer $i_1$, $i_2$, $k_1$ and $k_2$, then we have the following cases:

1. If $a \to_{y,\pi} x$ then $C = (\cdots b \cdots x \cdots y \cdots a \cdots z) \in \sigma\pi^{-1}$, $\pi = [\cdots y \cdots b \cdots z \cdots a \cdots x]$ and, $\tau = (y \; a \; x)$ is a transposition applicable to $\pi$. Then, $\sigma\pi^{-1}\tau^{-1} = \cdots(\cdots x \cdots y \cdots a \cdots z)(x \; a \; y) = \cdots(x \cdots z \cdots)(a \cdots)(y \cdots)$, with $C_1 = (x \cdots z \cdots)$, $C_2 = (a \cdots)$ and $C_3 = (y \cdots)$. Note that $|C_3| = d(x,y)$ odd, $|C_2| = d(y,a)$ and $|C_1| = d(a,z) + 1 + d(z,x)$. But $d(y,z) = d(y,a) + 1 + d(a,z)$ and $d(y,z)$ is even, then $d(y,a) + d(a,z)$ is odd. So, as $d(y,a)$ is odd and $d(a,z)$ is even then $C_2$ is odd. If $d(a,z)$ is odd and $d(y,a)$ is even then $C_1$ is odd, as $d(z,x)$ is even. Then, $\tau = (y \; a \; x)$ is a valid 2-move, which contradicts the hypothesis. So $a \to_{y,\pi} x$ is not true. Analogous arguments demonstrate that $b \to_{y,\pi} x$ is not true either.

2. If $a \to_{x,\pi} z$ then $C = (x \cdots y \cdots a \; z \; b \cdots) \in \sigma\pi^{-1}$, $\pi = [b \; a \cdots y \cdots z \cdots x \cdots]$ and $\tau = (a \; z \; x)$ is a transposition applicable to $\pi$, $a = (\sigma\pi^{-1})^{-1}(z) \in C$. Then, $\sigma\pi^{-1}\tau^{-1} = \cdots(x \cdots y \cdots a \; z \; b \cdots)\cdots(x \; z \; a) = \cdots(x \; b \cdots)(z)(a \cdots y \cdots)$, with $C_1 = (x \; b \cdots)$, $C_2 = (z)$ and $C_3 = (a \cdots y \cdots)$. Cycle $C_3$ has length $d(x,y) + d(y,a) + 1 = d(x,y) + d(y,z) - 1 + 1$. So, $y = (\sigma\pi^{-1})^k(x)$, $k$ odd, and by hypothesis, $z = (\sigma\pi^{-1})^l(y)$, $l$ even, then $C_3$ is odd. In this case, $\tau = (a \; z \; x)$ is a valid 2-move, also contradicting the hypothesis.

3. If $b \to_{x,\pi} z$ then $C = (x \cdots y \cdots a \; z \; b \cdots) \in \sigma\pi^{-1}$, $\pi = [b \; a \cdots y \cdots z \cdots x \cdots]$ and $\tau = (b \; a \; z)$ is a transposition applicable to $\pi$, $z = (\sigma\pi^{-1})(b)$. Then, $\sigma\pi^{-1}\tau^{-1} = \cdots(x \cdots y \cdots a \; z \; b \cdots)\cdots(z \; a \; b) = \cdots(z)(a \cdots x \cdots y \cdots)(b)$, with $C_1 = (z)$, $C_2 = (a \cdots x \cdots y \cdots)$ and $C_3 = (b)$. Cycles $C_1$ and $C_3$ have length 1, $C_2$ has odd length, because $C_2 = d(z,x) - 1 + d(x,y) + d(y,z) - 1$ and as $d(z,x)$ and $d(y,z)$ are even by hypothesis, then $d(z,x) - 1$, $d(y,z) - 1$ and $d(x,y)$ are odd. So, $\tau = (b \; a \; z)$ is a valid 2-move, contradicting the hypothesis.

4. If $b \to_{x,\pi} a$, then we have a case analogous to the $b \to_{x,\pi} z$ case and $\tau = (b \; a \; z)$ is a valid 2-move, contradicting the hypothesis.

5. If $a \to_{x,\pi} b$ then $C = (x \cdots y \cdots a \; z \; b \cdots) \in \sigma\pi^{-1}$, $\pi = [a \cdots b \cdots y \cdot \cdots z \cdots x \cdots]$, and $\tau = (b \; z \; x)$ is a transposition applicable to $\pi$. Then, $\sigma\pi^{-1}\tau^{-1} = \cdots(x \cdots y \cdots a \; z \; b \cdots)\cdots(x \; z \; b) = \cdots(x \; b \cdots y \cdots a \; z \cdots)\cdots$. Cycle $C' = (x \; b \cdots y \cdots a \; z \cdots)$ is composed by the same elements from $C$, that is, $C$ has length $d(x,y) + d(y,z) + d(z,x)$ that is odd. Then $\tau$ is a valid 0-move. Applying transposition $\tau_1 = (b \; y \; x)$ on $\tau\pi$, we obtain $\sigma\pi^{-1}\tau^{-1}\tau_1^{-1}$

$= \cdots (x\ b\ \cdots y\ \cdots a\ z\ \cdots) \cdots (x\ y\ b) = \cdots (x\ \cdots a\ z\ \cdots)(y\ \cdots)(b) \cdots$, with cycle $C'$ transformed on cycles $C_1 = (x\ \cdots a\ z\ \cdots)$, $C_2 = (y\ \cdots)$ and $C_3 = (b)$. Cycle $C_2$ has odd length, because it is composed by the elements between $x$ and $y$, $C_3$ has length 1 and $C_1$ has length $d(y,z) + 1 + d(z,x)$. As $d(y,z) + 1$ is odd, because $d(y,z)$ is even and as $d(z,x)$ is even then $C_3$ has length odd. Then, $\tau_1$ is a valid 2-move. Transposition $\tau_2 = (a\ z\ x)$ transforms $C_1$ on the following cycles: $C_1 \tau_2^{-1} = (x\ \cdots a\ z\ \cdots)(x\ z\ a) = (x\ \cdots)(z)(a\ \cdots)$ and $C_4 = (x\ \cdots)$, $C_5 = (z)$ and $C_6 = (a\ \cdots)$. Cycle $C_6$ has length $d(y,z) - 1$, that is odd. So, $\tau_2$ is a valid 2-move. $\qquad\square$

As could be seen on the previous theorem, there are oriented cycles that do not allow valid 2-moves. In order to avoid the creation of such cycles, we define *strongly oriented cycles*. Given $\pi$ and $\sigma$ over $E$, let us take $\alpha = (x\ \cdots y\ \cdots z\ \cdots)$ a $k$-cycle, $k \geq 3$, on $\sigma\pi^{-1}$, and odd $d(x,y)$. Cycle $\alpha$ is **strongly oriented** if $\alpha$ is oriented and there is at least a transposition $\tau$ that is a valid 2-move. The next lemma shows how to build a strongly oriented cycle from a non-oriented cycle.

**Lemma 5.** *Given $\pi$ and $\sigma$ over $E$, a 3-cycle $\tau = (u\ v\ w)$ with $v \rightarrow_{u,\pi} w$, $x$, $y$ and $z \in C$, such that $d(x,y)$ odd, $C = (x\ \cdots y\ \cdots z\ \cdots)$ a non-oriented $k$-cycle, $k \geq 3$, on $\sigma\pi^{-1}$, and $\tau$ and $C$ are crossing, then $\tau$ transforms $C$ on a strongly oriented cycle on $\sigma\pi^{-1}\tau^{-1}$.*

The following result shows how to create a strongly oriented cycle from two non-oriented cycles.

**Lemma 6.** *Given $\pi$ and $\sigma$ over $E$, with $y \rightarrow_{x',\pi} y' \rightarrow_{x',\pi} x$, $D = (x\ \cdots y\ \cdots)$ and $D' = (x'\ \cdots y'\ \cdots)$ two non-oriented cycles on $\sigma\pi^{-1}$, $D$ and $D'$ are not crossing but are linked and $d(x,y)$ is odd. Then $\tau$ formed by three among the four elements $x$, $y$, $x'$ and $y'$ such that $\tau$ is applicable to $\pi$ creates a strongly oriented cycle.*

Given $\pi$ and $\sigma$ over $E$, $C$ a $k_1$-cycle, $k_1 \geq 3$, $C'$ a $k_2$-cycle, $k_2 \geq 3$, on $\sigma\pi^{-1}$ such that $C$ is strongly oriented and $C'$ is non-oriented, then $C$ and $C'$ are **strongly crossing** if $C$ and $C'$ are crossing cycles.

**Lemma 7.** *Given $\pi$ and $\sigma$ over $E$. If on $\sigma\pi^{-1}$ there are strongly crossing cycles then we have two consecutive valid 2-moves.*

Cycle $C$ is **strongly non-interfering related to** cycle $C'$ if $C$ and $C'$ are non-interfering strongly oriented cycles.

**Lemma 8.** *Given $\pi$ and $\sigma$ over $E$, if there are $C$ and $C'$ on $\sigma\pi^{-1}$ such that $C$ is strongly non-interfering related to $C'$, then there are two consecutive valid 2-moves.*

The following lemma shows the transpositions that must be applied when the cycle decomposition of $\pi\sigma^{-1}$ has only non-oriented cycles, and at least one $k$-cycle, $k \geq 3$.

**Lemma 9.** *Given $\pi$ and $\sigma$ over $E$, with no oriented cycles on $\sigma\pi^{-1}$. If there is at least a non-oriented $k - $ cycle, $k \geq 3$, $C = (x \cdot\cdot y \cdot\cdot z \cdot\cdot)$, $d(x, y)$ odd, then there are $\tau_1$, $\tau_2$ and $\tau_3$ applied to $\pi$, $\tau_1\pi$ and $\tau_2\tau_1\pi$, respectively, such that $\tau_1$ is a valid 0-move and $\tau_2$ and $\tau_3$ are two consecutive valid 2-moves.*

*Proof.* We have two cases.

1. Take a non-oriented, $k_1$-cycle, $k_1 \geq 3$, $D = (u \cdot\cdot v \cdot\cdot w \cdot\cdot)$ such that

$$\pi^{i_1}(u) \to_{u,\pi} \pi^{i_2}(u) \to_{u,\pi} \pi^{i_3}(u) \to_{u,\pi} \pi^{i_4}(u) \to_{u,\pi} x$$

   Cycles $C$ and $D$ are crossing, and we will denote $y = \pi^{i_3}(u)$, $z = \pi^{i_1}(u)$, $v = \pi^{i_4}(u)$ and $w = \pi^{i_2}(u)$, for least positive integers $i_3$, $i_1$, $i_4$ and $i_2$. Take $\tau = (u \ \pi^{i_2}(u) \ \pi^{i_4}(u))$ with $\pi^{i_2}(u) \to_{u,\pi} \pi^{i_4}(u)$. Transposition $\tau$ is a valid 0-move because $\sigma\pi^{-1}\tau^{-1} = \cdot\cdot (x \cdot\cdot y \cdot\cdot z \cdot\cdot)(u \cdot\cdot v \cdot\cdot w \cdot\cdot)(v \ w \ u) = \cdot\cdot (x \cdot\cdot y \cdot\cdot z \cdot\cdot)(v \cdot\cdot u \cdot\cdot w \cdot\cdot)$ with $C' = (x \cdot\cdot y \cdot\cdot z \cdot\cdot)$, $D' = (v \cdot\cdot u \cdot\cdot w \cdot\cdot)$ and $\tau\pi = (u \cdot\cdot \pi^{i_1}(u) \cdot\cdot \pi^{i_4}(u) \cdot\cdot x \cdot\cdot \pi^{i_2}(u) \cdot\cdot \pi^{i_3}(u) \cdot\cdot)$. Cycle $C'$ is strongly oriented (Lemma 5), cycle $D'$ is non-oriented (Lemma 2), and $C'$ and $D'$ are crossing, so we have $C'$ and $D'$ strongly crossing. Then there are two consecutive valid 2-moves on $\sigma\pi^{-1}\tau^{-1}$ (Lemma 7).

2. Suppose that there is no cycle $D$ such that $C$ and $D$ are crossing following the conditions of item 1. Take a non-oriented $k_1$-cycle, $k_1 \geq 2$, $D = (u \cdot\cdot)$ and another non-oriented $k_2$-cycle, $k_2 \geq 2$, $F = (v \cdot\cdot)$. Take $u$, $v$, $w$ such that $u \to_{z,\pi} y$, $v \to_{y,\pi} x$, $w \to_{x,\pi} z$ and $u$, $w \in D$ and $v \in F$. So $\tau = (u \ v \ w)$ is such that $v \to_{u,\pi} w$ and $u \to_{z,\pi} y \to_{z,\pi} v \to_{z,\pi} x \to_{z,\pi} w$. Then, transposition $\tau$ is applicable to $\pi$ and is crossing with cycle $C = (x \cdot\cdot y \cdot\cdot z \cdot\cdot)$. So, $\tau$ transforms $C$ on a strongly oriented cycle $C'$ on $\sigma\pi^{-1}\tau^{-1}$ (Lemma 5). We have two cases (Lemma 3):

   (a) If $D$ and $F$ are linked cycles then $\tau$ creates an oriented cycle $D'$ on $\sigma\pi^{-1}\tau^{-1}$. Take $a = (\sigma\pi^{-1}\tau^{-1})^{-j_1}(u)$, $b = (\sigma\pi^{-1}\tau^{-1})^{j_2}(u)$ (on the same conditions of Lemma 4). Lemma 4 shows that an oriented cycle is not strongly oriented only if $a \to_{u,\tau\pi} b$ and $w \to_{u,\tau\pi} v$. But we have $v \to_{u,\tau\pi}$ on $D'$, and then $D'$ is strongly oriented. As $C'$ and $D'$ are strongly oriented cycles on the cycle decomposition of $\sigma\pi^{-1}\tau^{-1}$ and they are not crossing then $C'$ and $D'$ are strongly non-interfering and there are two consecutive valid 2-moves on $\sigma\pi^{-1}\tau^{-1}$ (Lemma 8).

   (b) If $D$ and $F$ are not linked cycles then $\tau$ creates a non-oriented cycle $D'$ on the cycle decomposition of $\sigma\pi^{-1}\tau^{-1}$ (Lemma 3). Cycles $C'$ and $D'$ do not change the crossing between cycle $C$ and transposition $\tau$ on the cycle decomposition of $\sigma\pi^{-1}\tau^{-1}$, so $C'$ and $D'$ are strongly crossing and there are two consecutive valid 2-moves on $\sigma\pi^{-1}\tau^{-1}$ (Lemma 7). $\square$

The following theorem shows which transpositions to apply when the cycle decomposition of $\sigma\pi^{-1}$ has only $k$-cycles, $1 \leq k \leq 2$, and at least two 2-cycles.

**Theorem 2 (Bafna and Pevzner).** *Given $\pi$ and $\sigma$ over $E$, if there are only $k$-cycles, $k \leq 2$, on $\sigma\pi^{-1}$ then we have a valid 0-move followed by a valid 2-move.*

**Algorithm.** *DistanceTransposition1.5*()

**Input:** $\pi$, $n = |\pi|$, $\sigma$

**Output:** $\tau_1, \cdots, \tau_k$, $d_\tau(\pi, \sigma) \leq k \leq 1.5 d_\tau(\pi, \sigma)$

$\quad j = 0$; $\pi_j = \pi$

$\quad$ **while** (there is a cycle $C$ on $\sigma\pi_j^{-1}$, $|C| \geq 3$) and ($\pi_j \neq \sigma$) **do**

$\quad\quad$ **while** there is an oriented cycle $C$ on $\sigma\pi_j^{-1}$ **do**

$\quad\quad\quad$ j++ {Lemma 4}

$\quad\quad\quad$ **if** there is a valid 2-move $\tau$ on $C$ **then**

$\quad\quad\quad\quad \pi_j = \tau\pi_{j-1}$

$\quad\quad\quad$ **else**

$\quad\quad\quad\quad \pi_j = \tau_1\pi_{j-1}$ Apply a valid 0-move $\tau_1$; {Lemma 4, case 5}

$\quad\quad\quad\quad$ j++; $\pi_j = \tau_2\pi_{j-1}$ Apply a valid 2-move $\tau_2$

$\quad\quad\quad\quad$ j++; $\pi_j = \tau_3\pi_{j-1}$ Apply a valid 2-move $\tau_3$

$\quad\quad\quad$ **end if**

$\quad\quad$ **end while**

$\quad\quad$ **while** (there is a non-oriented cycle $C = (x \cdot \cdot y \cdot \cdot z \cdot \cdot)$, $|C| \geq 3$, on $\sigma\pi_j^{-1}$) and

$\quad\quad$ ($\pi_j \neq \sigma$) **do**

$\quad\quad$ {Lemma 9}

$\quad\quad\quad$ **if** there is a cycle $D = (u \cdot \cdot v \cdot \cdot w \cdot \cdot)$, $|D| \geq 3$, $C$ and $D$ are crossing according

$\quad\quad\quad$ to the conditions of item 1 of Lemma 9 **then**

$\quad\quad\quad\quad$ j++; $\pi_j = \tau_1\pi_{j-1}$ Apply a valid 0-move $\tau_1$ {Lemma 7}

$\quad\quad\quad\quad$ j++; $\pi_j = \tau_2\pi_{j-1}$ Apply a valid 2-move $\tau_2$

$\quad\quad\quad\quad$ j++; $\pi_j = \tau_3\pi_{j-1}$ Apply a valid 2-move $\tau_3$

$\quad\quad\quad$ **else**

$\quad\quad\quad\quad$ Take two non-oriented cycles $D = (u \cdot \cdot)$ and $F = (v \cdot \cdot)$ according to

$\quad\quad\quad\quad$ conditions of item 2 of Lemma 9

$\quad\quad\quad\quad$ **if** $D$ and $F$ are linked cycles **then**

$\quad\quad\quad\quad\quad$ j++; $\pi_j = \tau_1\pi_{j-1}$ Apply a valid 0-move $\tau_1$ {Lemmas 4 and 8}

$\quad\quad\quad\quad\quad$ j++; $\pi_j = \tau_2\pi_{j-1}$ Apply a valid 2-move $\tau_2$

$\quad\quad\quad\quad\quad$ j++; $\pi_j = \tau_3\pi_{j-1}$ Apply a valid 2-move $\tau_3$

$\quad\quad\quad\quad$ **else**

$\quad\quad\quad\quad\quad$ j++; $\pi_j = \tau_1\pi_{j-1}$ Apply a valid 0-move $\tau_1$ {Lemmas 3 and 7}

$\quad\quad\quad\quad\quad$ j++; $\pi_j = \tau_2\pi_{j-1}$ Apply a valid 2-move $\tau_2$

$\quad\quad\quad\quad\quad$ j++; $\pi_j = \tau_3\pi_{j-1}$ Apply a valid 2-move $\tau_3$

$\quad\quad\quad\quad$ **end if**

$\quad\quad\quad$ **end if**

$\quad\quad$ **end while**

$\quad$ **end while**

$\quad$ **while** (there are $k$-cycles, $k \leq 2$ on $\sigma\pi_j^{-1}$ ) and ($\pi_j \neq \sigma$) **do**

$\quad\quad$ j++; $\pi_j = \tau_1\pi_{j-1}$ Apply a valid 0-move $\tau_1$ on two linked 2-cycles {Theorem 2}

$\quad\quad$ j++; $\pi_j = \tau_2\pi_{j-1}$ Apply a valid 2-move $\tau_2$ on the strongly oriented cycle

$\quad$ **end while**

Lemmas 4, 9 and Theorem 2 prove the correction of the algorithm *Distance-Transposition1.5* and lead to the following upper bound for $d_\tau(\pi, \sigma)$.

**Theorem 3.** $d_\tau(\pi, \sigma) \leq \frac{3}{4}((n + 1) - o_{odd}(\sigma\pi^{-1}, E))$.

Theorems 3 and 1 show the 1.5 ratio of the algorithm. This algorithm was implemented in Java, including: the basic operations on permutations, like cycle decomposition of a permutation, product of two permutations, and norm of a permutation; and the new operations acting on the cycle decomposition of $\sigma\pi_j^{-1}$, like finding a valid 2-move on an oriented cycle, a valid 0-move that are crossing with a non-oriented cycle, and the transpositions indicated on the proofs of the lemmas and theorems described on this section.

The space complexity of our implementation was $O(kn)$, $k = d_\tau(\pi, \sigma)$ and $n = |E|$, due to the $k + 1$ vectors to store the permutations and the $k$ vectors to store the transpositions. The time complexity is $O(n^8)$, due to the need for discovering crossing cycles on the cycle decomposition of $\sigma\pi_j^{-1}$.

# 4    Experiments and Discussion

As a case study for our theory, we executed the *DistanceTransposition1.5* algorithm for all permutations from length 2 to 11. These experiments were executed on a machine with Pentium 4 3GHz processor, 512Mb RAM and 40Gb rigid disk. To analyze the results, we compared the values produced by the approximation algorithm with the transposition distance, counting the number of permutations in which these values were different. In Table 1, columns 3 to 9 show the differences between $d_\tau(\pi, \sigma)$ and the value computed by many algorithms found on the literature, as well as the values computed by our algorithms.

We executed our algorithm using a heuristic for strictly decreasing permutations based on a previous result from Meidanis, Walter and Dias [13].

We can observe that our 1.5-approximation algorithm produced better results when compared to the BP algorithm without heuristics [18]. Our algorithm produced worst results when compared to BPh algorithm (Bafna and Pevzner

**Table 1.** Comparisons of the transposition distance with the results of the algorithms WDM-Walter, Dias and Meidanis [17], Ch-Christie [6] with heuristics (implemented by Walter, Curado and Oliveira [16]), H-Hartman [9] (implemented by Honda [11]), BP-Bafna and Pevzner [3] (implemented by Oliveira [18]), BPh-Bafna and Pevzner [3] with heuristics (implemented by Soares [19]) and the our proposed algorithms: af15-algebraic formalism with ratio 1.5 and afh15-algebraic formalism with ratio 1.5 and a simple heuristic.

| $|E|$ | number of permutations | WDM | Ch | H | BP | BPh | af15 | afh15 |
|---|---|---|---|---|---|---|---|---|
| 2 | 2 | 0 | 0 | 0 | 0 | 0 | 0 | 0 |
| 3 | 6 | 0 | 0 | 0 | 0 | 0 | 0 | 0 |
| 4 | 24 | 0 | 0 | 0 | 0 | 0 | 0 | 0 |
| 5 | 120 | 0 | 0 | 0 | 0 | 0 | 0 | 0 |
| 6 | 720 | 6 | 0 | 2 | 0 | 0 | 0 | 0 |
| 7 | 5040 | 72 | 0 | 108 | 1 | 0 | 1 | 0 |
| 8 | 40320 | 1167 | 40 | 1517 | 135 | 0 | 133 | 124 |
| 9 | 362880 | 14327 | 1182 | 25425 | 4361 | 490 | 3023 | 2977 |
| 10 | 3265920 | - | - | - | - | 17449 | 69353 | 69297 |
| 11 | 35925120 | - | - | - | - | 0 | 1235108 | 1234709 |

with heuristics), but this significant improvement obtained by the algorithm implemented by Soares [19] was due to the addition of a heuristic using the *branch-and-bound* technique, and it was not yet included on our implementation. Considering this, our results are very encouraging.

## 5    Conclusions and Future Work

In this work we presented an approximation algorithm using the algebraic formalism of Meidanis and Dias [12,15] to solve the problem of transposition distance. We proved an upper bound for the transposition distance that, together with a previously proved lower bound [12,14,15], allowed us to obtain the 1.5 ratio. Besides, we implemented this algorithm and did experiments with all permutations from lengths 2 to 11. When comparing the results produced by our algorithms with the results produced by other knows methods, we obtained better results. New directions of research are to find new theoretical results to improve the practical results, and to lower the ratio from 1.5 to 1.375, using computational strategies, as suggested by Elias and Hartman [7]. We also could lower the time complexity of our algorithms that, although acceptable in practice, is theoretically too high. Another interesting way of research is to find the transposition diameter. Finally we want to use the algebraic formalism to model other mutational events on genome rearrangements, which could contribute to create an unified approach involving different kinds of rearrangement events.

## References

1. Bader, D.A., Moret, B.M.E., Yan, M.: A linear-time algorithm for computing inversion distance between signed permutations with an experimental study. Journal of Computational Biology 8(5), 483–491 (2001)
2. Bafna, V., Pevzner, P.A.: Sorting by transpositions. In: Proceedings of the Sixth Annual ACM-SIAM Symposium on Discrete Algorithms, San Francisco, USA, January 1995, pp. 614–623 (1995)
3. Bafna, V., Pevzner, P.A.: Sorting by transpositions. SIAM Journal on Discrete Mathematics 11(2), 224–240 (1998)
4. Benoît-Gagné, M., Hamel, S.: A new and faster method of sorting by transpositions. In: Ma, B., Zhang, K. (eds.) CPM 2007. LNCS, vol. 4580, pp. 131–141. Springer, Heidelberg (2007)
5. Christie, D.A.: Sorting permutations by block-interchanges. Information Processing Letters 60(4), 165–169 (1996)
6. Christie, D.A.: Genome Rearrangement Problems. PhD thesis, Glasgow University (1998)
7. Elias, I., Hartman, T.: A 1.375-approximation algorithm for sorting by transpositions. In: Casadio, R., Myers, G. (eds.) WABI 2005. LNCS (LNBI), vol. 3692, pp. 204–215. Springer, Heidelberg (2005)
8. Hannenhalli, S., Pevzner, P.A.: Transforming men into mice (polynomial algorithm for genomic distance problem). In: Proceedings of the 36th Annual Symposium on Foundations of Computer Science (FOCS 1995), October 1995, pp. 581–592. IEEE Computer Society Press, Los Alamitos (1995)

9. Hartman, T.: A simpler 1.5-approximation algorithm for sorting by transpositions. In: Baeza-Yates, R., Chávez, E., Crochemore, M. (eds.) CPM 2003. LNCS, vol. 2676, pp. 156–169. Springer, Heidelberg (2003)
10. Hartman, T., Shamir, R.: A simpler and faster 1.5-approximation algorithm for sorting by transpositions. In: Proceedings of CPM 2003, pp. 156–169 (2003) (extended version)
11. Honda, M.I.: Implementation of the algorithm of Hartman for the problem of sorting by transpositions. Master's thesis, Department of Computer Science, University of Brasilia (in portuguese) (2004)
12. Meidanis, J., Dias, Z.: An alternative algebraic formalism for genome rearrangements. In: Sankoff, D., Nadeau, J.H. (eds.) Comparative Genomics: Empirical and Analyitical Approaches to Gene Order Dynamics, Map Alignment and Evolution of Gene Families, pp. 213–223. Kluwer Academic Publishers, Dordrecht (November 2000)
13. Meidanis, J., Walter, M.E.M.T., Dias, Z.: Transposition distance between a permutation and its reverse. In: Baeza-Yates, R. (ed.) Proceedings of the 4th South American Workshop on String Processing (WSP 1997), Valparaiso, Chile, pp. 70–79. Carleton University Press (1997)
14. Mira, C., Meidanis, J.: Algebraic formalism for genome rearrangements (part 1). Technical Report IC-05-10, Institute of Computing - University of Campinas (June 2005)
15. Mira, C.V.G., Meidanis, J.: Analysis of sorting by transpositions based on algebraic formalism. In: The Eighth Annual International Conference on Research in Computational Molecular Biology (RECOMB 2004) (March 2004)
16. Walter, M.E.M.T., Curado, L.R.A.F., Oliveira, A.G.: Working on the problem of sorting by transpositions on genome rearrangements. In: Baeza-Yates, R., Chávez, E., Crochemore, M. (eds.) CPM 2003. LNCS, vol. 2676, pp. 372–383. Springer, Heidelberg (2003)
17. Walter, M.E.M.T., Dias, Z., Meidanis, J.: A new approach for approximating the transposition distance. In: String Processing and Information Retrieval - SPIRE 2000, pp. 199–208 (2000)
18. Walter, M.E.M.T., Oliveira, E.T.G.: Extending the theory of Bafna and Pevzner for the problem of sorting by transpositions. Tendências em Matemática Aplicada e Computacional - TEMA - SBMAC 3(1), 213–222 (2002) (in portuguese)
19. Walter, M.E.M.T., Soares, L.S.N., Dias, Z.: Branch-and-bound algorithms for the problem of sorting by transpositions on genome rearrangements. In: Proceedings of the 26th Congress of the Brazilian Computer Society, XXXIII Seminário integrado de hardware e software – SEMISH, pp. 69–81 (2006)

# Using *BioAgents* for Supporting Manual Annotation on Genome Sequencing Projects

Célia Ghedini Ralha[1], Hugo W. Schneider[1], Lucas O. da Fonseca[1],
Maria Emilia M.T. Walter[1], and Marcelo M. Brígido[2]

[1] Department of Computer Science
University of Brasília, Campus Universitário Darcy Ribeiro
Caixa Postal 4466, Brasília-Brazil, ZipCode 70.910-900
{ghedini,hugows,lucasof,mia}@cic.unb.br
[2] Biology Institute, University of Brasília
Campus Universitário Darcy Ribeiro, Brasília-Brazil, ZipCode 70.910-900
brigido@unb.br

**Abstract.** Enormous volume of DNA sequences of organisms are continuously being discovered by genome sequencing projects around the world. The task of identifying biological function prediction for the DNA sequences is a key activity in genome projects. This task is done in the annotation phase, which is divided into automatic and manual. The automatic annotation has the objective of finding, for each DNA sequence identified in the project, similar sequences among millions, stored in public databases, by using approximated pattern matching algorithms. The manual annotation is done by the biologists, that use the results produced by the automatic annotation, and their knowledge and experience, to decide the function prediction to each DNA sequence. In this way, the biologists guarantee accuracy and correctness to each sequence function prediction. This work presents a new version of *BioAgents*, a multiagent system (MAS) for supporting manual annotation. The system simulates the biologists' knowledge and experience for annotating DNA sequences in genome sequencing projects. The MAS cooperative approach, allows to create different specialized intelligent agents that, working together, suggest proper manual annotation. *BioAgents* was defined with a three-layer architecture using the JADE framework with a ruler-based engine (JESS). We have done experiments with real data from three different genome sequencing projects: *Paracoccidioides brasilienses* fungus, *Paullinia cupana* (guaraná) plant and *Anaplasma marginale* rickettsia. The produced results were encouraging, which prove the usefulness of *BioAgents*.

**Keywords:** manual annotation, genome sequencing projects, multiagent system.

## 1 Introduction

The Human Genome Project (HGP) was one of the great feats of exploration in history, and its success encouraged the development of hundreds of genome

A.L.C. Bazzan, M. Craven, and N.F. Martins (Eds.): BSB 2008, LNBI 5167, pp. 127–139, 2008.
© Springer-Verlag Berlin Heidelberg 2008

projects around the world. The HGP, finished in April 2003, together with many other genome sequencing projects, have allowed great and fast development techniques both on molecular biology and bioinformatics areas [30]. Since 90's decade it's noteworthy the exponential growth in the volume of data generated by these genome sequencing projects. The management and analysis of these enormous volume of data is one of the recent most important research focus in computer science area, in which scientists are making great efforts to develop techniques and software to help the biologists to store and to analyse many types of biological sequence data generated by the projects.

From a computational point of view, a DNA sequence is a string, composed with the alphabet $\Sigma = \{A, C, G, T\}$, in which the characters corresponds respectively to the four DNA nucleotides - adenine, cytosine, guanine and thymine. Sequencing a DNA is simply to obtain the string of its nucleotides. A genome project is computationally supported by a pipeline composed by three phases: submission, assembly and annotation. A focus of study in the bioinformatics area is the improvement of the pipeline efficiency and correctness [12].

During the submission phase, the DNA sequences generated at the molecular biology laboratories are transformed into strings, that are stored on databases, and will be used on the next phase.

At the assembly phase, the sequences are grouped according to the probability that they have come from the same DNA region. Since the entire DNA can not be sequenced at once, due to limitations of the automatic sequencers, it must be replicated and broken on smaller fragments. Computational tools are used to group these fragments. A *contig* is a group formed by more than one sequence, having a consensus sequence to represent the group. A *singlet* is a group formed by an unique sequence, that could not be grouped with any other one. We will call these contigs and singlets simply by DNA sequences, that will be used on the next phase.

The annotation phase of a genome sequencing project has the objective of assigning biological function prediction for the DNA sequences produced by the assembly phase. The annotation phase is divided into two tasks, automatic and manual. The automatic annotation has the objective of finding similar sequences to each DNA sequence discovered on the genome project, using approximated comparison algorithms (*BLAST* [17] and *FASTA* [31]), and databases containing sequences and their corresponding function prediction (*GenBank* [20]). From a query sequence, an algorithm executing on a database finds a similar DNA sequence, which means that both have approximately the same strings. The hypothesis is that when two DNA sequences are similar, they probably perform the same roles on the cellular mechanisms. The automatic annotation, initially proposes a biological function prediction for each DNA sequence. The manual annotation is done by the biologists, that decide the function prediction to each sequence of the project, based on the outputs produced by the automatic annotation and using their knowledge and experience. In that way, the biologists guarantee accuracy and correctness to this task. But this work is time consuming, since the analysis involves many and different information sources. Thus, providing computational tools to assist the manual annotation task will certainly improve the final annotation.

Previously, we have presented the architecture and a first prototype of *BioAgents*, a system for supporting manual annotation on genome projects [27,28,29]. *BioAgents* tool was developed with a three layer architecture using JADE framework [18,19] and JESS inference engine [25], for simulating the task of manual annotation as done by biologists. The MAS approach allows the interaction of specialized software agents in the reach of an objective [32,33]. Specialized agents using different approximated comparison algorithms, which interact with each other to suggest a function prediction to a DNA sequence, may accomplish well the process of manual annotation.

In this article we present a new version of *BioAgents*, that includes a new protocol of interaction and a more efficient execution mode in separated threads, and besides presents new experiments.

The rest of this work is divided into four sections. In Section 2 we discuss some related work. In Section 3 we present the architecture and the new prototype of *BioAgents*. In Section 4 we describe the experiments and discuss the obtained results. At last, in Section 5, we conclude and suggest future work.

## 2   Related Work

Many projects on bioinformatics use techniques of artificial intelligence, such as MAS, data mining and learning machines. These techniques are employed on different processes belonging to the pipeline, including genome comparisons, analysis and inferring of function prediction of genes. As far as we know, there are no projects using MAS to the manual annotation phase on genome sequencing projects.

*BioMAS* system uses MAS for the automatic annotation phase of the herpes virus [21]. The focus is the extraction of information stored on the public databases and on the automatic annotation.

*Electronic Annotation-EAnnot* is a tool originally developed for the manual annotation of the human genome project [22]. The software combines tools to extract and analyse huge volumes of data of public databases to fastly generate automatic annotation and the inference of genes. *EAnnot* uses information stored in *messenger RNA-mRNA*, *Expressed Sequence Tags-ESTs* and protein alignments, and identify pseudogenes, among other characteristics.

The tool *Environment for Automatic Annotation and Comparison of Genomes - A3C* [24] is based on a MAS architecture divided into two levels. Level 1 has the objective of integrating tasks related to the annotation phase, having tools for the automatic annotations of proteins. Level 2 has algorithms for genomic comparisons, extracting useful information from level 1. The objective of A3C is to identify relationships among different organisms. This is done by obtaining particular characteristics of the investigated organism using the knowledge of other organisms already sequenced and studied.

The tool *Agent-based environmenT for aUtomatiC annotation of Genomes -ATUCG* is based on an agent architecture, and aims to support the biologists by using the concept of re-annotation [23]. In the re-annotation process, the information of the sequences already annotated are revised and compared to new models and data in order to obtain characteristics and information about the sequences, and annotating them again, if necessary.

## 3    *BioAgents* Improvements

As pointed in Section 1, *BioAgents* was developed to help biologists during the manual annotation phase of genome sequencing projects, that is a process in which the biologists' knowledge and experience is used to annotate genes. The system was developed to simulate the manual annotation done by biologists, using the outputs produced by the automated annotation phase, and interpreting these results according to the knowledge stored in *BioAgents*.

### 3.1    The Architecture

In this section we describe the architecture of *BioAgents*, which is divided into three layers: interface, collaborative and physical (Figure 1). The interface layer receives the requests and returns the results to users. The collaborative layer is the architecture core. It has specialized manager agents for executing particular algorithms, like *BLAST* and *FASTA*, that interact with analyst agents for treating specific databases, like *nr* [5] or *kog* [4]. Note that we defined specialized agents to deal with different algorithms and specific knowledge sources (KS). At last, this layer suggests annotations to be sent to the interface layer. The physical layer consists of different local databases containing the results of the automatic annotation.

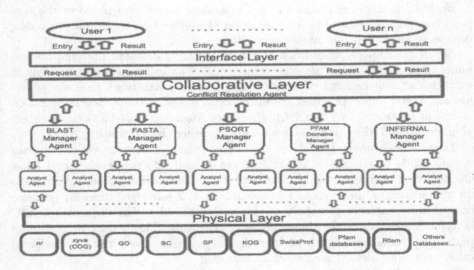

**Fig. 1.** The three layer architecture of *BioAgents* system

Following we detail the architecture layers:

- The *interface layer* is responsible for receiving the submitted requests, and for returning the results for the user. The user requests consist in sending a list of sequences to be annotated.
- The *collaborative layer* is responsible for the suggestion of the manual annotation that will be returned to the *interface layer*, using the results produced by the analysis on the databases of the *physical layer*. The *collaborative layer* is composed by the *conflict resolutions agent* (CR), by the *manager agents* (MR) and by the *analyst agents* (ANL).
  - The CR agent has the objective to submit the requests of the *interface layer* to the specialized MR agents. After receiving the results of the distinct MR agents, the CR agent decides the more appropriated suggestion to be sent to the *interface layer*. In our case study, we used *BLAST* and *FASTA* ANL agents.
  - A MR agent receives messages from the CR agent with tasks according to its expertise. A particular MR Agent verifies which databases and program results have been previously executed in the automatic annotation. This MR Agent allocates ANL Agents to perform particular analysis with particular programs and databases. The MR Agent then waits the suggestions of all the ANL Agents, using previously defined production rules to consolidate these suggestions. As each MR Agent is specialized on a particular tool, it is able to evaluate and to consolidate the results send by its ANL Agents.
  - Each ANL agent executes a particular program and uses a particular database. When a request is created by a MR Agent, each ANL agent defines a data structure, using a *parser* specific to the used database. This processing result with the suggestion is returned to MR Agent that ordered the request.
- The *physical layer* is responsible by the databases used for *BioAgents*. In all our case studies, we used the following data sources: *nr-GenBank* [16]; *GeneOntology* (GO) [7]; *Clusters of Orthologous Groups of proteins* (COG) [2] and the fungi databases of the nucleotide sequences of *Saccharomyces cereviseae* (SC) and *Schizosaccharomyces pombee* (SP). The databases needed to the comparisons must be installed on the system.

## 3.2   The Prototype

*BioAgents* architecture was partially re-written, particularly a more efficient execution mode using separated threads was developed. Like the first version, it is implemented in *Java* [15] with development environment *Eclipse SDK*, version 3.1.2 [3]. Again, the used framework for the agent development is *Java Agent DEvelopment Framework-JADE*, version 3.4.1 [13].

Figure 2 presents a *JADE*'s built-in *sniffer*, which is useful when debugging agents behaviors, since it displays the messages exchanged by the sniffed agents execution at a specific time. The *sniffer* is basically a FIPA-compliant agent with

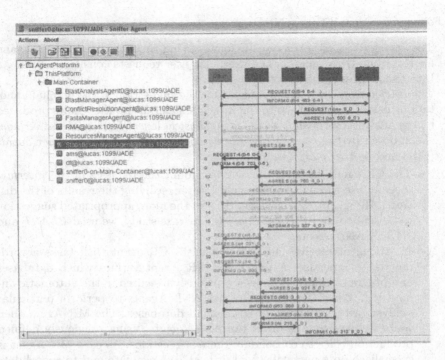

**Fig. 2.** *Screenshot* of agents execution using *JADE*'s built-in *sniffer*, displayed in the *sniffer* GUI

sniffing features using the asynchronicity of the ACL messages. In this figure, we show a *JADE*'s sniffer for a group of 11 agents, and we can see every message directed to agent/group or coming from agent/group. A deeper analysis of the outputs of the sniffer allowed us to detect a communication bottleneck among the agents. Then we decided to implement a new interaction protocol, using contract net, which improved the distribution and execution of the tasks.

The *parsers* used by the ANL agents were implemented by adapting some libraries of the *framework BioJava* version 1.4. *BioJava* offers some objects to manipulate biological sequences and *parsers* to files of sequences, among some other functionalities [6].

As in the first version, we have used the rule-based motor *Java Expert System Shell - JESS*, version 6.1 [14,25] to allow agents reasoning in *BioAgents* system. With *JESS* we defined the biologists knowledge through the use of production rules (declarative rules) according to the parameters defined on a specific genome project. In all experiments we used the same production rules based on *BLAST* and *FASTA* results, following the biologists recommendations. *JESS* was specially developed to be integrated to *Java* language, which makes easier the development of *Java* applications. The defined rules have been elaborated to recognize and to predict DNA functions, which characterise the manual annotation task, where the biologists knowledge has to be formalized, in order to infer and suggest the annotations.

## 4    Experiments and Discussion

In order to validate the new version of *BioAgents*, we used data from three genome sequencing projects developed at the MidWest Region of Brazil: Functional and Differential Genome from the *Paracoccidioides brasiliensis* (Pb) fungus [11], Genome Project of *Paullinia cupana* plant [9] and Genome Sequencing Project of the *Anaplasma marginale* rickettsia [8]. We used *BioAgents* to suggest annotations for both Genome Project Pb and Genome Project Guaraná using the results of *BLAST* and *FASTA*, and comparing the suggested annotations with the manual annotations previously done by the biologists. Specifically, for the Genome Project Pb, the analyzed data was extracted from *BLAST* executed with *nr*, *COG* and *GO* databases; and from *FASTA* with *Saccharomyces cereviseae* and *Schizosaccharomyces pombee* fungi databases. For the Genome Project Guaraná, we used *BLAST* executed with *nr*, *KOG* and *SwissProt* databases. The Genome Project Anaplasma was not yet manually annotated and we used *BioAgents* to support this task. For this project we used *BLAST* with *nr* and *Anaplasma marginalis St. Maries* [1] databases.

To analyse the outputs from *BLAST* and *FASTA*, *BioAgents* used two parameters, the *expectation-value (e-value)* and *score*. These parameters express the similarity between each sequence generated on the project with each sequence stored on the database. Both programs produce *alignments* between two sequences, which express their similarity by showing the correspondence among nucleotides from one sequence relative to the other. As lower is the *e-value* as lower is the error probability between the correspondences of both sequence of nucleotides, and as higher is the *score* more close are the sequences. The annotation of each sequence is based on the similarity between both sequences, and the hypothesis is that as much closer are the sequences as higher is the chance that both have the same biological function prediction.

Figure 3 shows the syntax of the two rules used by *JESS*. We note that these two rules were tested with the *MR* and *ANL* agents, using programs *BLAST* and *FASTA*. The rules described on this figure capture the following biological knowledge, which are pointed by (1), (2) and (3) in the figure:

- Verify if there are alignments having *e-value* less than or equal to $10^{-5}$ (value adopted by the biologists on the three genome projects);
- Among the alignments following the above restriction, select the lower *e-value*;
- If the *e-values* have the same values, select the alignment with the higher *score*.

From the Genome Project Pb, 6, 107 sequences were analyzed (Table 1). From these, 3, 774 genes were manually annotated by the biologists, and 2, 333 were not. Note that 3, 502 annotations were suggested by *BioAgents*, being 1, 547 correct when compared with the 3, 774 manual annotations of the Genome Project

```
(defglobal ?*maxEvalue* = 1.0E-5); (1)

(defmodule Evalue)

(defrule Exists_Evalue_Above_Limit
    "Activate GoodEvalueAnalysis module if there is at least one good evalue"
    (exists (BlastHit
                (HitEvalue ?evalue&:(<= ?evalue ?*maxEvalue*)) (2)
    ))
    =>
    (focus GoodEvalueAnalysis)
    (run)
)

(defmodule GoodEvalueAnalysis)

(defrule Best_Evalue
    "comment"
    (EvalueAnalysis (Evalue ?evalue1)(Score ?score1))
    ?fact <- (EvalueAnalysis (Evalue ?evalue2&:(>= ?evalue2 ?evalue1))
                (Score ?score2&:(< ?score2 ?score1))) (3)
    =>
    (retract ?fact)
)
```

**Fig. 3.** The set of *Jess* rules to analyse the outputs of *BLAST* and *FASTA*

**Table 1.** Results of *BioAgents* applied to the Genome Project Pb

| | |
|---|---|
| Number of genes | 6, 107 |
| Number of genes manually annotated | 3, 774 |
| Number of annotations suggested by *BioAgents* | 3, 502 |
| Number of annotations correctly indicated by *BioAgents* | 1, 547/3, 502 |
| Percentage of correct suggestions (related to the manual annotations) | 44.1% |
| Number of annotations suggested for genes not manually annotated | 336/2, 333 |

**Table 2.** Results of *BioAgents* applied on the Genome Project Guaraná

| | |
|---|---|
| Number of genes | 8, 597 |
| Number of genes manually annotated | 7, 725 |
| Number of annotations suggested by *BioAgents* | 6, 478 |
| Number of annotations correctly indicated by *BioAgents* | 2, 938/6, 478 |
| Percentage of correct suggestions (related to the manual annotations) | 45.35% |

Pb, which corresponds to 44.1% of correct suggestions. Observe that for the 2, 333 not manually annotated genes, 336 were suggested by *BioAgents*. According to the biologists, these are good results that can be improved as the agent knowledge bases are refined.

Considering the Genome Project Guaraná, 8, 597 sequences were analyzed (Table 2). From these, 7, 725 genes were manually annotated by the biologists

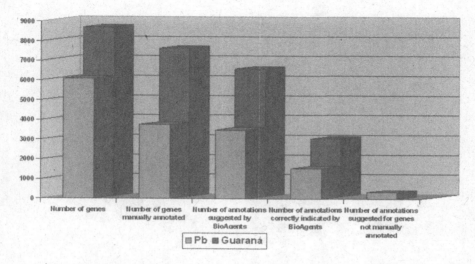

**Fig. 4.** Results of Genome Project Pb and Genome Project Guaraná

**Table 3.** Results of *BioAgents* applied on the Genome Anaplasma Project

| | |
|---|---|
| Number of *contigs* | 773 |
| Number of ORFs at the *contigs* | 1,541 |
| Media of ORFs on *contigs* | 1.993 |
| Number of annotations to ORFs (*contigs*) suggested by *BioAgents* | 1,361 |
| Number of *singlets* | 1,041 |
| Number of ORFs on *singlets* | 1,673 |
| Media of ORFs on *singlets* | 1.607 |
| Number of annotations to ORFs (*singlets*) suggested by *BioAgents* | 1,398 |
| Number of ORFs | 3,214 |
| Number of ORF annotations suggested by *BioAgents* | 2,759 |
| Percentage of suggestions | 85.84% |

and 872 were not. Note that 6,478 annotations were suggested by *BioAgents*, being 2,938 correct when compared with the 7,725 manual annotations, which corresponds to 45.35% of correct suggestions.

For the Genome Project Anaplasma, *BioAgents* suggested 2,759 annotations for a total of 3,214 ORFs (Table 3), which corresponds to 85.84% of suggestions. This is an expected result since one of the used database was from the same already annotated organism *Anaplasma marginalis St. Maries.*

Figure 4 shows the results of Genome Project Pb and Genome Project Guaraná according to Tables 1 and 2. Figure 5 show the results of the Genome Project Anaplasma according to Table 3. Figure 6 show the results of the three experiments. Based on the obtained results, we consider that *BioAgents* can really help the biologists on the manual annotation phase of genome sequencing projects.

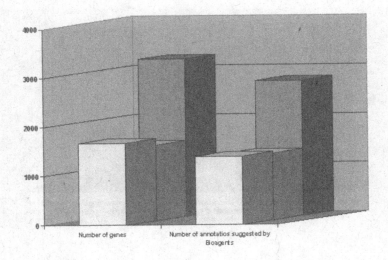

**Fig. 5.** Results of Genome Project Anaplasma

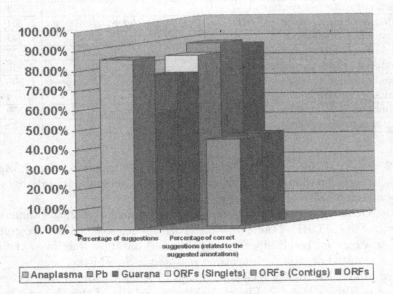

**Fig. 6.** Percentage results of the three experiments

# 5   Conclusions and Future Work

In this article we presented a new version of *BioAgents*, a multiagent system to support the manual annotation in genome projects, that includes a new protocol of interaction and a more efficient execution mode in separated threads. The annotation process, done by biologists on genome sequencing projects, is based on heterogeneous and dynamic environment. It uses different and distributed databases, with the data being continuously modified, which fits well to the multiagent approach. *BioAgents* has agents specialized on distinct tasks, so that they can act independently, using specific rules.

Besides, we discussed the use the new version of *BioAgents* in three different genome sequencing projects: *Paracoccidioides brasilienses* (Pb) fungus, *Paullinia cupana* (guaraná) plant and *Anaplasma marginale* rickettsia. Using a few production rules, we obtained 44.1%, and 45, 35% of correct suggestions, respectively on Genome Project Pb and Genome Project Guaraná, computed from the number of correct suggestions from *BioAgents* when compared with the manual annotations already done on these two projects. Besides, *BioAgents* suggested 336 annotations for not manually annotated sequences of the Project Genome Pb. For Genome Project Anaplasma, *BioAgents* suggested 2, 759 annotations for 3, 214 ORFs, which represents 85.84% of manual annotations for the ORFs. This percentage was expected since *Anaplasma marginalis St. Maries* and *nr* were used as databases for the suggestions. These results were considered very promising by the biologists that analyzed these data.

Manual annotation is time and people consuming and its quality may be variable according to the annotation expertise team. *BioAgents* may help to speed up the annotation process and to avoid conflicts among human annotations. In this direction, an improvement in the expertise of the system, expressed through the rules, may produce a reliable, reproducible and portable annotation tool.

The majority of the related work treat the automatic annotation, like *BioMAS* system and *Environment for Automatic Annotation and Comparison of Genomes - A3C*. Other works, like *Agent-based environmenT for aUtomatiC annotation of Genomes - ATUCG*, focus on the task of re-annotation. *Electronic Annotation- EAnnot* treats manual annotation, specifically for the HGP. As far as we know, *EAnnot* does not have a reasoning mechanism to suggest annotation.

Future work include the distributed implementation for the agents, in order to reduce the time execution, and the improvement of the *interface layer*, providing public access to the researchers that want to use the system. We intend to use *BioAgents* in another genome project, the Genome Project Jararaca, that shortly will start its manual annotation [10]. The improving of the knowledge of $MR$ and $ANL$ agents is necessary to get a higher accuracy for the suggestions proposed by our system. This could be done including other methods and databases, like *HMMER/PFAM*, and identification of non-coding RNAs.

## Acknowledgements

We would like to gratefully acknowledge Richarson S. Lima for his contribution to the first version of *BioAgents* [26]. We also would like to thank the molecular biology laboratory of the University of Brasília for providing the data for the experiments.

## References

1. Anaplasma marginalis St. Maries,
   http://www.ncbi.nlm.nih.gov/sites/
   entrez?Db=genome&Cmd=ShowDetailView&T
2. Clusters of Orthologous Groups of proteins (COG),
   http://www.ncbi.nlm.nih.gov/COG/
3. Eclipse SDK, http://www.eclipse.org
4. kog database, http://www.ncbi.nlm.nih.gov/COG/grace/shokog.cgi
5. nr database, http://www.ncbi.nlm.nih.gov/blast/blast_databases.shtml
6. Framework BioJava, http://biojava.org/wiki/Main_Page
7. GeneOntology (GO), http://www.geneontology.org/
8. Genome Project Anaplasma,
   https://www.biomol.unb.br/anaplasma/servlet/IndexServlet
9. Genome Project Guaraná, https://dna.biomol.unb.br/GR/
10. Genome Project Jararaca,
    https://helix.biomol.unb.br/jararaca/servlet/IndexServlet
11. Genome Project Pb, https://dna.biomol.unb.br/Pb-eng/
12. The IGS Annotation Engine, http://ae.igs.umaryland.edu/
13. Java Agent DEvelopment Framework - JADE, http://jade.tilab.com
14. Java Expert System Shell - JESS, http://www.jessrules.com/jess/index.shtml
15. Java Language, http://java.sun.com
16. nr-genbank, http://www.ncbi.nlm.nih.gov/Genbank/
17. Altschul, S.F., Gish, W., Miller, W., Myers, E.W., Lipman, D.J.: Basic local alignment search tool. J. Mol. Biol. 215(3), 403–410 (1990)
18. Bellifemine, F., Caire, G., Poggi, A., Rimassa, G.: JADE - a white paper. White Paper 3, TILAB - Telecom Italia Lab (September 2003)
19. Bellifemine, F., Caire, G., Trucco, T., Rimassa, G.: Jade Programmer's Guide (June 2007), http://jade.tilab.com/doc/programmersguide.pdf
20. Benson, D.A., Karsch-Mizrachi, I., Lipman, D.J., Ostell, J., Wheeler, D.L.: Genbank. Nucleic Acids Res. 36 (Database issue) (January 2008)
21. Decker, K., Zheng, X., Schmidt, C.: A multi-agent system for automated genomic annotation. In: AGENTS 2001: Proceedings of the 5th international conference on Autonomous agents, pp. 433–440. ACM, New York (2001)
22. Ding, L., Sabo, A., Berkowicz, N., Meyer, R.R., Shotland, Y., Johnson, M.R., Pepin, K.H., Wilson, R.K., Spieth, J.: EAnnot: A genome annotation tool using experimental evidence. Genome Research 14(12), 2503–2509 (2004)
23. do Nascimento, L.V., Bazzan, A.L.C.: An agent-based system for re-annotation of genomes. In: III Brazilian Workshop on Bioinformatics (WOB), pp. 41–48 (2004)
24. dos Santos, C.T., Bazzan, A.L.C.: Using the A3C system for annotation of keywords - a case study. In: III Brazilian Workshop on Bioinformatics (WOB), pp. 175–178 (2004)

25. Hill, E.F.: Jess in Action: Java Rule-Based Systems. Manning Publications Co., Greenwich (2003)
26. Lima, R.S.: Sistema multiagente para anotação manual em projetos de sequenciamento de genomas. Master's thesis, Department of Computer Science, University of Brasília (2007), http://monografias.cic.unb.br/dspace/handle/123456789/28/browse-title
27. Lima, R.S., Ralha, C.G., Walter, M.E.M.T., Brígido, M.M.: A multiagent system to help manual annotation on genome sequencing projects. In: IWGD 2005: Proceedings of the International Workshop on Genomic Databases (2005), http://www.biowebdb.org/iwgd05/proceedings/multiagent-system.pdf
28. Lima, R.S., Ralha, C.G., Walter, M.E.M.T., Schneider, H.W., Pereira, A.G.F., Brígido, M.M.: BioAgents: A multiagent system for manual annotation on genome sequencing projects. In: IWGD 2007: Proceedings of the International Workshop on Genomic Databases (2007), http://bsb2007.inf.puc-rio.br/index.php?pg=home
29. Lima, R.S., Ralha, C.G., Walter, M.E.M.T., Schneider, H.W., Pereira, A.G.F., Brígido, M.M.: BioAgents: Um sistema multiagente para anotação manual em projetos de seqüenciamento de genomas. In: ENIA 2007: 6th Brazilian Meeting on Artificial Intelligence, Brazil, pp. 1302–1310 (2007), http://www.sbc.de9.ime.eb.br/
30. Liolios, K., Tavernarakis, N., Hugenholtz, P., Kyrpides, N.: The Genomes On Line Database (GOLD) v.2: a monitor of genome projects worldwide. Nucleic Acids Research 34, 332–334 (2006) (Database-Issue)
31. Pearson, W.R., Lipman, D.J.: Improved tools for biological sequence comparison. Proceedings of the National Academy of Sciences of the USA 85, 2444–2448 (1988)
32. Weiss, G.: Multiagent Systems: A Modern Approach to Distributed Artificial Intelligence. The MIT Press, Cambridge (July 2000)
33. Wooldridge, M.: Introduction to MultiAgent Systems. John Wiley & Sons, Chichester (June 2002)

# Application of Genetic Algorithms to the Genetic Regulation Problem

Maria Fernanda B. Wanderley[1], João C.P. da Silva[1],
Carlos Cristiano H. Borges[2], and Ana Tereza R. Vasconcelos[2]

[1] Departamento de Ciência da Computação, Instituto de Matemática, Universidade
Federal do Rio de Janeiro, Caixa Postal 68.530, CEP 21941-590,
Rio de Janeiro, RJ, Brazil
{mfbw,jcps}@ufrj.br
[2] Laboratório Nacional de Computação Científica, Laboratory of Bioinformatics,
Av. Getúlio Vargas, 333, CEP 25651-075, Petrópolis, RJ, Brazil
{cchb,atrv}@lncc.br

**Abstract.** Gene expression is the process of decoding the information in
a DNA sequence into a protein. In this process, an enzyme called RNA-
polymerase transcribes DNA into messenger-RNA, which is translated
into protein. The determinant factors to decide which protein belongs to
each cell and how much of it will be produced are the concentration of
mRNA, and the frequency mRNA is translated. Operators and regulators, called transcription factors, control the transcription process. The
gene regulation network consists of determining how and which transcription factors are positioned in some DNA sequence. In this work, we
explore the ability of genetic algorithms to search in complex spaces to
find predictions of possible units of genetic information. We propose four
approaches to solve this problem, trying to identify the pertinent set of
parameters to be used. We use *E. coli* sigma 70 promoters as a study of
case.

**Keywords:** Gene Regulation Network, Genetic Algorithm.

## 1 Introduction

One of the main concepts of molecular biology is that the actions and properties
of each cell are determined by the proteins it contains [9]. *Gene expression* is
the process of decoding the information in a particular DNA sequence into a
particular protein. In this process, an enzyme called RNA polymerase *transcribes*
DNA into mRNA (*messenger RNA*) which is *translated* into protein [9]. The
determinant factors to decide which protein belongs to each cell and how much
of it will be produced are the concentration of mRNA, the frequency at which
mRNA is translated, and protein stability. It is important to observe that the
synthesis of proteins affects the synthesis of DNA and RNA, since there are
special proteins that catalyze their synthesis.

There are three kinds of genes at DNA [9]: the *structurals*, which codify a
protein; the *operators*, which control the structural genes; and the *regulators*,

A.L.C. Bazzan, M. Craven, and N.F. Martins (Eds.): BSB 2008, LNBI 5167, pp. 140–151, 2008.

which control the operator genes. The operators and the regulators, which can be *repressors* or *activators*, are called *transcription factors* (TF) because they control the *transcription of DNA into RNA*. The repressors control the transcription by codifying a protein that connects to the operator gene preventing RNA-polymerase to bind at the *promoter region*, which indicates where the transcription should start. The activators work in a similar way, by binding at the operator gene to stimulate the process of transcription.

The gene regulation network [9] consists of determining how and which transcription factors are positioned in some DNA sequence. These factors determine whether some protein will or will not be produced, how much of the protein will be produced, and when the production of the protein from RNA transcribed from DNA should be stopped. The configuration of these factors is called *unit of genetic information* (UGI), and determining the location of those sites in a DNA sequence is an important task to understand the gene regulation process.

In this work, we propose to use genetic algorithms (GAs) to determine possible candidates for UGIs in a DNA sequence. We analyze different ways for encoding UGIs to be used in GAs, several fitness functions, crossover and mutation rates, and the impact of using elitism in the selection operation, trying to identify the pertinent set of parameters to be used in the prediction of UGIs. We use the *E. coli* sigma 70 promoter as the study of case since it is a well-known organism.

The idea of using GAs to solve this problem arose because of the capacity of GAs to perform searches in poorly known or irregular search spaces [10], seeming to be really appropriate for the problem. We have as our objective to create an adequate codification and measurement so that a naive GA can be efficient.

Other similar works have already been done using genetic algorithms. However, their approach was different from the one we present in this work. While we propose the use of PATSER scores combined with GAs to find sets of TF that could form UGIs, in [1] GAs were used to find the best position weight matrix (PWM) for putative binding sites motif and [13] combined GAs with greedy method in order to find transcription factor binding sites (TFBS) in a set of promoter sequences.

This work is organized as follows: In Sec. 2, we present some basic aspects of genetic regulation. In Sec. 3, we discuss the sequence and transcription factors used in our work, as well as the score function used to construct the fitness functions to GAs. Also, we propose strategies to use GAs in genetic regulation. In Sec. 4, we present some results, comparing the proposed strategies. In Sec. 5, we conclude this paper and offer suggestions for future research.

## 2    Genetic Regulation

A molecule of DNA is a double strand of nucleotides composed of a nitrogenous base (A-adenine, G-guanine, C-cytosine and T-thymine), a sugar (deoxyribose)

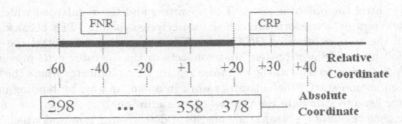

**Fig. 1.** Representation of one of many DNA transcription mechanisms. The transcription initiation site is represented by +1. The downstream, represented by positive number, indicates the direction of transcription. The upstream is represented by negative numbers. Note that the coordinate of the transcription factor FNR is -40, while the coordinate of transcription factor CRP is +30 (Position Precedence Principle). When considering a 450 base pair long DNA sequence (Sec. 3), the relative position +1 corresponds to the absolute position 358.

and a phosphate group. In this work, we will represent DNA as an oriented line (Fig. 1). The *start site* or *transcription-initiation site* represents the base pair where the transcription process initiates and, by convention, is denoted by +1. Base pairs that go in the direction of the transcription, said to be *downstream*, are represented as positive numbers and those in the opposite direction, said to be *upstream*, are represented as negative numbers [9].

In the Jacob and Monod model [9], repressors and activators, called *transcription factors*, and *E. coli* RNA-polymerase work together to regulate transcription initiation. A *protein-binding sequence* is a sequence of bases in DNA where some transcription factor binds to prevent (in case of a repressor) or to stimulate (in case of an activator) RNA-polymerase to bind at the promoter region to initiate the transcription process. So, determining the position of the binding sites in DNA is an important information to understand the genetic regulation process.

In [2], [3] some important characteristics of the UGIs were presented. One such characteristic is the required presence of a binding sequence at the region between -60 and +20. These sites are called *proximal sites* (highlighted in Fig. 1). Another important characteristic is the existence of a pattern of position followed by the operators and regulators, called the *Proximal Precedence Principle*, which states that the proximal operators are located at the right of the promoter (downstream), while the regulators are at its left (upstream).

To remote sites (outside the range of -60 and +20), the precedent relation applied is the *Positional Precedence Principle*. According to this principle, a transcription factor $A$ precedes a transcription factor $B$ if $C_A < C_B$, where $C_A$ is the coordinate of the base located at the center of $A$ and $C_B$ is the coordinate of the nucleotide located at the center of $B$. For example, in Fig. 1 the transcription factor $FNR$ precedes the transcription factor $CRP$. These principles will be used to analyze the results obtained.

# 3 Applying Genetic Algorithms to the Genetic Regulation Problem

## 3.1 Sequence and Transcription Factors

In our study, we used a 450 base pair long DNA sequence of the operon *fixA-fixB-fixC-fixX-yaaU* of the *E. coli K12* genome to determine which transcription factors, and their positions, appear in that sequence. We considered that the absolute position 358 in this sequence corresponds to the relative position +1 of the transcription initiate site (see Fig. 1).

The list of 35 transcription factors considered is presented in Table 1. The search space size of possible UGI candidates, considering this 450 base pair-long sequence and these 35 transcription factors, is of the order of $6.8 \times 10^{16}$.

Each transcription factor has an associated weight matrix (Table 1), used by the PATSER program [8] to score subsequences of the given sequence in the regulation region. The objective is to measure how close each subsequence matches the pattern described by the matrix. This means that for a weight matrix of size $m$ and a given sequence of size $l$, we have $(l - m + 1)$ subsequences to score.

The value in the weight matrix can be derived experimentally or from the alignment matrix [11]. In the latter case, the alignment matrix is constructed from a set of aligned sequences such that each position contains the number of

**Table 1.** Transcription Factors

| Transcription Factor | Alignment matrix size | Transcription Factor | Alignment matrix size |
|---|---|---|---|
| AraC | 26 | Lrp | 19 |
| ArcA | 17 | MalT | 16 |
| ArgR | 25 | MarA | 23 |
| CaiF | 29 | MelR | 18 |
| CpxR | 24 | MetJ | 18 |
| CRP | 30 | ModE | 24 |
| CysB | 22 | NarL | 16 |
| CytR | 22 | NtrC | 29 |
| DnaA | 20 | OmpR | 16 |
| FadR | 29 | OxyR | 17 |
| FIS | 23 | PhoB | 25 |
| FNR | 16 | PurR | 16 |
| FruR | 16 | Rob | 23 |
| Fur | 25 | SoxS | 19 |
| GadX | 16 | TorR | 18 |
| GlpR | 18 | TyrR | 18 |
| IHF | 25 | XylR | 29 |
| LexA | 16 | | |

Alignment Matrix

```
A A G G T A
A T G G C C
A T T A G A
A C G G G T
```

|   |   |   |   |   |   |   |
|---|---|---|---|---|---|---|
| A | 4 | 1 | 0 | 1 | 0 | 2 |
| C | 0 | 1 | 0 | 0 | 1 | 1 |
| G | 0 | 0 | 3 | 3 | 2 | 0 |
| T | 0 | 2 | 1 | 0 | 1 | 1 |

A T G G G A => Consensus

Weight Matrix

|   |      |      |      |      |      |      |
|---|------|------|------|------|------|------|
| A | 1.2  | 0    | -1.6 | 0    | -1.6 | 0.59 |
| C | -1.6 | 0    | -1.6 | -1.6 | 0    | 0    |
| G | -1.6 | -1.6 | 0.96 | 0.96 | 0.59 | -1.6 |
| T | -1.6 | 0.59 | 0    | -1.6 | 0    | 0    |

A    G    T    A    G    A    => Test sequence

1.2  -1.6 +  0  +  0  + 0.59 + 0.59 = 0.78

**Fig. 2.** Alignment matrix is constructed by, given a set of alignment sequences, determining the frequency of each nucleotide in the correspondent position. The weight matrix is constructed using the formula (1). The score of the test sequence is the sum of the weight of each correspondent letter in the sequence, which in the example equals 0.78 [8].

times a nucleotide (A, C, T or G) is observed at that position (Fig. 2), generating a consensus sequence corresponding to the alignment.

Each element in the weight matrix is obtained using the correspondent element in the alignment matrix as follows: First, we add pseudo-counts in proportion to *a priori* probability of the corresponding nucleotides and then divide it by the total number of sequences used in the alignment plus the total number of pseudo-counts (in our case, 1). The resulting frequency is normalized by *a priori* probability for the corresponding nucleotides, usually 0.25 for each base. The final quotient is converted to an element of the weight matrix by taking its natural logarithm. Formally, the weight $m_{i,j}$ correspondent to the nucleotide $i$ at position $j$ is defined as:

$$m_{i,j} = \ln \frac{(n_{i,j} + p_i)/(N+1)}{p_i} \tag{1}$$

where $n_{i,j}$ represents the number of times that the nucleotide $i$ is observed at the position $j$ of the alignment, $p_i$ represents *a priori* probability of the nucleotide $i$, and $N$ represents the total number of the sequences used in the alignment.

The score of a subsequence is calculated aligning it along the weight matrix and summing the correspondent weight for the each nucleotide aligned at each position. An example of alignment and weight matrices can be seen in Fig. 2.

## 3.2   Genetic Algorithms

*Genetic algorithms* (GAs) are a class of algorithms based on Darwin's theory, the basic idea of which is to find an approximate solution for a problem through an evolutionary process that selects the fittest solution among others [5]. The basic genetic algorithm can be described by the following steps:

1. Randomly create an initial population, which represents a set of possible solutions of the problem;
2. Evaluate the individuals of the population, using a fitness function that indicates how "adapted to the environment" an individual is (meaning, how near from a solution an individual is);
3. Generate a new population applying operators, such as selection, crossover, and mutation, to the current one;
4. Repeat steps 2-3 until a stop condition is reached.

Several parameters need to be set prior to using GAs. Some examples are: (i) how to encode the individuals, (ii) which is the suitable fitness function used to measure how fit an individual is to the problem, (iii) which crossover and mutation rates to use, and (iv) whether to use elitism (which means to keep one or more of the best individuals from the current population to the next one).

### 3.3 Proposed Strategies

We will present here four strategies to represent individuals and to apply GAs to the Genetic Regulation Problem. Our objective is to find a solution (or solutions) for this problem by maximizing the scores related to position and some transcription factor at a pre-determined sequence. None restriction were made in order to respect the obligation of the presence of at least one factor at the proximal site nor to prevent the overlap of factors. Our objective was to see if GA was able to generate UGIs without restrictions.

As follows, $TF_i$ represents a transcription factor from Table 1, $POS_i$ represents the position of the transcription factor $TF_i$ on the 450 bp-long DNA sequence used, and $SCR(TF_i, POS_i)$ represents the score of $TF_i$ at the position $POS_i$ given by PATSER [8].

In the first strategy, the individuals were represented as binary strings of 90 bits, the first 36 represented 6 transcription factors and the rest of the bits were used to represent the positions of those factors on the 450 bp-long DNA sequence. The individuals are represented in the following way: $TF_1 \ldots TF_6$ $POS_1 \ldots POS_6$. An example of an individual represent by this strategy, after decoding from its binary form, is [empty, empty, NarL, NarL, CaiF, CpxR, 150, 163, 322, 71, 217, 154]. The evaluation function is given by summing the scores given by PATSER [8] for the codified factors and correspondent positions. If the factors or positions codified on the individual were not valid or did not have a positive score, then no value was summed on the evaluation function. Mathematically, the evaluation function can be expressed by:

$$EF_1 = 1 + SCORE(TF_1, POS_1) + \ldots + SCORE(TF_6, POS_6) \qquad (2)$$

One difficulty of this strategy is the number of invalid transcription factors and positions that it can generate. Using those 6 bits to represent transcription factors, we can generate $2^6 = 64$ different transcription factors but there are only 35 factors to be used; therefore, 29 of the generated elements are invalid. The same happened for the positions, where we have $2^9 = 512$ generated positions but we have only 450 positions to address.

In the second strategy, we tried to repair this problem, keeping the codification of the individual and changing the evaluation function, to consider the number of invalid factors generated ($NTF$). A factor is considered to be an $NTF$ if the number codified at the individual does not map to a transcription factor or if its position does not have a positive score associated. In this new function, the total sum of scores is divided by the $NTF$ plus one (to prevent a division by zero).

$$EF_2 = (1+SCORE(TF_1, POS_1)+\ldots+SCORE(TF_6, POS_6))/(1+NTF) \quad (3)$$

After preliminary tests, this evaluation function proved to be more suitable and, thus, it was used by the next two strategies as well.

In the next two strategies, we restricted the number of transcription factors to 4, in order to reduce the search space and try to find better solutions. So, the number of bits necessary to represent an individual decreases to 60. In the third strategy, we also changed the order of representation of the factors and positions, so the individuals were represented as $TF_1 \ POS_1 \ldots TF_4 \ POS_4$. An example of an individual in this strategy, after decoding from its binary form, is [$CaiF$ 217, $FIS$ 64, $IHF$ 29, $GlpR$ 273]. As we will see, this new representation increased the search efficiency because the crossover operator became less disruptive, decreasing the probability of harming an individual with good evaluation. Another difference between this approach and the others is the fact that this new codification generates only integer numbers between 0 and 35 to represent transcription factors and integer numbers between 0 and 450 to represent positions, where only 0 did not represent a factor or a position.

Notwithstanding, the third strategy solved the issue of invalid factors and positions, the number of generated positions that did not have positive scores associated still was quite large, on average, 95.04% of them. In the fourth strategy, this problem is solved and only positions with positive scores to each factor are generated.

In this last strategy, the genes of the individual that represent positions do not generate integer numbers between 0 and 450, but a real number on the range $[0, 1]$. In this case, an example of an individual, after decoding from its binary form, could be [$NarL$ 0.9501, $CaiF$ 0.5760, $CaiF$ 0.231, $CytR$ 0.398]. To evaluate the individual, this real number is mapped on the number of positive scores of the transcription factor that corresponds to this position. This process allows a dynamic mapping process, since the number of positions with positive score is different for each one of the factors.

For example, suppose that a factor has $POS_{PS}$ positions representing the number of positions that have a positive score given by PATSER. The table position ($POS_{TP}$), that contains the score to be used in the evaluation function is given by:

$$POS_{TP} = 1 + round(POS * (POS_{PS} - 1)) \quad (4)$$

where $POS$ represents the value position codified on the individual.

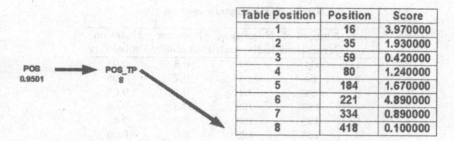

| Table Position | Position | Score |
|:---:|:---:|:---:|
| 1 | 16 | 3.970000 |
| 2 | 35 | 1.930000 |
| 3 | 59 | 0.420000 |
| 4 | 80 | 1.240000 |
| 5 | 184 | 1.670000 |
| 6 | 221 | 4.890000 |
| 7 | 334 | 0.890000 |
| 8 | 418 | 0.100000 |

**Fig. 3.** Mapping between $POS$ and $POS_{TP}$. $POS = 0.9501$ is the position codified at the individual and $POS_{TP} = 8$ is the position of the table that contains the real TF position on the sequence. In this case, $POS_{PS} = 8$. The table with the scores was generated by PATSER for the transcription factor $DnaA$.

Fig. 3 shows how the mapping between the real number codified on the individual and the table position is made.

All strategies are summarized in Table 2.

**Table 2.** Summary of the strategies

| Strategy | Individual | Individual Size | Evaluation Function |
|:---:|:---:|:---:|:---|
| 1 | $TF_1 \dots TF_6 \ POS_1 \dots POS_6$ | 90 | $EF_1 = 1 + SCR(TF_1, POS_1) + \dots$ $+ SCR(TF_6, POS_6)$ |
| 2 | $TF_1 \dots TF_6 \ POS_1 \dots POS_6$ | 90 | $EF_1 = (1 + SCR(TF_1, POS_1) + \dots$ $+ SCR(TF_6, POS_6))/(1 + NTF)$ |
| 3 | $TF_1 \ POS_1 \dots TF_4 \ POS_4$ | 60 | $EF_1 = (1 + SCR(TF_1, POS_1) + \dots$ $+ SCR(TF_4, POS_4))/(1 + NTF)$ |
| 4 | $POS_{TP} = 1 + round(POS*$ $(POS_{PS} - 1))$ | 60 | $EF_2 = (1 + SCR(TF_1, POS_1) + \dots$ $+ SCR(TF_4, POS_4))/(1 + NTF)$ |

## 4 Results

For each of the strategies explained above, we performed tests with the parameters of Table 3. All tests used roulette-wheel selection, one-point crossover and simple mutation, and were made with and without elitism; on those tests that used elitism, the number of individuals preserved were 2.

After all tests had been finished, the second strategy was the one with the worst results with respect to satisfying the restrictions of have a TF at the proximal site and no overlap between TFs. This occurred because the number of invalid factors and positions codified on the individual was large and then the search was inefficient. The fourth strategy was the best one in that it solved the question of invalid factors and positions that happened with the other strategies.

**Table 3.** Parameters used on tests

| Test | Number of Generations | Number of Individuals | Crossover Probability | Mutation Probability |
|------|------|------|------|------|
| 1 | 64 | 64 | 0.8 | 0.05 |
| 2 | 64 | 64 | 0.7 | 0.05 |
| 3 | 64 | 64 | 0.6 | 0.05 |
| 4 | 128 | 128 | 0.8 | 0.05 |
| 5 | 128 | 128 | 0.7 | 0.05 |
| 6 | 128 | 128 | 0.6 | 0.05 |

**Table 4.** Results obtained in tests of the 1st strategy

| | Strategy 1 | | | | | |
|------|------|------|------|------|------|------|
| | Without elitism | | | With elitism | | |
| Test | Best Score | Mean | Standard Deviation | Best Score | Mean | Standard Deviation |
| 1 | 42.2500 | 24.7250 | 11.5928 | 42.9900 | 24.4710 | 7.8988 |
| 2 | 27.0700 | 17.2510 | 4.5389 | 48.9200 | 30.1850 | 11.1643 |
| 3 | 39.4400 | 25.0010 | 11.7540 | 46.0700 | 27.0450 | 10.6533 |
| 4 | 59.5000 | 45.5700 | 11.7213 | 65.0200 | 38.8730 | 13.4272 |
| 5 | 59.5000 | 38.9090 | 12.7814 | 69.2300 | 43.1420 | 16.6664 |
| 6 | 64.9600 | 40.4340 | 16.6992 | 67.3400 | 38.0850 | 15.9563 |

**Table 5.** Results obtained in tests of the 2nd strategy

| | Strategy 2 | | | | | |
|------|------|------|------|------|------|------|
| | Without elitism | | | With elitism | | |
| Test | Best Score | Mean | Standard Deviation | Best Score | Mean | Standard Deviation |
| 1 | 14.0967 | 9.2805 | 3.3830 | 18.8750 | 10.1772 | 4.0064 |
| 2 | 10.4050 | 7.8567 | 2.1874 | 46.0000 | 18.5172 | 11.5516 |
| 3 | 12.5467 | 8.7242 | 2.7211 | 19.8150 | 11.6220 | 3.4320 |
| 4 | 29.9350 | 19.8903 | 7.0213 | 59.1500 | 23.1940 | 14.5267 |
| 5 | 23.1000 | 16.8688 | 4.2398 | 35.4850 | 18.6510 | 7.5850 |
| 6 | 32.9000 | 18.0770 | 8.2292 | 45.8600 | 18.9105 | 10.8298 |

Each test proposed in Table 3 was executed 10 times, on a Core2Duo, 1.8GHz, with 2.0 GB of RAM memory, and took approximately 5 seconds in the best case and approximately 20 seconds in the worst case. The results that we obtained are shown in Tables 4, 5, 6 and 7 (which was the best one).

On the average, the results with elitism were better than the ones without it. Of the six tests analyzed, the first three, with a population of 64 individuals and 64 generations, presented results worse than the ones obtained by tests 4 to 6, with a population of 128 individuals and 128 generations, because with a larger population it is possible to explore a bigger sample of the search space. For tests

**Table 6.** Results obtained in tests of the 3rd strategy

| | Strategy 3 | | | | | |
| --- | --- | --- | --- | --- | --- | --- |
| | Without elitism | | | With elitism | | |
| Test | Best Score | Mean | Standard Deviation | Best Score | Mean | Standard Deviation |
| 1 | 38.3600 | 21.0270 | 6.4477 | 64.7900 | 28.3620 | 14.6940 |
| 2 | 40.5500 | 24.2740 | 9.8917 | 38.3400 | 24.9690 | 7.3078 |
| 3 | 37.3200 | 19.7090 | 7.1399 | 54.9000 | 28.2460 | 12.9417 |
| 4 | 71.8200 | 34.7350 | 17.3403 | 47.1400 | 34.2110 | 9.5571 |
| 5 | 65.4000 | 40.0560 | 16.3459 | 65.8600 | 37.9360 | 14.6278 |
| 6 | 57.2000 | 34.4800 | 13.1154 | 65.8400 | 40.3160 | 14.8843 |

**Table 7.** Results obtained in tests of the 4th strategy

| | Strategy 4 | | | | | |
| --- | --- | --- | --- | --- | --- | --- |
| | Without elitism | | | With elitism | | |
| Test | Best Score | Mean | Standard Deviation | Best Score | Mean | Standard Deviation |
| 1 | 71.8200 | 49.1950 | 13.4897 | 84.1500 | 52.7940 | 15.2225 |
| 2 | 64.4100 | 57.2060 | 7.5431 | 66.7400 | 47.5560 | 16.6195 |
| 3 | 63.6700 | 46.8780 | 11.0031 | 66.4400 | 48.8960 | 14.9455 |
| 4 | 84.1500 | 59.2260 | 14.3054 | 74.6500 | 66.7930 | 10.4447 |
| 5 | 84.1500 | 57.5220 | 14.4115 | 79.0300 | 64.4940 | 9.2419 |
| 6 | 86.4500 | 66.3950 | 12.9878 | 76.4500 | 66.8450 | 7.0611 |

**Table 8.** Statistics of the individuals generated by strategy 4 (without elitism)

| | Strategy 4 without elitism | | | |
| --- | --- | --- | --- | --- |
| Test | Number of individuals on final population | Individuals with proximal site | Individuals without overlapping | Individuals with proximal site and no overlapping |
| 1 | 64 | 4.68% | 95.31% | 4.68% |
| 2 | 64 | 10.93% | 95.31% | 10.93% |
| 3 | 64 | 7.81% | 96.87% | 7.81% |
| 4 | 128 | 21.87% | 96.87% | 21.87% |
| 5 | 128 | 4.68% | 82.03% | 4.68% |
| 6 | 128 | 14.06% | 59.37% | 10.93% |

from 1 to 3, a greater crossover probability was more effective, while in the last three tests a lower probability was better.

In a preliminary analysis of the results, we verified whether there were individuals that had overlapping factors and that did not have at least one factor at the proximal site. In Table 8, we show the percentage of individuals that satisfy these requisites for strategy 4. We chose not to make any kind of restriction because one of our main objectives was to observe whether the genetic algorithm was able to generate individuals that could satisfy the biological requisites pointed out in [2], [3]. Besides, some individuals, such as [*CaiF* 164, *CytR* 18, *CaiF* 217, *CaiF* 274], found UGIs that have transcription factors at nearby positions (differing by 2 bp) to the ones in the TRACTOR database [4], [6], [7], [12].

The presence of transcription factors on the proximal site is not guaranteed but is observed with some individuals of the population. A factor is at the proximal site if its central nucleotide position is between positions -60 and +20, with respect to the promoter. In the sequence used in this work, the positions -60 and +20 correspond to the absolute positions 298 and 378 (Sec. 3). For example, the individual [*CaiF* 274, *Fur* 23, *CaiF* 217, *GadX* 343] does not have overlapping factors and has a factor at the proximal site, *GadX*. This TF has size 16 (see Table 1), so its central nucleotide is at position 343.

## 5   Conclusions and Future Works

In this work we proposed to generate possible candidates for UGI using genetic algorithms from the information given by the PATSER program [8]. Some difficulties were found because of the low number of positions that had a positive evaluation compared with the number of possible positions in the DNA sequence we used. This made us propose another strategy to deal with the position and so the fourth strategy was the one with the best performance. We also verified that elitism is very important to genetic algorithm success in this case. The solution space of this problem is complex and if we had not used elitism, individuals with good evaluation could have been lost when we applied crossover or mutation, decreasing the mean evaluation of the population.

In future works, we intend to: (i) propose a new crossover operator to solve the issue of invalid factors and positions generated after using this operator, (ii) propose a new mutation operator, (iii) create an evaluation function that penalizes individuals with overlapping, (iv) generate individuals respecting the requirement of at least one factor at the proximal site, (v) use an elitism operator that preserves these individuals, and (vi) modify the stop condition of the algorithm in order to achieve better results.

## References

1. Chang, X., Zhou, W., Zhou, C., Liang, Y.: Prediction of Transcription Factor Binding Sites Using Genetic Algorithm. In: 1st IEEE Conference on Industrial Electronics and Applications, May 24-26, 2006, pp. 1–4 (2006)
2. Collado-Vides, J.: A linguistic representation of the regulation of transcription initiation. i. an ordered array of complex symbols with distinctive features. BioSystems, 87–104 (1993)
3. Collado-Vides, J.: A linguistic representation of the regulation of transcription initiation. ii. distinctive features of sigma 70 promoters and their regulatory binding sites. BioSystems 29, 105–128 (1993)
4. Espinosa, V., Gonzalez, A., Huerta, A., Vasconcelos, A.T., Collado-Vides, J.: Comparative Studies of Transcriptional Regulation Mechanisms in a group of gamma-proteobacterial Genomes. J. Mol. Biol. 354, 184–199 (2005)

5. Goldberg, D.E.: Genetic Algorithms in Search, Optimization and Learning. Addison-Wesley, Massachusetts (1989)
6. Gonzalez, A., Espinosa, V., Vasconcelos, A.T., Perez-Rueda, E., Collado-Vides, J.: TRACTOR_DB: a Database of Regulatory Networks in Gamma-Proteobacterial Genomes. Nucleic Acids Res. 33, D98–D102 (2004)
7. Hernandez, M., Gonzalez, A., Espinosa, V., Vasconcelos, A., Collado-Vides, J.: Complementing computationally predicted regulatory sites in Tractor_DB using a pattern matching approach. Silico Biology 5, 0020 (2004)
8. Hertz, G.Z., Stormo, G.D.: Identifying dna and protein patterns with statistically significant alignments of multiple sequences. Bioinformatics 15(7), 563–577 (1999)
9. Lodish, H., Berk, A., Zipursky, L., Matsudaira, P., Baltimore, D., Darnell, J.: Molecular Cell Biology, 4th edn. W.H. Freedman, [S.l] (2000)
10. Michalewicz, Z.: Genetic Algorithms + Data Structures = Evolution Programs, 3rd edn. Springer, Berlin (1996)
11. Stormo, G.D., Hartzell, G.W.: Identifying protein-binding sites from unaligned dna fragments. Proceedings of the National Academy of Sciences of the United States of America 86(4), 1183–1187 (1989)
12. Tractor db, http://www.tractor.lncc.br/
13. Wang, W., Chang, X., Zhou, C.: Combining Greedy Method and Genetic Algorithm to Identify Transcription Factor Binding Sites. In: Sixth International Conference on Hybrid Intelligent Systems, 2006. HIS 2006, p. 15 (December 2006)

# Tests for Gene Clusters Satisfying the Generalized Adjacency Criterion

Ximing Xu and David Sankoff

Department of Mathematics and Statistics,
University of Ottawa, Ottawa, Canada K1N 6N5
{xxu060,sankoff}@uottawa.ca

**Abstract.** We study a parametrized definition of gene clusters that permits control over the trade-off between increasing gene content versus conserving gene order within a cluster. This is based on the notion of generalized adjacency, which is the property shared by any two genes no farther apart, in the linear order of a chromosome, than a fixed threshold parameter $\theta$. Then a cluster in two or more genomes is just a maximal set of markers, where in each genome these markers form a connected chain of generalized adjacencies. Since even pairs of randomly constructed genomes may have many generalized adjacency clusters in common, we study the statistical properties of generalized adjacency clusters under the null hypothesis that the markers are ordered completely randomly on the genomes. We derive expresions for the exact values of the expected number of clusters of a given size, for large and small values of the parameter. We discover through simulations that the trend from small to large clusters as a function of the parameter theta exhibits a "cut-off" phenomenon at or near $\sqrt{\theta}$ as genome size increases.

## 1 Introduction

Criteria for identifying common spatial groupings, such as synteny blocks or gene clusters, in two or more genomes entail a trade-off between increased content versus stricter order: if we require genes, motifs, segments, anchors or other elements (for which we will use the generic terms *markers*) of the group to be ordered identically within different genomes, so that we can have great confidence that these are genuine, evolutionarily conserved or functionally determined configurations, only relatively small groups are likely to satisfy this restrictive condition, so that the analysis misses large common genomic regions that only suffer small, perhaps insignificant, disruptions of common order. On the other hand, by allowing unrestricted scrambling of markers within the common groups (e.g., $r$-windows [2], max-gap [1] or "gene teams" [3]), we may be able to detect larger, more loosely structured groupings, but at least in the first analysis, must forgo accounting for local genome rearrangement, missing an important aspect of evolutionary history, and we relinquish the possibility of pinpointing extensive local conservation of order within the group.

We previously presented a parametrized definition of gene clusters that allows us to control the emphasis placed on conserved order within a cluster [6] and

A.L.C. Bazzan, M. Craven, and N.F. Martins (Eds.): BSB 2008, LNBI 5167, pp. 152–160, 2008.

hence to systematically explore the details of the content/order trade-off. The basis for this is the notion of generalized adjacency, which is the property shared by any two markers no farther apart, in the linear order of a chromosome, than a fixed threshold. Then a cluster in two or more genomes is just a maximal set of markers, where in each genome these markers form a connected chain of generalized adjacencies. Increasing the size of the threshold relaxes the degree of common ordering required, within a cluster, in the different genomes.

Nevertheless, for any fixed threshold, evolutionary rearrangements continue to disrupt the orders of markers on chromosome and will create, alter or destroy generalized adjacency clusters. Since even pairs of randomly constructed genomes may have some generalized adjacency clusters in common, the question arises of whether the number or size of these clusters is significantly larger than the random case. To answer such questions in this paper, we study the statistical properties of generalized adjacency clusters under the null hypothesis that the $n$ markers are ordered completely randomly on the genomes (N.B. it suffices to randomize just one of the genomes, since relabeling markers can convert one of the genome to a canonical order, e.g., $1, 2, \ldots, n$, without changing the number, location and size of clusters).

## 2    Definitions

Our definition of generalized adjacency clusters is illustrated in Figure 1.

**Definition 1.** *Let $V_X$ to be the set of markers in the genome $X$. These markers are partitioned among a number of total orders called* **chromosomes**. *For markers $g$ and $h$ in $V_X$ on the same chromosome in $X$, let $gh \in E_X$ if the number*

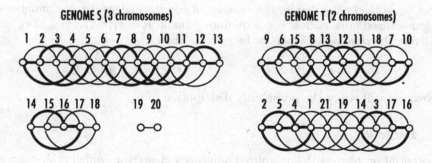

**Generalized Adjacency Clusters:**

θ= 2 : {2,4,5}, {6,8}, {11, 12 13}, {16, 17}
θ= 3 : {1,2,4,5}, {6,7,8,9,10, 11, 12 13}, {14, 16, 17}
θ= 4 : {1,2,3,4,5}, {6,7,8,9,10, 11, 12 13}, {14, 16, 17}

**Fig. 1.** Graphs constructed from two genomes using parameter $\theta = 3$. Thick edges determine generalized adjacency clusters. Clusters listed for $\theta = 2$ and $\theta = 4$ as well.

*of genes intervening between g and h in X is less than θ, where θ ≥ 1 is a fixed* **neighbourhood parameter**.

*Consider the graphs $G_S = (V_S, E_S)$ and $G_T = (V_T, E_T)$ with a non-null set of vertices in common $V = V_S \cap V_T$. We say a subset of $C \subseteq V$ is a* **generalized adjacency cluster** *if it consists of the vertices of a maximal connected subgraph of $G_{ST} = (V, E_S \cap E_T)$.*

This definition of clusters decomposes the markers in the two genomes into identical sets of disjoint generalized adjacency clusters of size greater or equal to 2, and possibly different sets of singletons belonging to no cluster, either because they are in $V$, but not in $E_S \cap E_T$, or because they are in $V_S \cup V_T \setminus V$. For simplicity, we do not attempt to deal with duplicate markers in this paper, and we also assume $V_S = V_T = V$. In practice, depending on the relative emphasis to be placed on order rearrangement versus marker insertion/deletion, we can delete all markers in $V_S \cup V_T \setminus V$ *before* calculating $E_S$ and $E_T$, so as to exclude the effect of the markers unique to $S$ or unique to $T$.

When $\theta = 1$, a cluster has exactly the same marker content and order (or reversed order) in both genomes. When $\theta = \infty$, the definition returns simply all the synteny sets, namely the sets of markers in common between two chromosomes, one in each genome.

## 3   The Number of Generalized Adjacencies in Common in Two Random Genomes

Each genome can be represented as a permutation of the first $n$ positive integers. We denote by $I$ the *reference genome* $1, 2, \ldots, n$ and by $R$ the *random genome* sampled from all $n!$ possible genomes, each with probability of $\frac{1}{n!}$.

Let $n_2 = |E_I \cap E_R|$ denote the number of common edges, i.e. the number of the generalized adjacencies. For a random genome $R = r_1, r_2, \ldots, r_n$, if $r_h = i$, we define the *position* of $i$ in $R$ to be $g_i = h$. Then

$$|E_I \cap E_R| = |\{1 \leq i < j \leq n \mid j - i \leq \theta, |g_i - g_j| \leq \theta\}|.$$

Next we will study the probability distribution of $n_2$.

### 3.1   Large $\theta$

A potential problem with generalized adjacency clustering, which it shares with other methods such as max-gap, is that beyond certain values of $\theta$, instead of large clusters being statistically significant, the absence of such clusters becomes significant. We examine these cases first, before analyzing the more useful, smaller values of $\theta$.

1. $\theta \geq n - 1$. In this case $n_2 = |E_I| = |E_R| = \binom{n}{2}$, so that $P[n_2 = \binom{n}{2}] = 1$.
2. $\theta = n - 2$
   (a) If $\{g_1, g_n\} = \{1, n\}$, probability $\frac{2}{n(n-1)}$, $n_2 = \binom{n}{2} - 1$,

(b) If $|(g_1, g_n) \cap \{1, n\}| < 2$, $n_2 = \binom{n}{2} - 2$.

Thus $P[n_2 = \binom{n}{2} - 1] = \frac{2}{n(n-1)}$ and $P[n_2 = \binom{n}{2} - 2] = \frac{(n-2)(n+1)}{n(n-1)}$

3. $\theta = n - k$ where $k$ is a positive integer and smaller than $\frac{n}{2}$. In this case,

$$|E_I| = |E_R| = k(n-k) + \frac{(n-k)(n-k-1)}{2}.$$

Now, $|E_I \cap E_R| \geq |E_I| - \frac{k(k-1)}{2}$, because the number of the pairs $(g_i, g_j)$, $i \neq j$ satisfying both $|i - j| \leq \theta$ and $|g_i - g_j| > \theta$ cannot be greater than $\frac{k(k-1)}{2}$. Then for $k$ small relative to $n$,

$$n_2 \geq \binom{n}{2} - 2\binom{k}{2}$$

## 3.2 Small $\theta$

$\theta = 1$. The definition of generalized adjacency reduces to the ordinary notion of adjacency. In this case the exact expression for the probability distribution of $n_2$ is known and its limiting distribution is Poisson with parameter 2 [4,5].

$\theta \geq 2$. We now present our main analytical results. We first examine the expected value $\mathbf{E}(n_2)$ of the number of adjacencies common to $I$ and $R$.

**Proposition.** For $\theta \geq 1$,

$$\mathbf{E}(n_2) = 2\theta^2 - \frac{4n\theta^3 - \theta^2(1+\theta)^2}{2n(n-1)},$$

so that for a given $\theta$

$$\lim_{n \to \infty} \mathbf{E}(n_2) = 2\theta^2$$

*Proof.* Counting the total number of edges in $E_I$, we have

$$|E_I| = (n-\theta)\theta + \sum_{i=1}^{\theta-1} i = n\theta - \binom{\theta+1}{2}$$

Each of these edges has probability

$$p = \frac{2(n-2)!}{n!} \sum_{i=1}^{\theta} (n-i)$$

of occurring in $E_R$. Thus

$$\mathbf{E}(n_2) = |E_I| p$$

$$= 2\theta^2 - \frac{4n\theta^3 - \theta^2(1+\theta)^2}{2n(n-1)}. \qquad \square$$

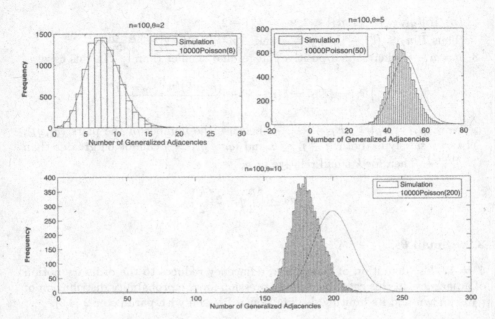

**Fig. 2.** Empirical distributions of the number of generalized adjacencies compared to the related Poisson distribution for $\theta = 2, 5$ and $10$

We can say more about the limiting behaviour of $n_2$. Indeed, we may state (proof omitted):

**Proposition.** For $\theta \geq 1$, $n_2$ converges in distribution to a Poisson distribution with parameter $2\theta^2$.

We generated $10,000$ random permutations on $1, \ldots, 100$ and calculated $n_2$ for various values of $\theta$. In Figure 2, we compare the simulated distribution of $n_2$ (with means indistinguishable from $2\theta^2 - \frac{4n\theta^3 - \theta^2(1+\theta)^2}{2n(n-1)}$ in each case) to the Possion distribution with parameter $2\theta^2$, for $\theta = 2, 5$ and $10$. For fixed $n$, the difference is larger as $\theta$ increases, though as $n$ increases the Poisson is the limiting distribution.

## 4    Clusters of Larger Size

We use $n_k$ to denote the number of connected components of size $k$ in $E_I \cap E_R$, with no disjointness requirement or restriction against the component being contained in a larger cluster. We have already studied the distribution of $n_2$ in Section 3. We now consider the expectation of $n_3$. Extending the approach we used in the Proposition in Section 3.2, we can list all the connected components of size 3 in genome $I$ and calculate the probability it is also in $R$. Adding all the probabilities together, we find

$$\mathbf{E}(n_3) = \frac{\theta^2}{n}(5\theta^2 - 2\theta - 1) + O(\frac{1}{n^2})$$

Similarly, with additional effort, we find that

$$\mathbf{E}(n_4) = \frac{\theta^2}{n^2}(\frac{124}{9}\theta^4 - \frac{95}{6}\theta^3 - \frac{8}{9}\theta^2 + \frac{29}{6}\theta + \frac{1}{9}) + O(\frac{1}{n^3})$$

but the number of different kinds of components of size 5 precludes extending our method, based on listing all possibilities, to $n_5$ and beyond.

### 4.1   Testing

Despite the fact that we have only partial results for $n_k$, we can still use standard statistical methods to test for the relatedness of two genomes or the significance of a generalized adjacency cluster, especially if $\mathbf{E}(n_4)$ is small.

## 5   The Maximum Size Generalized Adjacency Cluster

The ideal statistic to use to test the relatedness of genomes or to detect clusters would be the size of the largest cluster $k_{\max}$. While analytical techniques have not produced useful information about the distribution of $k_{\max}$, it is a straightforward matter to simulate random genomes and estimate this distribution empirically. Figure 3 shows the cumulative distribution functions for $k_{\max}$

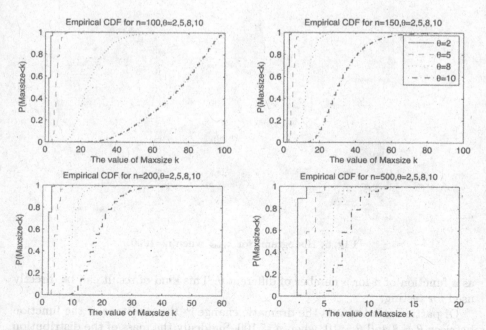

**Fig. 3.** Empirical cumulative distribution functions for $k_{\max}$ as a function of $n$ and $\theta$

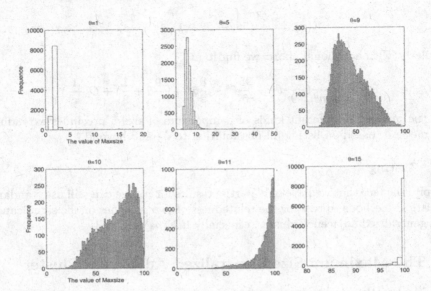

**Fig. 4.** Histograms for $k_{\max}$ when n=100

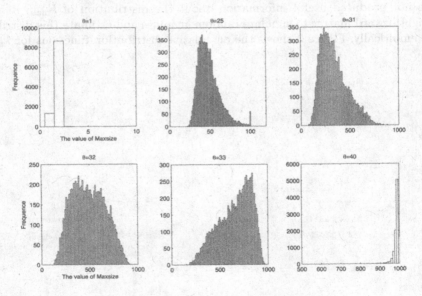

**Fig. 5.** Histograms for $k_{\max}$ when n=1000

as a function of $n$ for a number of different $\theta$. This kind of result can be directly used for testing.

Of particular interest is the dramatic change in the structure of the function between $\theta = 8$ and $\theta = 10$, when $n = 100$. Suddenly the mass of the distribution

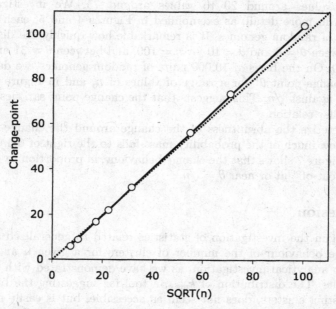

**Fig. 6.** Change-point for $k_{max}$ distribution as a function of $\sqrt{n}$. Dotted diagonal represents exact square root of $n$.

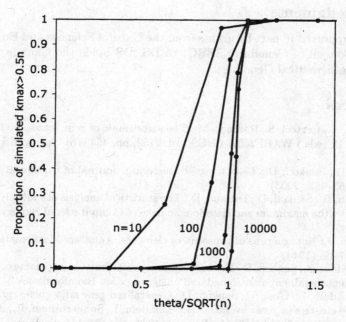

**Fig. 7.** Cut-off for maximum size cluster

shifts from values around 20 to values around 75. We investigated this phenomenon in more detail, as exemplified in Figures 4 and 5, each based on 10,000 pairs of random genomes. It is remarkable how quickly the distribution changes between $\theta = 9$ and $\theta = 10$ for $n = 100$, and between $\theta = 31$ and $\theta = 33$ for $n = 1000$. On the basis of 10,000 pairs of random genomes, we determined the mean change-point $\theta^*$ for a range of values of $n$, and in Figure 6 plotted these points against $\sqrt{n}$. This suggests that the change-point satisfies $\theta^* = \sqrt{n}$ or some similar relation.

To characterize the abruptness of the change around the change-point, we calculated how much of the probability mass falls to the right of $0.5n$, for each value of $\theta$. Figure 7 shows that the change behaviour, in proportion to $\sqrt{n}$, tends to a sharp "cut-off" at or near $\theta = \sqrt{n}$.

## 6  Discussion

We have begun the investigation of statistics related to generalized adjacency clusters. The behaviour of the number of clusters for a given $n$ and $\theta$ seems amenable to analytical investigation, as we have demonstrated with a number of new results. The distribution of $k_{max}$, a tool for suggesting the biologically most interesting clusters, does not seem as accessible, but is easily simulated. Knowledge of the cut-off behaviour serves to delimit the region for meaningful tests to $\theta$ suitably less than $\sqrt{n}$.

## Acknowledgments

Research supported in part by grants from the Natural Sciences and Engineering Research Council of Canada (NSERC) to DS. DS holds the Canada Research Chair in Mathematical Genomics.

## References

1. Bergeron, A., Corteel, S., Raffinot, M.: The algorithmic of gene teams. In: Guigó, R., Gusfield, D. (eds.) WABI 2002. LNCS, vol. 2452, pp. 464–476. Springer, Heidelberg (2002)
2. Durand, D., Sankoff, D.: Tests for gene clustering. Journal of Computational Biology 10, 453–482 (2003)
3. Hoberman, R., Sankoff, D., Durand, D.: The statistical analysis of spatially clustered genes under the maximum gap criterion. Journal of Computational Biology 12, 1081–1100 (2005)
4. Wolfowitz, J.: Note on runs of consecutive elements. Annals of Mathematical Statistics 15, 97–98 (1944)
5. Xu, W., Alain, B., Sankoff, D.: Poisson adjacency distributions in genome comparison: multichromosomal, circular, signed and unsigned cases. Bioinformatics 24 (2008)
6. Zhu, Q., Adam, Z., Choi, V., Sankoff, D.: Generalized gene adjacencies, graph bandwidth and clusters in yeast evolution. In: Mandoiu, I., Sunderraman, R., Zelikovsky, A. (eds.) ISBRA 2008. LNCS (LNBI), vol. 4983, pp. 134–145. Springer, Heidelberg (2008)

# Identity Transposon Networks in *D. melanogaster*

Alcides Castro-e-Silva[1], Gerald Weber[1], Romuel F. Machado[1],
Elizabeth F. Wanner[2], and Renata Guerra-Sá[3]

[1] Department of Physics
**alcides@iceb.ufop.br**
[2] Department of Mathematics,
[3] Department of Biological Sciences,
Federal University of Ouro Preto, Ouro Preto-MG, Brazil

**Abstract.** Transposable elements, or transposons, are DNA segments
that are repeated within the same genome and are an important component of the genomes of most species. It is generally believed that they
play an important role in evolution and genome restructuring. In this
work we built a network based on a score which represents the transposon identity. This score is calculated by comparing all currently known
*D. melanogaster* transposons to each other using a Neddleman-Wunsch
alignment algorithm. We then use this score to build networks with transposons having a minimal value of identity. We start with networks of
transposons with total identity (all have score one) to networks where
they may have any identity score (all have non-negative score). The number of successful comparisons as a function of the minimal score shows
an abrupt transition for minimal scores at 0.25 which can be associated
to general properties of repetitions usually found in genomes. We also
show that this score leads to a transition in the topology of transposon
networks from scale-free to almost fully-connected.

Current advances in genomic sequencing generated huge amounts of data from
many species to a great degree of detail. It is now possible to access complete
genomes and chromosome sequences, genes and transcriptions factors and protein relations just to mention a few but important examples. The ever increasing
details of these databases stresses the fact that it is important to understand
how their elements are related and how they interact. Interaction networks, such
as protein-protein interactions, may emerge from combining elements of these
databases. None of these networks are independent, they can interact with other
networks to several degrees and on various scales, i.e., we may have a network of
networks and so on. Analysing the scale of the interaction network is one possible way to grasp the complexity of the vast amount of information provided by
these networks. The study of interconnected elements is called graph theory and
the classical mathematical theory was developed by Erdös and Rényi [1]. Graph
theory was reborn in 1999 with the work of Barabasi and Albert who introduced the concept of scale-free networks [2,3]. Basically, the difference beetween
Erdös-Barabasi graphs relies on equilibrium concepts. The networks studied by
Erdös were called random networks, in this class of graphs the number of nodes

A.L.C. Bazzan, M. Craven, and N.F. Martins (Eds.): BSB 2008, LNBI 5167, pp. 161–164, 2008.

are constant and the links are distributed with a certain probability over those nodes. Such procedure creates equilibrium networks since all nodes have the same statistical characteristics. On the other hand in the Barabasi model, the nodes (and its links) are added to a initial core, and the network grows (therefore called growing networks). Here we have a non-equilibrium graph since the nodes are not statistically equivalent and they have different *ages* since the nodes are introduced at different stages of network growth. Another important feature of Barabasi model are the rules of how the links are established: the probability of a new node to connect to an old one is proportional to the number of connections of the old node already has. This is called *preferential attachment* which is also known as *the rich get richer*. Growing networks with preferential attachment lead to scale-free networks that is a special case of graph characterised by a power-law of distribution of connectivities. Following the work of Barabasi, it was discovered that many biological networks display scale-free properties such as the protein interaction of the gene regulatory and the metabolic system [4].

In this work we investigate the network of transposable elements or transposons of *D. melanogaster* [5,6]. We show that this similarity network has a scale-free power law. Since preferential attachment is the only known method to create scale-free networks this is indicative of some sort of growing mechanism should responsible for the transposition of such repetitive elements. Indeed this growing mechanism is at the very heart of the appearance of multiple copies of transposons in genome.

We calculated the global alignment score use a standard Needleman-Wunsch algorithm to compare all currently known 6003 transposons of *D. melanogaster* [7]. We used a score of $i = 2$ for two identical nucleotides, $n = -1$ for non-identical nucleotides and $g = -2$ for gaps. The alignment score $S$ resulting from the Needleman-Wunsch algorithm takes a maximum value of $i^N$ when both sequences of length $N$ are identical. We use this to define a relative alignment score $s = S/i^{N_{\min}}$ [$N_{\min} = \min(N_1, N_2)$] for two sequences of length $N_1$ and $N_2$, such that it becomes normalised to one for the case of fully identical sequences. Complete non-similarity sequences yield a value of $s$ close to zero, or even negative due to the negative alignment score for non-identical bases or gaps. To speed up the calculation, we have restricted the alignment to sequences whose length satisfy

$$\frac{|N_1 - N_2|}{\max(N_1, N_2)} < 0.5. \tag{1}$$

For the known transposons of *D. Melanogaster* we performed a total of $4.6 \times 10^6$ alignments. The complete identity, $s = 1$, is found for transposons which occur at different location within a genome or chromosome but have not yet suffered any further mutation. This indicates situations where the transposition has occurred only recently during the evolution.

Our networks are formed by nodes (transposons) and a link beetween two transposons is added if the normalised score $s$ is larger than a minimum score $s_m$. For instance, with $s_m = 1$ we obtain a network formed by transposons which are fully identical. In Fig. 1 we show the number of transposons in a network as function of the minimum score $s_m$. We observe a steep transition at around

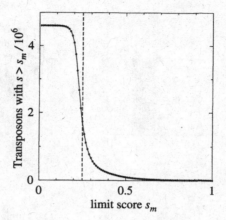

**Fig. 1.** Number transposons with normalised score $s$ larger than a minimum score $s_m$. The transition around $s_m = 0.25$ is shown by vertical dashed line.

$s_m = 0.25$ where the number of transposons in the network are reduced by two orders of magnitude. This type of transition is known to occur in the repeat analysis of short sequences in genomes [8]. In this type of analysis, the genome is divided into small subsequences of a given length and each subsequence is compared to all other subsequences of same length. For very short subsequences there are no unique sequences in the genome, however the transition for non-unique sequences to all sequence becoming unique happens over an interval of just very few nucleotides [8]. The transition shown in figure 1 is of similar origin. Even very dissimilar transposons share a number of similar subsequences due to the occurrence of repetitions in the genome [8], therefore these repetitions give rise to the large number of scores smaller than 0.25.

We also calculated the distribution of connectivity $P(k)$. This distribution is a histogram that shows how many nodes have $k$ connections, results are shown in Fig. 2 for minimal score $s_m$ equal to 0.1, 0.25, 0.4 and 0.9. For $s_m > 0.25$ we observe the characteristic power-law form $P(k)$ corresponding to scale-free networks. This power-law is shown as a guide-to-the-eye straight line in log-log plot. The power law distribution yields two basics features of the network regarding the connectivity: (a) there is no characteristic node and (b) there are few nodes with high connectivity (called hubs) and many nodes with low connectivity.

Work is in progress where we study the particular features of specific transposon families, such as the abundant INE-1 family as well as transposon classes such as LTR retrostranposons. Also, we are currently using genetic algorithms to optimise the Needleman-Wusch score to enhance the specificity of transposon alignment.

We thank the Brazilian agencies Fapemig and CNPq for financial support.

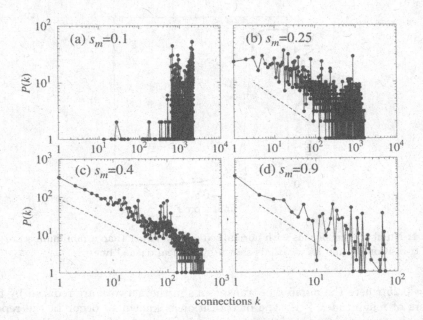

**Fig. 2.** Distribution of connectivities of Transposons identity for several scores (log-log plots). The power-law signature of scale-free behaviour, shown as guide-to-the-eye dashed lines, is present only for minimal scores $s_m$ larger than 0.25.

# References

1. Erdős, P., Rényi, A.: On the evolution of random graphs. Publ. Math. Inst. Hung. Acad. Sci. 5, 17–61 (1960)
2. Barabási, A., Albert, R.: Emergence of scaling in random networks. Science 286(5439), 509 (1999)
3. Barabasi, A., Oltvai, Z.: Network biology: understanding the cell's functional organization. Nature Reviews Genetics 5(2), 101–113 (2004)
4. Jeong, H., Tombor, B., Albert, R., Oltvai, Z., Barabasi, A., et al.: The large-scale organization of metabolic networks. Nature 407(6804), 651–654 (2000)
5. Bartolome, C., Maside, X., Charlesworth, B.: On the abundance and distribution of transposable elements in the genome of Drosophila melanogaster. Molecular Biology and Evolution 19(6), 926–937 (2002)
6. Rizzon, C., Marais, G., Gouy, M., Biémont, C.: Recombination rate and the distribution of transposable elements in the Drosophila melanogaster genome. Genome Research 12, 400–407 (2002)
7. Durbin, R., Eddy, S.R., Krogh, A., Mitchison, G.: Biological sequence analysis: probabilistic models of proteins and nucleic acids. Cambridge Univ. Press, Cambridge (2000)
8. Whiteford, N., Haslam, N., Weber, G., Prügel-Bennett, A., Essex, J.W., Roach, P.L., Bradley, M., Neylon, C.: An analysis of the feasibility of short read sequencing. Nucl. Acids. Res. 33(19), e171 (2005)

# Prediction of Protein-Protein
# Binding Hot Spots:
# A Combination of Classifiers Approach

Roberto Hiroshi Higa[1,2] and Clésio Luis Tozzi[2]

[1] Embrapa Informática Agropecuária
Empresa Brasileira de Pesquisa Agropecuária - EMBRAPA, CP 6041
13083-970 - Campinas, SP, Brazil
roberto@cnptia.embrapa.br
http://www.cnptia.embrapa.br
[2] Departamento de Engenharia de Computação e Automação Industrial
Faculdade de Engenharia Elétrica e de Computação, CP 6101
Universidade Estadual de Campinas - UNICAMP
13083-970, Campinas, SP, Brazil
{rhhiga,clesio}@dca.fee.unicamp.br
http://www.fee.unicamp.br

**Abstract.** In this work we approach the problem of predicting protein
binding hot spot residues through a combination of classifiers. We consider a comprehensive set of structural and chemical properties reported
in the literature for characterizing hot spot residues. Each component
classifier considers a specific set of properties as feature set and their
output are combined by the mean rule. The proposed combination of
classifiers achieved a performance of 56.6%, measured by the F-Measure
with corresponding Recall of 72.2% and Precision of 46.6%. This performance is higher than those reported by Darnel et al. [4] for the same
data set, when compared through a t-test with a significance level of 5%.

**Keywords:** hot spots, combination of classifiers, protein interaction,
binding sites.

## 1 Introduction

Protein-protein interactions play a key role in most of biological process, being of
great importance for living cells. Although the principles governing this process
is still not fully understood, it is well-known that binding energy is not evenly
distributed among interface residues, with a large contribution coming from only
a small subset of the interface residues [10]. These residues are referenced as
binding hot spots.

The recent interest in protein-protein interface as drug targets [2] has highlighted the importance of identifying hot spots systematically. Usually, this is
done through site-directed mutagenesis experiments like alanine scanning technique [10], whose aim is to evaluate the impact on the binding energy caused

A.L.C. Bazzan, M. Craven, and N.F. Martins (Eds.): BSB 2008, LNBI 5167, pp. 165–168, 2008.

by mutations to alanine of specific interface residues; but, they can demand a significant experimental effort. In this scenario, the interest for cheaper and faster computational hot spot prediction methods grows. Such a computational method can help biologists to keep the experimental effort focused only on those interface residues presenting better chance to be hot spots.

In this work, we use a comprehensive set of structural and chemical properties to predict binding hot spot residues through a strategy of combination of classifiers.

## 2   Material and Methods

We use a data set compiled by Darnell et al. [4]. This choice is based on the fact that this data set has been processed in order to reduce as much as possible the presence of low quality and/or redundant structures. We also had to remove from the data set 15 residues for which we could not calculate the corresponding conservation score property. The following set of properties was selected in order to characterize interface residues:

- Amino acid type of the interface residue, represented by the two indexes proposed by Hagarty et al. [6];
- Residue conservation score of the interface residue and the average score of its neighbor residues, calculated by using the software rate4site [11] and MSA of homologue sequences from Swissprot/Uniprot Knowledgebase release 9.6 [1];
- Solvent accessible surface area - ASA in isolation and in complex for the interface residue and for its neighbor residues, calculated by using program *volbl*, included in the software package *alpha shapes* [8];
- Atomic packing scores computed for intra chain neighbors and for inter chain neighbors, defined by the occupied volume around the interface residue;
- Inter chain atomic contacts [9]; and
- Computational $\Delta\Delta G$ value, computed by using the Kortemme and Baker model [7].

In order to set up a reference for comparison with the one obtained for the combination of classifiers, we trained and tested a set of classifiers - linear, quadratic, parzen and SVM, considering the entire set of the above mentioned properties. Then, in order to build the combination of classifiers, we trained and tested the same set of classifiers considering each subset of properties individually, with amino acid type and residue conservation score considered together. For each subset of properties, the classifier which achieved the higher performance was selected for combination. Ties were broken by given preference to the simpler classifier, considering the following order of complexity: linear, quadratic, parzen and SVM. To combine their output, we evaluated different combination rules - vote, maximum, minimum, product, mean and median - choosing those one which achieved the best performance.

We used the following measures to assess the classification performance [4]: Precision, Recall, F-Measure and Accuracy, all estimated by a leave-one-out procedure [12]. Due to the the unbalanced distribution of samples between classes, we randomly re-sampled the majority class to obtain a balanced data set and reported performances corresponding to the average over 20 repetitions of the procedure. We also used a one-tailed paired t-test [3], with a significance level of 5% for comparing performance between methods. For implementation of the combination of classifiers, we used the public domain matlab toolbox PRTools [5].

## 3   Results and Discussion

Initially, we evaluated the performance of different classification methods using the feature vector composed by the whole set of parameters. We considered linear, quadratic, Parzen and SVM models, estimating their performances according to the procedure presented in section 2. The best performance was achieved by a SVM classifier using a radial basis function (RBF) kernel with dispersion parameter $\gamma=2.6$ and the regularization parameter C=2. That corresponds to a F-Measure of 64.6% ($\pm$6.1), corresponding to a Recall of 67.6% ($\pm$7.3) and a Precision of 61.9% ($\pm$5.5).

Also, according to the procedure presented in section 2 the following set of component classifiers was selected for combination: a linear classifier using the computational $\Delta\Delta G$ as feature set, a Fisher classifier using the atomic contacts parameters as feature set, a quadratic classifier using the ASA parameters as feature set, a linear classifier using the atomic packing parameters as feature set and a SVM classifier using the AAindex and the residue conservation score parameters as feature set. From these, the best performance was achieved by the quadratic classifier using the ASA parameters, corresponding to a F-Measure of 68.5% ($\pm$3.0) and an overall accuracy of 65.6% ($\pm$3.2).

Next, we considered the following set of combination rules: vote, maximum, minimum, product, mean and median. Since the best performance was achieved by mean and product rules, we opted for assuming mean as the combination rule. For this rule, we obtained a F-Measured of 70.6% ($\pm$3.6), corresponding to a Recall of 72.4% ($\pm$4.6), a Precision of 71.3% ($\pm$2.1) and an overall accuracy of 71.7% ($\pm$3.9). This performance is clearly higher than that achieved by the SVM classifier using the whole set of properties. Notice that it is also higher than that achieved by the best component classifier: quadratic classifier using ASA parameters as feature set.

In order to compare our results with the one reported by Darnell et al. [4], we evaluated the combination of classifiers using the re-sampled data set for training and the entire data set for testing. As for this application it is also interesting to evaluate the performance of the classifier which uses only structural and chemical parameters, we reported the performance for combinations of classifiers using two different subset of properties: one using only structural properties (Str) and other which also uses the computational $\Delta\Delta G$ (Str+En) property. The combination of classifiers using Str achieved a F-Measure of 52.4% ($\pm$2.2), corresponding to a Recall of 70.2% ($\pm$3.1), a Precision of 41.8% ($\pm$1.9) and an overall accuracy of 69.3% ($\pm$1.6). Furthermore, the combination of classifiers using Str+En achieved a F-Measure of 56.6% ($\pm$2.5), corresponding to a Recall of 72.2% ($\pm$4.0), a

Precision of 46.6% (±2.0) and an overall accuracy of 73.4% (±1.5). By using a t-test with significance level of 5%, the F-Measure achieved by *Str+En* is higher than those reported by Darnell et al. [4].

## 4   Concluding Remarks

The prediction of protein-protein binding hot spot has been investigated by a strategy of combining classifiers and a set of structural, chemical and energy based properties. We report a performance of 56.6%, measured by the F-Measure, corresponding to a Recall of 72.2% and a Precision of 46.6%. By using a t-test with significance level of 5%, this performance is higher than that reported by Darnell et al. [4] using the same data set.

## References

1. Apweiler, R., Bairoch, A., Wu, C.H., et al.: UniProt: The Universal Protein Knowledgebase. Nucl. Acid. Res. 32, D115–D119 (2004)
2. Arkin, M.R., Wells, J.A.: Small-Molecule Inhibitors of Protein-Protein Interactions: Progressing Towards the Dream. Nature Reviews, Drug Discovery 3, 301–317 (2004)
3. Bussab, W.O., Morettin, P.A.: Basic Statistics, 5th edn. Editora Saraiva, São Paulo, Brazil (2002) (in Portuguese)
4. Darnell, S.J., Page, D., Mitchell, J.C.: An Automated Decision-Tree Approach to Predicting Protein Interaction Hot Spots. Proteins 68, 813–823 (2007)
5. Duin, R.P.W., Juszczak, P., Paclik, P., et al.: PRTools4, a Matlab Toolbox for Pattern Recognition, Delft University of Technology (2004)
6. Hagerty, C.G., Munchnik, I., Kulikowski, C.: Two Indices Can Approximate Four Hundred and Two Amino Acid Properties. In: Proc. of 1999 IEEE Int. Simp. Intell. Control./Intell. Syst. and Semiotics, Cambridge, MA, pp. 365–369 (1999)
7. Kortemme, T., Baker, D.: A Simple Physical Model for Binding Energy Hot Spots in Protein-Protein Complexes. Proc. Natl. Acad. Sci. USA 99, 14116–14121 (2002)
8. Liang, J., Edelsbrunner, H., Fu, P., Sudhakar, P.V., et al.: Analytical Shape Computation of Macromolecules: I. Molecular Area and Volume through Alpha Shape. Proteins 33, 1–17 (1998)
9. Mancini, A.L., Higa, R.H., Oliveira, A., et al.: STING Contacts: A Web-Based application for Identification and Analysis of Amino Acid Contacts within Protein Structure and Across Protein Interfaces. Bioinformatics 20(13), 2145–2147 (2004)
10. Moreira, I.S., Fernandes, P.A., Ramos, M.J.: Hot Spots - A Review of the Protein-Protein Interface Determinant Amino-Acid Residues. Proteins 68, 803–812 (2007)
11. Pupko, R., Bell, R.E., Mayrose, I., et al.: Rate4Site: An Algorithmic Tool for the Identification of Functional Regions in Proteins by Surface Mapping of Evolutionary Determinants Within Their Homologues. Bioinformatics 18(Supl.1), S71–S77 (2002)
12. Webb, A.: Statistical Pattern Recognition. Wiley, Chichester (2002)

# AGN Simulation and Validation Model

Fabrício M. Lopes[1,3], Roberto M. Cesar-Jr[1], and Luciano da F. Costa[2]

[1] Instituto de Matemática e Estatística, Universidade de São Paulo, Brazil
{fabriciolopes,roberto.cesar}@vision.ime.usp.br
[2] Instituto de Física de São Carlos, Universidade de São Paulo, Brazil
luciano@ifsc.usp.br
[3] Universidade Tecnológica Federal do Paraná, Brazil
fabricio@utfpr.edu.br

**Abstract.** An important question in computational biology is how genes are regulated and interact through gene networks. Some methods for the identification of gene networks from temporal data were proposed. An important open problem regards how to validate such resulting networks. This work presents an approach to validate such algorithms, considering three main aspects: (1) AGN model generation and simulation; (2) gene network identification; (3) validation of identified network.

## 1 Introduction

In a biological context, the cells can be viewed as networks of molecules connected by chemical reactions. The development of massive data collection techniques, as cDNA microarrays and SAGE, allows the simultaneous verification of cell's components estate in multiples instances of time. Computational methods have been extensively used to analyze and to interpret this amount of generated data. In particular, genetic regulatory networks (GRN) [1] are used to indicate how the genes are regulated and consequently give insights about the activity of live organisms in molecular level. Some methods were proposed for the identification of gene networks [2,3,4,5].

However, there is an important problem: how to validate the network identification results? In this way, we have developed a new approach to generate artificial gene networks (AGN) and to simulate temporal expression data from them (Section 2). Figure 1 gives an overview of the present work. Furthermore,

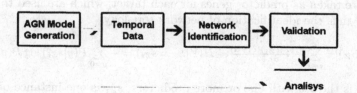

**Fig. 1.** Pipeline of the proposed framework

A.L.C. Bazzan, M. Craven, and N.F. Martins (Eds.): BSB 2008, LNBI 5167, pp. 169–173, 2008.

a network identification method [2] (Section 3) was incorporated, and the identified networks are validated based on AGN model (Section 4). In Section 5, are presented preliminary results. This paper is concluded in Section 6.

## 2  AGN Model Generation and Simulation

Two theoretical models of complex networks [6,7,8], corresponding to the scale-free Barabási-Albert (BA) and the uniformly-random Erdös-Rényi (ER), have been considered in our network generation approach. More specifically, the generation starts with a network size $N$ (i.e. number of nodes) and a average degree $k$. The BA networks were grown starting with $m_0$ nodes, to which additional nodes with $m = k$ edges each were successively attached preferentially to the degree of the existing nodes. The ER structures were generated by implementing edges between every pair of nodes with fixed probability $p$. In order to ensure similar average degrees, we imposed the condition $p = \frac{k}{N-1}$.

Therefore, an AGN is formed by a set of $N$ genes, $g_1, g_2, ..., g_N$, which may assume a value from a discrete set $Y$ (in this work, $Y = \{0, 1\}$). The edges are defined as a mapping function $\Psi(g_i) = \{p_{1i}, p_{2i}, ..., p_{ki}\}$, in which $p_{ki}$ (predictors) represents the genes that have input edges to $g_i$ (target). For each target it is built a table containing all possible predictor's combination values. For each $g_i$ a value $v \in Y$ is randomly defined. These rule tables define the simulation of the dynamical expression, i.e given the initial values of the $N$ genes and the number of transitions $T$, the dynamics starts from $t_0$ (initial values) and each target's state at $t_i$ $0 < i < T$ is obtained observing the predictors states at $t_{i-1}$ and its rule table. As a result, we have the simulated temporal data with $T$ instants of time (transitions), which are used for the network identification process presented in the following section.

## 3  Network Identification

The identification method used in this work is described in [2], in which gene network identification is modeled as a series of feature selection problems, one for each gene. Therefore, the *Sequential Forward Floating Selection* (SFFS) [9] algorithm was performed for each target gene in order to select the $S_Z$ set that minimizes the criterion function (mean conditional entropy) (1). The selected features are taken as predictor genes for each target, which are used to link the genes and thus the identification of network topology.

$$E[H(Y|S_Z)] = \sum_{i=1}^{c} \frac{H(Y|s_{Zi})(o_i + \alpha)}{\alpha c + T}, \quad H(Y|S_Z = s_{Zi}) = - \sum_{y=0}^{1} P(y|s_{Zi}) \log P(y|s_{Zi}) \quad (1)$$

where $S_Z$ is the set with one or more predictors, $s_{Zi}$ is one instance of $S_Z$ and $c = |Y|^{|S_Z|}$ is the possible number of instances of $S_Z$. The term $o_i$ is the number of occurrences of instance $s_{Zi}$ in temporal data and $\alpha$ is the penalty weight for no observed instances ($\alpha = 1$ in the present work).

# 4   Validation

Considering both models: BA and ER, the AGNs were represented in terms of their respective adjacency matrices $K$, such that each edge from node $i$ to node $j$ implies $K(j,i) = 1$, with $K(j,i) = 0$ otherwise. In order to quantify the similarity between two given networks $A$ (AGN) and $B$ (identified network), we adopted the similarity measurements presented in [10], which are calculated as follows:

$$g(A,B) = \sqrt{R_1 R_0}, \qquad R_1 = \frac{b_1}{A_1}, \qquad R_0 = \frac{b_0}{A_0} \qquad (2)$$

We consider the geometrical average $g(A,B)$ between the ratios of correct ones $(R_1)$ and correct zeros $(R_0)$, observing that matrix $A$ contains $A_0$ zeros and $A_1$ ones, and matrix $B$ contains $b_0$ zeroes coinciding with the zeroes of $A$ and $b_1$ coinciding ones. Observe that both coincidences and differences are taken into account by these indices, implying the maximum similarity to be obtained for indices values near 1.

# 5   Experimental Results

In all experiments, the two network architectures BA and ER with 100 nodes were used. The average degree varied from 1 to 5 and the number of transitions varied from 10 to 250 in steps of 20.

Figure 2 presents the network identification results by increasing the number of transitions. Clearly we can observe an improvement in the results using a larger number of transitions. However, the experiments indicated that some temporal signals do not present variations after fewer observations of time.

In order to avoid this effect, time signals were generated using from 1 to 9 different initializations with random initial values, which were concatenated in one single temporal signal. Figure 3 presents the median results considering all variations of transitions and average degrees. Based on our observations, an improvement was confirmed by the results for increasing number of initializations, specially in BA-model (c) presenting excellent correct network recovery: 95%.

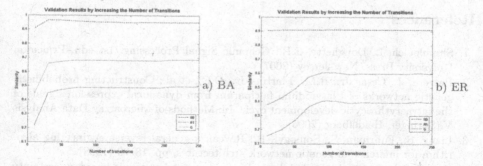

**Fig. 2.** Network identification rate considering the increasing number of transitions

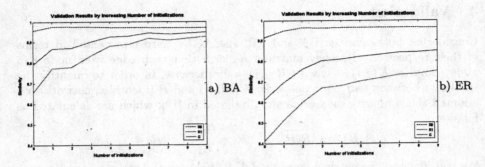

**Fig. 3.** Network identification rate considering the number of initializations

## 6   Conclusion

The proposed framework is based on a AGN model that allows to simulate temporal expression data from it. The data was analyzed by a network identification method and its results validated by the AGN model. The results indicate that the number of transitions is very important and that the use of concatenations of temporal signals represents an important procedure to obtain better results for the network identification, mainly because normally biological experiments produce replicas that can be used by computational methods.

The next stage of this work is to implement complex network measurements [8] and then to analyze network structures like hubs and communities. Other relevant improvement is to change the rule tables by joint probability functions, including some uncertainty in the creation of simulated data.

## Acknowledgments

Luciano da F. Costa thanks CNPq (308231/03-1) and FAPESP (05/00587-5) for sponsorship. This work was supported by FAPESP, CNPq and CAPES.

## References

1. Shmulevich, I., Dougherty, E.R.: Genomic Signal Processing, 1st edn. Princeton University Press, New Jersey (2007)
2. Barrera, J., Cesar Jr., R.M., Martins Jr., D.C., et al.: Constructing probabilistic genetic networks of Plasmodium falciparum from dynamical expression signals of the intraerythrocytic development cycle. In: Methods of Microarray Data Analysis V. Springer, Heidelberg (2006)
3. Liang, S., Fuhrman, S., Somogyi, R.: Reveal: a general reverse engineering algorithm for inference of genetic network architectures, pp. 18–29 (1998)
4. Shmulevich, I., et al.: Probabilistic boolean networks: a rule-based uncertainty model for gene regulatory networks. Bioinformatics 18(2), 261–274 (2002)

5. Mendes, P., Sha, W., Ye, K.: Artificial gene networks for objective comparison of analysis algorithms. Bioinformatics 19(Suppl. 2), 122ii–129 (2003)
6. Albert, R., Barabási, A.L.: Statistical mechanics of complex networks. Rev. Mod. Phys. 74(1), 47–97 (2002)
7. Newman, M.E.J.: The structure and function of complex networks. SIAM Review 45(2), 167–256 (2003)
8. da F. Costa, L., Rodrigues, F.A., et al.: Characterization of complex networks: a survey of measurements. Advances in Physics 56(1), 167–242 (2007)
9. Pudil, P., Novovičová, J., Kittler, J.: Floating search methods in feature selection. Pattern Recogn. Lett. 15(11), 1119–1125 (1994)
10. da F. Costa, L., et al.: Predicting the connectivity of primate cortical networks from topological and spatial node properties. BMC Systems Biology 1, 1–16 (2007)

# A Practical Evaluation of BioProvider
## (Extended Abstract)

Maira Ferreira de Noronha[1], Sergio Lifschitz[1], and Antonio Basilio de Miranda[2]

[1] PUC-Rio Depto Informatica, Rio de Janeiro, Brazil
{maira,sergio}@inf.puc-rio.br
[2] FIOCRUZ, DBBM, Rio de Janeiro, Brazil
antonio@fiocruz.br

**Abstract.** We present here an instantiation of BioProvider, a tool that efficiently provides data for biological applications, tailored to the way BLAST demands data. We briefly discuss some of the factors that may influence data availability and performances.

## 1 Introduction

One of the most important tasks for the analysis of molecular biology data is sequence comparison. Biological applications such as BLAST [3] and Smith-Waterman [5] are the preferred and most popular tools for sequence comparison. This work evaluates a data management oriented tool aiming at delivering biological data efficiently to multiple biological applications.

This tool, called BioProvider [4], is inspired on typical DBMS services. On the one hand, it allows *ad-hoc* management of memory buffers and, on the other hand, the control of application's process scheduling. All communications are done through a device driver [2]. It is a non-intrusive approach that enables users to keep running their original applications while our tool provides the optimized data access and availability.

This paper evaluates a specific instantiation of BioProvider for running with BLAST programs. The practical results obtained with BLAST indicate that our database approach for developing BioProvider is well adapted for biological applications and sequence data management.

## 2 BLAST Buffer Management and BioProvider

This work is mainly concerned with providing data access to biological applications in a way similar to what database management systems (DBMS) do for generic data and queries. The BioProvider proposal [4] introduces a general approach for dealing with biological data, particularly biological sequences. In order to evaluate our ideas, we will discuss here an instantiation of BioProvider that works with BLAST - Basic Local Alignment Search Tool (e.g. [3]).

By taking the BLAST characteristics into account, our work in [1] suggested an ad-hoc buffer management strategy for BLAST. The idea involves the usage of

A.L.C. Bazzan, M. Craven, and N.F. Martins (Eds.): BSB 2008, LNBI 5167, pp. 174–177, 2008.

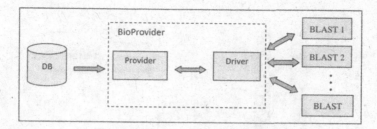

**Fig. 1.** The BioProvider Architecture

memory structures for sequence storage, named *rings*. These consist of memory buffers organized circularly, where database sequences are uploaded from disk. Buffer pages substitution follows a FIFO-like page replacement policy. While present within this ring, data may be shared by all the running processes that are in the second stage of the BLAST algorithm. Buffer pages are refreshed when all active processes have read the corresponding information.

BioProvider explores, then, the way the biological data, such as sequences, are provided to the application processes. This tool extends our previous works [1,2] enabling a non-intrusive implementation that considers ring and multiple buffer management, besides scheduling strategies, using a database approach. We present here a particular instantiation of BioProvider for BLAST-like programs. A broader view of BioProvider is presented in [4].

We have implemented the linux device driver as a kernel module. However, BioProvider could as well have been implemented in other operating system platforms, as the application code remains unchanged. Figure 1 illustrates Bio-Provider and its interaction with BLAST and the sequences database.

BioProvider has been implemented firstly for Linux with kernel versions 2.6 and 2.4, and tested with Linux Fedora and RedHat distributions. The most important modules of the tool are the *provider* program, the *driver* implementation and a *killer* program that ends the provider process. Due to similarities on the sequence file formats of the recent versions of NCBI BLAST (2.0 and later) [3] and the open source WU-BLAST 1.4 [6], BioProvider can be used with both, without any particular customization.

## 3   Some Implementation Results

The tests were run on a 3 Ghz Pentium 4 machine with 512 megabytes of RAM and Linux Fedora 4 operating system. The 50 query sequences used in the tests where obtained from 3 different databases: *ecoli.aa*, *ptaa* and *swissprot*, available at [3]. These sequences were compared with the *nr* protein databases.

To evaluate the performance of multiple BLAST processes running concurrently, tests with different computer memory and ring sizes were done. In each test, 50 BLAST processes were created, starting in fixed intervals of time, one after another, where the *nth* process used the *nth* sequence of the group of

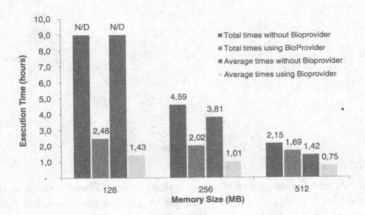

**Fig. 2.** Memory Size Factor, Test 1

sequences. This was done in order to simulate an environment where, from time to time, users run BLAST processes. The data analyzed in our tests were the average and total execution time of the BLAST processes.

In order to analyze the impact of the memory size in performances, tests were done varying the RAM memory available in the computer. The same tests were performed without BioProvider. However, when the RAM memory was 128 megabytes, the tests without BioProvider could not finish after over 30 hours of execution and we have canceled it. Figure 2 shows the test results comparing BLAST process performances with and without BioProvider.

Memory size was shown to be a very important factor in the performance of BLAST processes, as the smaller the memory, the worst the performance. On the other hand, the processes were less influenced from memory size when Bio-Provider was used. Therefore, the smaller the memory, the bigger the advantage of BioProvider. Besides allowing the execution of BLAST processes in otherwise forbidding situations, BioProvider reduced the total and average time of process execution in 56% and 73% respectively in a machine with 256 megabytes of RAM memory, and 21% and 48% in a machine with 512 megabytes.

Tests were also performed to analyze the impact of the ring size in the overall performance. The results obtained are depicted in Figure 3. It can be observed that, as expected, process performance declines when the ring is too big since memory shortage occurs for the running processes. At the same time, a small loss of performance can be perceived when the ring size is too small. This can be explained by the need of more ring updates for BLAST processes to continue reading. BioProvider reduced the total execution time of the processes between 8% and 21%, and the average execution time between 28% and 48%.

We have studied many other parameters that include the query sequences, their similarity with the sequence databases, as well as their lengths. We have analyzed also the impact of the number of sequences per block and, consequently, the size of the blocks as well. Due to the lack of space, we refer the reader to [4] for a detailed evaluation on these and other factors.

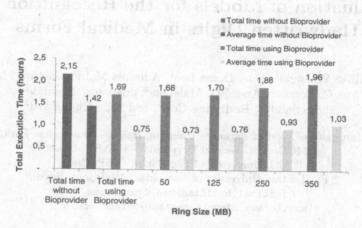

**Fig. 3.** Ring Size Factor, Test 2

## 4 Conclusions

We discuss here an instantiation of BioProvider that was implemented to efficiently deliver data to BLAST. Some tests executed with BioProvider showed many situations where it is possible to improve BLAST performances. It was also possible to verify the influence of some factors on BLAST using BioProvider. The source code for BioProvider as well as usage instructions can be found at http://www.inf.puc-rio/~blast.

## References

1. Lemos, M., Lifschitz, S.: A Study of a Multi-Ring Buffer Management for BLAST. In: 1st IEEE International Workshop on Biological Data Management (BIDM), pp. 5–9 (2003)
2. Mauro, R.C., Lifschitz, S.: An I/O Device Driver for Bioinformatics Tools: the case for BLAST. Genetics and Molecular Research (GMR) 4(3), 563–570 (2005)
3. NCBI BLAST, http://www.ncbi.nlm.nih.gov/BLAST/
4. de Noronha, M.F.: Execution Control and Data Avaliability for Biological Sequences Applications: the case for BLAST, MSc Dissertation, PUC-Rio Departamento de Informatica (September 2006) (in portuguese)
5. Smith, T.F., Waterman, M.S.: Identification of Common Molecular Subsequence. Journal of Molecular Biology 147, 195–197 (1981)
6. WU-BLAST, http://blast.wustl.edu

# Evaluation of Models for the Recognition of Hadwritten Digits in Medical Forms

Willian Zalewski[1], Huei Diana Lee[1], Adewole M.J.F. Caetano[2,*],
Ana C. Lorena[2], André G. Maletzke[3], João José Fagundes[4],
Cláudio Saddy[4], Rodrigues Coy[4], and Feng Chung Wu[1]

[1] State University of West of Paraná – Unioeste, Itaipu Technological Park, Brazil
[2] CMCC, ABC Federal University – UFABC, Brazil
[3] ICMC, University of São Paulo – USP, Brazil
[4] FCM, State University of Campinas – Unicamp, Brazil
{willzal,hueidianalee}@gmail.com,
{ana.lorena,adewole.caetano}@ufabc.edu.br

**Abstract.** Medicine has benefited widely from the use of computational
techniques, which are often employed in the analysis of data generated
in medical clinics. Among the computational techniques used in these
analyses are those from Knowledge Discovery in Databases (KDD). In
order to apply KDD techniques in the analysis of clinical data, it is often
necessary to map them into an adequate structured format. This paper
presents an extension in a methodology to map medical forms into structured datasets, in which a sub-system for handwritten digit recognition
is added to the overall mapping system.

**Keywords:** Machine learning, digit recognition, medical forms.

## 1 Introduction

In Medicine, data are often disposed in medical reports and printed forms containing information like the patient's history and symptoms, which difficult a direct analysis by computational algorithms. There are several reasons why these
data are unavailable in an adequate format, among which are the inexistence
of computers in medical ambulatories, the common sense in Medicine that the
use of printed documents makes the relationship with the patient less imper-
sonal and the necessity to maintain printed records. In previous work, a new
methodology for mapping medical forms into the attribute-value representation
was proposed and successfully employed in a medical case study [1].

This work presents an extension to the proposed methodology, where classification models for handwritten digit recognition are added to the overall mapping
system.

---

* Financial support of PDTA-PTI/BR.

A.L.C. Bazzan, M. Craven, and N.F. Martins (Eds.): BSB 2008, LNBI 5167, pp. 178–181, 2008.

## 2   Methodology for Automatic Mapping of Forms

The proposed methodology for mapping medical forms was organized in three main steps: (1) generation of forms and database (DB) construction, (2) construction of patterns about the forms and (3) mapping of forms and DB fulfill. All steps of this methodology were integrated to a system named *Form Mapping System* (ForMappSys). Step (1) involves constructing forms, by a user-friendly interface, containing numerical and multiple choice fields from previously defined attributes. The forms have also reference marks and identifications, which provide support for later steps (Figure 1). In Step (2), each form generated in the previous step is digitalized and is used to acquire information about the localization of fields in the respective form. This step allows a robust and efficient recognition of different forms, with, for example, distinct fields' compositions and also containing noise from the digitalization process. In Step (3), the mapping of the filled form is performed, using the patterns obtained from the forms and fields extracted in the previous step. Only marked fields are mapped to the DB.

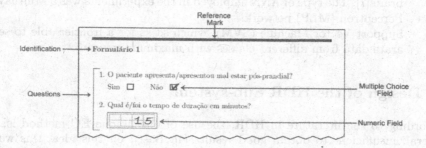

**Fig. 1.** Form example

## 3   Handwritten Digit Recognition

The problem of recognizing handwritten characters has been studied for decades and several techniques have been proposed in order to solve this problem [2]. The strategy generally followed by handwritten digit recognition (HDR) systems can be divided into three steps:

1. Pre-processing: minimizing problems that may negatively interfere in the recognition process;
2. Extraction of characteristics: the extraction of characteristics (EC) step is of great importance to obtain good results. The methods proposed for this search to minimize the variability of patterns in a same class and stand out differences of patterns among distinct classes. They are generally classified in two categories: structural characteristics and statistics characteristics.
   - **Structural EC methods** are based in a structural analysis of the image, that is, how the pixels in an image are arranged to compose the lines in the characters. The following structural characteristics were

considered in this work: Intersection with straight lines, Junctions and End points [3,4].

- **Statistical EC methods** allow obtaining global information about the character image, that is, how the pixels of a character are distributed. The methods considered in this work are: Radial codification, Contour profiles, Chaincode direction, Gradient direction, Zoning, Projection histograms [2,3,4,5].

3. Classification: consists in the application of techniques to determine from which character class the character represented by the set of characteristics extracted in the previous step belongs. Among the most employed techniques in handwritten digit classification are:

- The Nearest Neighbor (NN), which stores all training data and classifies a new data point according to the class of its nearest neighbor in the training dataset [6].
- Artificial Neural Networks (ANNs), which are computational systems inspired in the structure, processing method and learning ability of the brain [7]. The type of ANN employed in the experiments was a Multilayer Perceptron (MLP) network.
- Support Vector Machine (SVM), which seeks for a frontier able to separate data from different classes with maximum margin.

## 4    Design of the HDR Sub-system

According to the literature in HDR, the use of one unique EC method is, in general, insufficient to obtain good results [4]. Based on this idea, this work investigated the combination of multiple characteristics extractors, in particular of structural and statistical characteristics from the images. The combination of different sets of characteristics allows to minimize disadvantages of some methods by complementing them with properties of other methods [3]. In this first study, a subset of 1000 images was randomly selected from the MNIST DB. This dataset

**Table 1.** Cross-validation results

| EC Method | NN | MLP | SVM |
|---|---|---|---|
| ChainCode Direction | 63.4 (4.9) | 68.1 (4.1) | 70.0 (3.7) |
| Contour Profile | 92.7 (2.4) | 96.4 (1.9) | 97.0 (1.6) |
| Gradient Direction | 62.0 (3.7) | 72.9 (4.2) | 70.1 (3.8) |
| Intersections With Straight Lines | 61.6 (4.9) | 69.1 (4.8) | 50.2 (4.7) |
| Projection Histogram | 87.8 (3.4) | 90.3 (2.7) | 90.8 (2.4) |
| Radial Codification | 55.2 (4.7) | 59.1 (4.2) | 60.4 (4.2) |
| Zoning | 83.1 (3.6) | 82.1 (3.7) | 81.9 (3.3) |
| End Points | 47.3 (5.1) | 55.9 (3.9) | 52.6 (4.4) |
| Junctions | 22.1 (3.8) | 30.0 (3.9) | 32.1 (4.1) |
| All | 97.7 (1.3) | 99.3 (0.8) | 99.1 (1.0) |

was further evaluated with the 10-fold cross-validation methodology. Table 1 presents the accuracy results and Standard deviation rates achieved in this first set of experiments. Based in the results, the MLP technique was chosen for building the final classification model of the HDR sub-system.

## 5   Case Study

A model form was built using the ForMappSys system. This form is composed of five multiple choice questions and four questions with numerical answers. Fifty copies of the model form were made, filled *ad libitum* using a standard black pen by ten collaborators.

Considering all forms, only one of the 250 multiple choice questions was not correctly mapped by ForMappSys system. Herewith, it is possible to evidence a 99.6% of accuracy in mapping multiple choice fields. For the 504 digits manually written in the forms, the accuracy of classification was of 96.23%.

## 6   Conclusion and Future Work

Specialists of the domain consider the results promising. The analysis of the results showed that a large part of the filled digits in the forms were correctly classified. Future work includes selecting relevant attributes from the digits' characteristics and combining classifiers to increase the reliability of the predictions.

## References

1. Maletzke, A.G., Lee, H.D., Zalewski, W., Edson, R.F.V., Matsubara, T., Coy, C.S.R., Fagundes, J.J., Góes, J.R.N., Chung, W.F.: Mapeamento de informações médicas descritas em formulários para bases de dados estruturadas [in portuguese], Brasil, pp. 1–10 (2007)
2. Trier, O.D., Jain, A.K., Taxt, T.: Feature extraction methods for character recognition - a survey. Pattern Recognition 29, 641–662 (1996)
3. Heutte, L., Paquet, T., Moreau, J.-V., Lecourtier, Y., Olivier, C.: A structural/ statistical feature based vector for handwritten character recognition. Pattern Recognition Letters 19, 629–641 (1998)
4. Arica, N., Yarman-Vural, F.: An overview of character recognition focused on off-line handwriting. IEEE Trans. Syst. Man and Cybern. Part C: Appl. and Rev. 31, 216–233 (2001)
5. Wang, X., Xie, K.: A novel direction chain code-based image retrieval. In: Proc. 4th Int. Conf. on Computer and Information Technology, pp. 190–193 (2004)
6. Lee, Y.: Handwritten digit recognition using k- nearest neighbor, radial-basis functions, and back-propagation neural networks. Neural Comp. 3(3), 440–449 (1991)
7. Haykin, S.: Neural Networks - A Compreensive Foundation. Prentice-Hall, Englewood Cliffs (1999)

# Author Index

# Lecture Notes in Bioinformatics

Vol. 3737: C. Priami, E. Merelli, P. Gonzalez, A. Omicini (Eds.), Transactions on Computational Systems Biology III. VII, 169 pages. 2005.

Vol. 3695: M. R. Berthold, R.C. Glen, K. Diederichs, O. Kohlbacher, I. Fischer (Eds.), Computational Life Sciences. XI, 277 pages. 2005.

Vol. 3692: R. Casadio, G. Myers (Eds.), Algorithms in Bioinformatics. X, 436 pages. 2005.

Vol. 3680: C. Priami, A. Zelikovsky (Eds.), Transactions on Computational Systems Biology II. IX, 153 pages. 2005.

Vol. 3678: A. McLysaght, D.H. Huson (Eds.), Comparative Genomics. VIII, 167 pages. 2005.

Vol. 3615: B. Ludäscher, L. Raschid (Eds.), Data Integration in the Life Sciences. XII, 344 pages. 2005.

Vol. 3594: J.C. Setubal, S. Verjovski-Almeida (Eds.), Advances in Bioinformatics and Computational Biology. XIV, 258 pages. 2005.

Vol. 3500: S. Miyano, J. Mesirov, S. Kasif, S. Istrail, P.A. Pevzner, M. Waterman (Eds.), Research in Computational Molecular Biology. XVII, 632 pages. 2005.

Vol. 3388: J. Lagergren (Ed.), Comparative Genomics. VII, 133 pages. 2005.

Vol. 3380: C. Priami (Ed.), Transactions on Computational Systems Biology I. IX, 111 pages. 2005.

Vol. 3370: A. Konagaya, K. Satou (Eds.), Grid Computing in Life Science. X, 188 pages. 2005.

Vol. 3318: E. Eskin, C. Workman (Eds.), Regulatory Genomics. VII, 115 pages. 2005.

Vol. 3240: I. Jonassen, J. Kim (Eds.), Algorithms in Bioinformatics. IX, 476 pages. 2004.

Vol. 3082: V. Danos, V. Schachter (Eds.), Computational Methods in Systems Biology. IX, 280 pages. 2005.

Vol. 2994: E. Rahm (Ed.), Data Integration in the Life Sciences. X, 221 pages. 2004.

Vol. 2983: S. Istrail, M.S. Waterman, A. Clark (Eds.), Computational Methods for SNPs and Haplotype Inference. IX, 153 pages. 2004.

Vol. 2812: G. Benson, R.D.M. Page (Eds.), Algorithms in Bioinformatics. X, 528 pages. 2003.

Vol. 2666: C. Guerra, S. Istrail (Eds.), Mathematical Methods for Protein Structure Analysis and Design. XI, 157 pages. 2003.